CW00740799

SOVIET T-62
MAIN BATTLE TANK

SOVIET T-62
MAIN BATTLE TANK

James Kinnear and Stephen L. (Cookie) Sewell

OSPREY PUBLISHING
Bloomsbury Publishing Plc
Kemp House, Chawley Park, Cumnor Hill, Oxford OX2 9PH, UK
29 Earlsfort Terrace, Dublin 2, Ireland
1385 Broadway, 5th Floor, New York, NY 10018, USA
E-mail: info@ospreypublishing.com
www.ospreypublishing.com

OSPREY is a trademark of Osprey Publishing Ltd

First published in Great Britain in 2021

© Jim Kinnear and Stephen L. Sewell, 2021

ISBN: HB 9781472848222; eBook 9781472848215; ePDF 9781472848192; XML 9781472848208

21 22 23 24 25   10 9 8 7 6 5 4 3 2 1

Index by Zoe Ross
Originated by PDQ Digital Media Solutions, Bungay, UK
Printed and bound in India by Replika Press Private Ltd.

Front cover: Upper image: An early production T-62 on Red Square for the November Parade in 1965 (see page 17). Lower image: A company of mixed variant T-62M tanks (see page 70). All images on front and back cover are courtesy of the authors.

PICTURE CREDITS

All pictures, including those on the cover, are from the author's collections unless otherwise noted. In particular, the authors would like to express their appreciation to Andrey Aksenov, John Ham, Alexander Koshavtsev, Alexander Morzhitsky and Sergei Popsueivich and Igor Zheltov. Artworks are by Andrey Aksenov and are credited where they appear. Thanks also go to the Museum of Russian Military History, Padikovo, and the Muzei Tekhniki (Vadim Zadorozhny Museum) at Arkhangelskoe, both located in the suburbs of Moscow, for permission to photograph their preserved T-62 tanks in detail.

NOTE ON THE TRANSLATION AND PRONUNCIATION OF RUSSIAN LANGUAGE

The Russian alphabet has more characters than the Latin-based English language, and the Russian language is also grammatically complex, and subject to varying translations depending on context, gender, time period and nationality of the translator. Therefore, it is not always possible to directly translate Russian terms or names into English, and the various means of doing so are contentious and often arbitrary. Translations of some Russian terms have also been simplified in this book without the contentious pronunciation accents, as although perceived correct by those with an academic but no practical experience of the language, use outside a dry academic environment makes the subsequent English translation of a living Russian language difficult to read. An example is Ob'iekt (object) that has been simplified as Obiekt for consistency with previously published books. As these books are technical histories rather than studies of Russian grammar, the authors trust that this simplification of translation and terminology makes the books easier to read than would be the case if all the accents were included.
Osprey Publishing supports the Woodland Trust, the UK's leading woodland conservation charity.

To find out more about our authors and books visit **www.ospreypublishing.com**. Here you will find extracts, author interviews, details of forthcoming events and the option to sign up for our newsletter.

CONTENTS

INTRODUCTION

Zhosef Ya. Kotin, head of the Leningrad group of tank factories and design bureaus. Here shown as a general-lieutenant, he believed that all the Red Army and later Soviet Army needed was heavy tanks.

Aleksandr A. Morozov, head of the Kharkov group. He believed in revolutionary designs but too often his vision exceeded the technical capabilities of the times.

The T-62 main battle tank was noted for four main achievements:

- it was the first Soviet tank to mount a high-power 115mm smoothbore gun;
- it was the first Soviet tank to use armour-piercing fin-stabilized discarding sabot (APFSDS) ammunition;
- it was only produced in the Soviet Union and not licensed for production in Warsaw Pact countries as with the T-34, T-54 and T-55 (although the DPRK received a conditional licence to produce their version of the tank); and
- it was the last 'simple' tank produced as an example of the first generation of post-war Soviet tanks.

At the time of its early service in the Soviet Army, the T-62 became an iconic 'bogeyman' tank to NATO and the West and caused a great deal of research to be placed into defeating its ammunition and also countering it on the battlefield. While just over 19,000 series production T-62 tanks were built over its 11-year production run, after less than a decade in Soviet Army service it was released for export, and served in a number of countries for many years after the fall of the Soviet Union. China had captured an early example during a border incident in 1969 and, after reverse engineering the tank, decided it served them no real purpose to produce it. But the Democratic People's Republic of Korea (DPRK) did like the tank and, with a limited licence to produce the tank, built over a thousand copies as the Ch'onma in six versions, and also used the T-62 as the basis for its next tank, the Pokpo'ong.

The T-62 tank was at the time of its introduction just what the Soviet Army wanted as it was little different in operation and maintenance from its T-54 and T-55 predecessors, and having few sophisticated systems it was easily mastered by raw recruits over a five-month training schedule. But the T-62 had a rocky road to existence as a new generation of Soviet technocrats wanted a far more exotic design with more advanced technology features; suffice it to say that in the hands of the Russians the T-62 actually outlived its successor.

In combat the tank did not quite live up to its potential tank-killing capability as the Soviet Union never of course engaged NATO, and in the hands of third-world surrogates the tanks suffered high attrition rates due to misuse and poor training. But the tank soldiered on even in Russian service long after the later T-72 and T-80 tanks had begun to be scrapped in large numbers in the post-Soviet era. One nuance of the T-62 design was that with its lower-powered engine and wide-ratio five-speed transmission it was found to be better suited for use in mountainous terrain, which is one reason why the T-62 was widely used during the decade-long Soviet war in Afghanistan. The T-62 was many years later used with some considerable skill by the Russians as late as August 2008, during the short war in South Ossetia against Georgia.

As with the T-55 before it, the T-62 underwent a number of upgrades to increase its armour protection, firepower and performance, including a through-the-bore anti-tank guided missile capability.

As with the previous books in this series (on the T-10, T-54 and T-55), this book is based on existing research undertaken by Russian armour historians and veterans of the Soviet tank industry now available in the unclassified world. To this day Soviet and Russian post-World War II state archives are essentially barred to Western researchers, so the efforts of these individuals are greatly appreciated. Most of them will be identifiable from the bibliography of the sources used in the research for this book. As with any such work, the result is based on the collective efforts of many individuals who provided archive and photographic material, as well as correcting errors and omissions. Thanks in particular go to Andrey Aksenov, Aleksandr Koshavtsev, Yuri Pasholok, Sergei Popsuevich and Igor Zheltov. Credit must also be given to acknowledged experts in the field such as Christopher Foss. Major kudos must be given to Steve Zaloga for his pioneering research and work on the study of Soviet and Russian tanks. All of them have provided both information and advice on approaching this subject.

Leonid N. Kartsev, chief designer at Nizhny Tagil from 1953 to 1969. His designs evolved from past tank designs, and while not as advanced as those of Morozov, were far more desirable to the Soviet Army.

FAR LEFT The T-62 Model 1961 tank as produced, showing the 115mm U-5TS gun it was created to mount.

LEFT This view shows the parentage of the T-62 based on its T-55 predecessor.

CHAPTER ONE

'REVOLUTIONARY' VERSUS 'EVOLUTIONARY' – MOROZOV VERSUS KARTSEV

THE CHANGE IN SOVIET THINKING

In the early 1950s the Soviet military-industrial complex began to evolve into a far more scientifically driven organization that was focusing on both technical and quantitative superiority. Lend-Lease American equipment during World War II had shown the Soviets to be technically quite backwards in certain areas such as VHF radio sets and gun stabilizers in the M4 medium tank and multi-axle drive systems and all-wheel braking as used in the GMC CCKW and Studebaker 6x6 cargo trucks. This fed into their doctrinal concept of working on a replacement for any system as soon as one was accepted for service and went into mass production.

To that end the Soviet Union deployed a large number of scientific research institutes (Nauchno-Issledovatel'skiy Institut – NII), with All-Union (Vsesoyuznyy – VNII) and Central (Tsentral'niy – TsNII) ones being the most powerful. One of the most influential was VNII-100, the former prototype armour design centre, which was part of the Leningrad armoured vehicle complex run by Zhosef Kotin. Most armour designs needed their blessing to move towards development. Also a major factor was NII-48, the scientific research institute for armour, which tested and developed various forms of homogeneous, cast and composite protection for armoured vehicles.

But designs also had to be approved by an increasing number of governmental agencies in Moscow in order to advance. These included the most influential one – the Scientific Technical Committee of the State Committee on Defence Technology (NTK GKOT), which was an adjunct of the Council of Ministers of the USSR (SM SSSR) and the Central Committee of the Communist Party. There was a similar group in the Main Directorate for Armoured Vehicle Technology (NTK GBTU), the Main Directorate for Artillery Technology (NTK GAU), and the Main Directorate for Tank Production of the Ministry of Transport Machinery Production, better known as 'Glavtank'. But the Ministry of Defence, the Commanding General of the Ground Forces, and the Commanding General of Tank Troops also had a say in the final decision.

Underlying all of the above was the emergence of localized political factions, which the Soviets colloquially referred to as 'clans' in the tribal sense of the word. In the tank industry these crystallized as the 'Leningrad Clan' who backed Kotin and his people; the 'Kharkov Clan' whose Ukrainian members stood behind Aleksandr Morozov and his design bureau; and the 'Urals Clan' represented by those standing with Leonid Kartsev.

THREE CLANS, THREE POINTS OF VIEW

In the mid 1950s, each 'clan', as mentioned above, had staked out a specific point of view in regard to tank development: traditionalist, revolutionary, and evolutionary.

The traditionalist view was that of Zhosef Kotin and his group, which included Leningrad, Chelyabinsk, and to some degree VNII-100. Kotin had been convinced since the late 1930s that all the USSR needed was heavy tanks, starting with his KV series and then through the IS tanks to the then-current T-10 heavy tank. But Kotin ignored the fact that Western countries had developed new types of ammunition such as high explosive anti-tank and armour-piercing discarding sabot that permitted medium tanks like the M48 or Centurion to knock out heavy tanks fitted with monolithic armour protection, like that used by the T-10, at typical combat ranges.

The revolutionary approach favoured by Aleksandr Morozov was to leap ahead of possible adversaries by adopting radical new technology and concepts they had not envisioned. He began this with the first tank of his own design, the T-44 medium tank, and continued refining it as the T-54, with its powerful 100mm gun making it the best armed tank on the battlefield at the time of its introduction. Being equipped with a transverse engine to keep its short, compact components in a densely packed hull and turret, and a reliable diesel engine that was at the time only beginning to be examined

The Obiekt-140.

Obiekt-165 was a new design with a bigger turret to better accommodate the D-54T gun and its bulky ammunition. But while better with superior ergonomics for the turret crew was still not a significant step forward.

for use in NATO countries, made it a leap ahead of those tanks, in theory.

The evolutionary concept favoured by Leonid Kartsev was to build upon what had been proven in combat and in service and add capabilities as they matured or were shown to be fully viable in testing. He used this approach when he developed first a tank with a single-axis main gun stabilizer (T-54A) and then a two-axis stabilizer (T-54B), as well as add-on night combat capability with infrared searchlights and sights, and underwater driving for fording rivers with the OPVT-54B system. Since these were evolutionary changes based on known systems, they were also easily retrofitted to previous tanks then in service. All of these items proved reliable in service with proper training of crews and were popular with the Soviet Army leadership.

While the traditionalist approach was essentially moribund (Khrushchev stated on many occasions there was no more need for heavy tanks but Kotin considered that the army would still have a requirement), the other two views would form the root of competition and even minor conflict between Kharkov and Nizhny Tagil design centres until the break-up of the Soviet Union in 1991.

THE SEARCH FOR THE NEW MAIN BATTLE TANK BEGINS

In November 1951 Aleksandr Morozov was finally able to leave Plant No. 183 – the Ural Railway Wagon Production Factory (Uralvagonzavod – UVZ) – and return to take over the design bureau (Section 60) at Plant No. 75 in Kharkov. Many of his fellow designers – evacuated to Nizhny Tagil and UVZ in October 1941 – returned with him. While he managed to persuade Moscow to let him retain control of medium tank design and production, with UVZ only having a satellite function, this was not seen as conducive to the best approach to new designs. He recommended his favourite deputy, Yakov I. Baran, to take over Section 520 (the tank design bureau) at UVZ but instead the elderly A. V. Kolesnikov was named as the interim chief designer.

Kartsev had worked under Morozov since arriving in Nizhny Tagil from engineering school. They developed an interesting relationship that would define both of them until Morozov's death in 1976. Sometimes it was paternalistic, with Morozov treating Kartsev like a son; sometimes they were compatriots, and on occasion opponents; but it was always cordial in the end. Both of them did fully agree on one point: they disliked Zhosef Kotin who they considered a sycophant and political toady.

In 1953 the powers that be decided to pick a permanent new chief designer for UVZ. With the recommendation of plant manager I. V. Okunev, the selection was the now 31-year-old Leonid Kartsev. He made the rounds in Moscow for approval and, as a result, was notified he was the new chief designer on 3 March 1953 – two days before Stalin died.

Kartsev took over a design bureau numbering 120 personnel, many of whom were new graduates of various engineering academies. According to his memoirs, while he was sorting out the best personnel to make assignments, the NKVD (Narodny Kommisariat Vnutrenikh Del or People's Commissariat for Internal Affairs) paid him a visit and informed him too many of his designers were 'Yevray' – Jews. They wanted to round them up and remove them but Kartsev, backed up by Okunev, refused. Before the NKVD could take any action, Lavrenti Beria, the notorious head of the NKVD, was denounced by Nikita Khrushchev, arrested (by the Soviet Army) and subsequently shot, with the NKVD losing much of their power and influence and such warrants being cancelled. With his work force now safe, Kartsev could then concentrate on making the best assignments for his personnel.

Their first major challenge – other than perfecting the T-54 tanks then in production at the plant – was the development of the New Medium Tank (Novy Sredny Tank or NST). This began with a concept discussed at a meeting of the Ministry of Transportation Machinery (MTrM) on 20 May 1952, and formalized in Joint Resolution No. 4169-1631 of the Council of Ministers of the USSR (SM SSSR) and the Central Committee of the Communist Party (TsK VKP(b), later TsK KPSS) on 9 September 1952. The primary component of this new design was based on the use of a new high-power 100mm rifled gun, designated the D-54T. This gun was proposed by F. F. Petrov at Plant No. 9 and was to provide a massive increase in muzzle velocity and armour penetration.

The effort by Nizhny Tagil was centred on fitting the D-54T into a standard T-54 Model 1951 tank chassis, initially designated Obiekt-139 and later Obiekt-141; Kharkov proposed a wholly new vehicle to mount the gun designated Obiekt-430. This was a radical design in which a number of new concepts were proposed, specifically including a composite armour glacis with armour-fibreglass-armour panels to form the glacis and an opposed piston four-cylinder (eight-piston) two-cycle air-cooled diesel engine, designated the 4TD, to power it. This was formally authorized on 28 March 1953 by Resolution No. 928-398 of the SM SSSR.

While the UVZ plant proceeded with both Obiekt-139 and Obiekt-141 – one of many differences being the stabilizer system fitted to the D-54TS gun – early on Kartsev noted that the particularly long rounds (1,100mm) would be extremely difficult for the loader to handle in the turret of a standard T-54 tank. Therefore he proposed a new design with a larger turret to ease the problem and hopefully increase the rate of fire.

Based on the results of an initial concept meeting on 10 March 1953, both Plant No. 75 and the UVZ presented formal proposals which were accepted by the SM SSSR and authorized on 29 September 1953 by Resolution No. 2498-2031. Morozov continued to press his concept tank as Obiekt-430, but Kartsev now proposed a new design dubbed Obiekt-140. Plans and concepts were due on 1 January 1954.

Kartsev received formal permission to proceed with Obiekt-140 on 2 April 1954 per Resolution No. 598-265 of the SM SSSR. But he was having problems with the work as the chief of the experimental design shop was none other than Yakov Ionovich Baran. 'Yasha' Baran was not happy to have been left in Nizhny Tagil and there was apparently friction between Baran and Kartsev on design thinking and concepts. His proposed layout for Obiekt-140 looked quite similar to what Kharkov was offering as Obiekt-430: a low machine with six road wheels per side, three return rollers, a new type of OMSh track, and other modifications. It used a similar power plant, but coupled to a hydro-mechanical semi-automatic transmission (in that it used a fluid coupling but still needed a clutch as in the later T-80), as a standard T-54, albeit with the engine rolled forward approximately 50 degrees to lower the height of the engine deck.

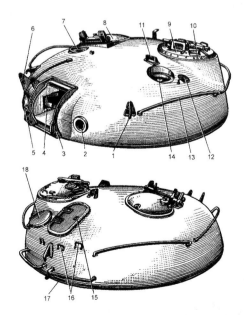

The new turret design for Obiekts-165 and 166. The big difference over the T-54 and T-55 designs was the smoother shape and the port in the rear of the turret for casing ejection.

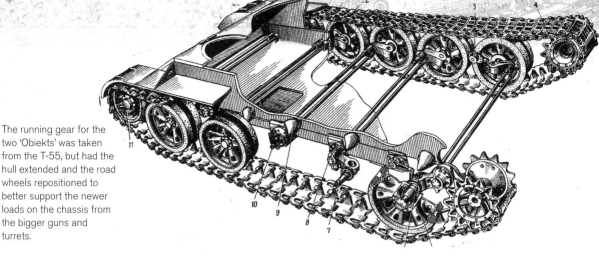

The running gear for the two 'Obiekts' was taken from the T-55, but had the hull extended and the road wheels repositioned to better support the newer loads on the chassis from the bigger guns and turrets.

Using a somewhat flimsy excuse of health problems, 'Yasha' Baran was granted a compassionate transfer back to Kharkov on 29 November 1954, and his departure heralded the end of the Kharkov era in Nizhny Tagil. Kartsev appointed his classmates I. A. Nabutovskiy and V. N. Venediktov to take over the project. Valeriy Venediktov served the same position with Kartsev as Baran had to Morozov and, from this point on, was his chief designer and partner in future tank projects.

Both designs were assessed at a meeting of the MTrM and Ministry of Defence (MO) on 22 December 1954. Their opinion was that Plant No. 75's Obiekt-430 was the better design but the design from the UVZ was more viable and could be built faster; both projects were authorized to continue.

On 30 December 1955, a meeting was held by the NTK GBTU in which both projects and work on their prototypes were examined. Both were recommended to continue, but in April 1956 the UVZ was given a critique (rumoured to be promoted by Morozov to downplay their efforts) to check the operation of the transmission, engine cooling, crew ergonomics, etc. of the Obiekt-140 tank.

While work on Obiekt-140 was progressing, Kartsev and his team decided to build a completely new prototype tank design on their own initiative that they felt would better answer the NST requirements. This tank used many essential items from the T-54 series of tanks such as the engine, transmission, five road wheels per side without return rollers, but a much larger turret and a hull-length increase of 386mm. The hull had to have lateral extensions to permit the new turret to fit but still remain within railway loading limits as required for all medium tanks. This new tank was designated Obiekt-142.

But the Baran-designed Obiekt-140 was still having massive problems, and in November 1957 Kartsev requested the termination of the project.

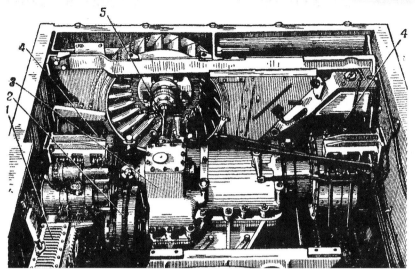

TOP The engine bay layout was nearly identical, but the larger fan required that the unit be canted backwards and a bulge placed in the rear lower plate to accommodate the design.

BELOW LEFT The layout as noted remained the same with the 'guitara' transfer case on the right side and the middle fuel tank forward of it.

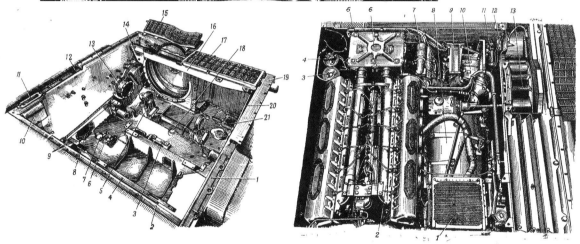

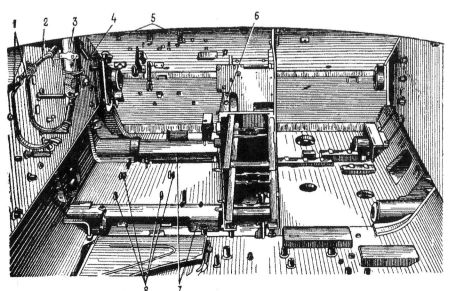

ABOVE The engine and mechanical component layout was identical to that of the T-55: engine forward and to the left, air cleaner to its right, 'guitara' on the right, transmission in the rear centre with final drives on each side, and the radiator and oil cooler in their same places.

LEFT The bow of the tank was virtually identical to the T-55 but did not have a machine gun port as the vehicle was considered a 'tank destroyer' and hence did not require one.

The stretched and reorganized hull floor pan shows the bulge for the fan and the relocated and redesigned escape hatch.

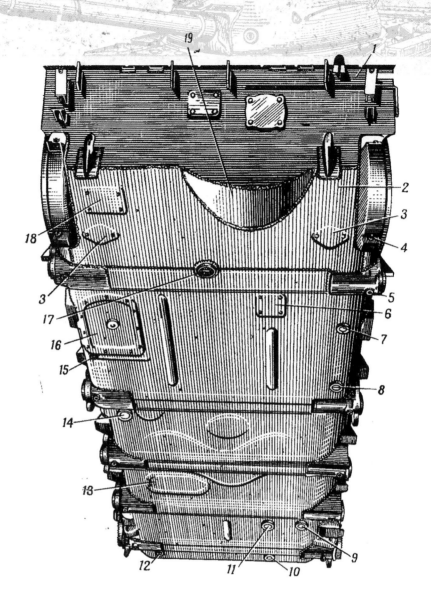

Beside the problems manifested during testing of the first two prototypes, he cited the fact that, per intelligence reports on Western developments, the tank's monolithic armour protection would not stop either HEAT (high explosive anti-tank) or APDS (armour-piercing discarding sabot) rounds from penetrating it. He did not see it as a major advance on either the T-54 or the new T-55 about to enter production.

The Obiekt-140 prototype would meantime be developed via another generation of prototypes to become the basis for the future amorphously designated T-62, which went from 'medium tank' to 'tank destroyer' to 'main battle tank' as its development for series production navigated the internal politics of the day.

LEFT A comparison of the suspension layout of the T-55 (left) and T-62 (right). Road wheels are one – gap – four and three – gap – two.

BELOW An early production T-62 on Red Square for the November Parade in 1965.

CHAPTER TWO
THE DEVELOPMENT OF THE T-62 MEDIUM TANK

MAKING THE BEST OF AN UNHAPPY SITUATION

While Kartsev was completely honest in his evaluation of the UVZ-designed Obiekt-140, this turned out to be a politically damaging move as it handed the advantage to Kharkov. On 6 June 1958, the SM SSSR passed Resolution No. 609-294 which terminated both Obiekt-140 and Obiekt-142, while authorizing the continuation of work on Obiekt-430, even though that tank was suffering a tremendous amount of development difficulties that offset its proposed advantages. Kartsev continued working on Obiekt-142, but with some changes. As it had proved to be almost impossible to operate the gun with the long ammunition rounds in the existing turret volume, the tank was now given a wholly new domed cast turret developed and produced at ChKZ in Chelyabinsk, replacing the flatter cast design used on Obiekt-140 and Obiekt-142. The new version, now designated Obiekt-165, featured a large number of changes. The overall length of the tank hull was increased, with the hull floor and engine compartment redesigned, the torsion bar positions lowered 23mm; the overall track widened 60mm; and three variants of aluminium and steel road wheels were developed. The turret race was enlarged to accommodate the new turret, which featured a new turret traversing mechanism, and a strengthened turret travel position lock. The tank also had a second glacis-mounted 7.62mm SGMT machine gun as on the T-54 tank but which had been deleted on the T-55. The Obiekt-165 was, with the exception of the main armament, the future T-62 tank. Two experimental and five pre-production Obiekt-166 tanks were built, with successful testing resulting in the Obiekt-165 being adopted for service by Minister of Defence Order No. 7 dated 9 January 1962 as the T-62A. Series production of the T-62A was planned to start from September 1963; however, there were difficulties with developing an effective armour-piercing round for the U-8TS tank gun. During testing, it was also discovered that, on firing, the release of high-pressure gases via the muzzle brake led to clouds of dust or snow, temporarily obscuring the vision of the turret crew. There were also some difficulties with the original 100mm D-54TS gun stabilizer system, which despite several variants being attempted was never cured. These factors, together with the existence of an alternative, smoothbore 115mm U-5TS for the new tank design, led to the cancellation of the T-62A tank in November 1963.

The new Obiekt-165/166 Model as proposed was basically a much-improved version of the T-55 tank, from which the new tank borrowed a great number of components. While working on this design, Kartsev proposed to the artillery designer, F. F. Petrov, that he might consider a new version of the 100mm D-54TS gun modified as a smoothbore weapon. This was in response to official praise for the new 100mm T-12 'Rapira' smoothbore anti-tank gun which had proven particularly effective in service. While proposals had been made to fit the 'Rapira' to T-55 tanks, it was quickly noted that its 1,200mm-long unitary round was physically impossible to manoeuvre inside the turret. Kartsev asked if it was possible to bore-out the D-54TS (as that gun fit into their new tank design) into a smoothbore, which Petrov agreed was technically possible while maintaining good barrel integrity. This produced a weapon some 15mm larger in bore but able to use the same propellant charge to achieve high muzzle velocity. The proposed gun – the 115mm U-5TS – received the project name 'Molot' (hammer). The new gun was the first smoothbore tank gun in the world to be introduced as a production weapon. The development of the 115mm U-5TS was accompanied by the first development of armour-piercing fin-stabilized discarding sabot (APFSDS) ammunition, which massively increased muzzle velocity to nearly 1,600m/s and armour penetration to 228–380mm (for APFSDS rounds) or 440mm (for cumulative rounds) against vertical armour plate. After the initial development work was approved, the new tank received the GABTU designation Obiekt-166.

The Soviet Ministry of Defence liked the concept and authorized UVZ to proceed with the improved T-55 design on 31 December 1958. Two weeks later, on 13 January 1959, Kartsev then proposed using only the new 115mm smoothbore tank gun in the Obiekt-165 (Obiekt-166) as its main armament in lieu of the 100mm D-54TS.

Obiekt-140 in the storage yard at Kubinka. Its main disadvantage, other than being only a minor improvement on the T-54, was the large and heavy round used for the high-power D-54T gun.

The Obiekt-140's competitor was the Obiekt-430 from Kharkov. While internally it had the same basic layout as Obiekt-140, it used the 4TD four-cylinder eight-piston two-cycle diesel engine that was unsuccessful.

Back in Kharkov, Morozov was not happy with this turn of events, as it would produce a new tank with a larger-calibre gun before his own design could be fully developed. As a result, he pressed hard for the ongoing Kharkov-designed Obiekt-430 to be the only new medium tank project accepted for development. The Soviet Ministry of Defence was faced with two rival design teams at Nizhny Tagil and Kharkov, both of which had experienced delays and technical difficulties with Kharkov pushing their design as the preferred new 'universal' tank. The NTK GBTU found a Solomon-like solution by authorizing further development of both the Obiekt-165 and the Obiekt-166, but as 'tank destroyers' rather than tanks. This was a temporary decision to further develop a combat vehicle that could support T-54 and T-55 tanks and destroy enemy tanks beyond the range limitations of these tanks. This was formalized by Resolution No. 831-371 of the SM SSSR on 21 July 1959. Even so, in a letter dated 31 August 1959, N. A. Kucherenko from the State Council on Defence Technology referred to Obiekt-166 as a tank. The T-62 'tank destroyer' later became a 'tank' after massive lobbying from Nizhny Tagil plant towards the authorities, on the simple basis that production of a more mainstream design as a tank would generate large production numbers, hence employment and income, whereas a reincarnation of the SU-122-54 in the 'tank destroyer' role would not. The T-62 being considered as a 'tank destroyer' was not developed in isolation, with other concurrent developments on the theme including the SU-100M and the SU-152 'Taran' vehicles.

Testing of the – at the time still rival – Obiekt-165 and Obiekt-166 designs continued through 1960 and 1961 with firing trials of the respective guns in the two tanks and firing testing on their hull and turret sets. The latter showed similar results to firing against the T-55. But both tanks

RIGHT An Obiekt-166 prototype in the Kubinka Museum, which became the T-62 Medium Tank. With over 19,000 T-62 tanks built, the tank became the NATO 'bogeyman' for many years.

BELOW Obiekt-432, the prototype of all future Soviet tanks with a three-man crew and an autoloader for the main gun. While it had a better engine design in the five-cylinder ten-piston 5TDF, it took until 1969 to get all of the bugs out of the design. Its delayed introduction necessitated the T-62 as a gap-filler.

suffered from a relatively low rate of fire due to one change that had been made to the tanks. Firing testing showed that, even with a mid-barrel-located bore evacuator to purge propellant gases from the turret, after three rounds fired the turret was filled with toxic smoke and the crew began to suffer due to lingering propellant gas in the shell casings.

As a result, Kartsev added an automatic shell casing ejector to the design, which attenuated both the cartridge handling and toxic smoke residue issues. This grabbed the casing out of the breech when ejected, automatically opened a port in the back of the turret, and violently ejected the casing, which landed some 7 metres behind the tank. Thereafter, the gun automatically assumed a set-loading angle to simplify loading the new round. Once the new round was in and the loader closed the breech, the gun returned to its last elevation before firing, with the overall process taking up to 15 seconds. The unitary rounds were heavy (19–22kg depending on type) and long (up to 1,100mm) so the loader could not rapidly load and ram the rounds into the breech.

At the same time as development was ongoing, the State Committee on Defence Technology (GKOT) demanded that both Obiekt-165 and 166 be fitted with the new nuclear radiation liner ('podboy') as used in the T-55A to protect the crew. Experimental work on this design was undertaken with the Obiekt-166P prototype. But while the liners could be fitted into the tanks, the reduction in available room inside the tanks prevented smooth operation of the vehicle and gunnery. After a final test report in December 1962 the idea was dismissed, albeit with some tanks later being fitted with 'nadboy' external linings. The tank crews were instead provided with anti-radiation suits.

The final stage in the development of Obiekt-166 and its acceptance over the Obiekt-165 as the future Nizhny Tagil tank design came in October 1961. The deciding vote was cast by a rather unlikely actor – Twice Hero of the Soviet Union and Marshal of Ground Troops V. Ya. Chuikov. He was something of a legend in the Red Army and was famous for his defence of Stalingrad as commander of the 62nd Army. He fervently supported Stalin's dictum of 'Ne Shagu Nazad' (not one step backward) in defence. As a result, the Red Army had held the city, albeit with frightful casualties – the 62nd Army absorbed some six to seven rifle divisions (that would have numbered 81,000 men at full strength) but which never had an available for duty strength over 33,000. For their efforts the 62nd Army became the 8th Guards Army and Chuikov became a national hero. By January 1961 he had advanced to marshal and was the commanding general of the Soviet Ground Forces.

During his time in Germany after the war, senior British liaison officers with BRIXMIS had identified three character traits that defined Chuikov. First, he was a dedicated believer in the Stalinist view of control of the Soviet Union and its way of life, and loyal to a fault to the leadership. Second, he was hardnosed to a fault as noted by his dogged defence of Stalingrad in 1942. And third, while he was not an alcoholic he was an extremely hard drinker when given the chance and prone to nasty hangovers the next day, which his subordinates learned to fear and avoid.

The latter particular trait was apparently the case on the day in 1961 when Chuikov received a briefing that the British had developed the 105mm L7

rifled tank gun, and that both the US and Federal Republic of Germany were going to mount said weapon in their new tanks, the M60 and Leopard 1, with the British also planning to so-retrofit their Centurion tanks. (He was also told the gun was going into the new French AMX-30, but that was a mistake as the French had developed their own unique 105mm smoothbore gun design.)

The upshot was that Chuikov was furious that NATO forces had potentially more powerful tank guns with longer range and more capable ammunition choices than he had available. With Kartsev and others present he asked if there was a larger-calibre gun available for Soviet tanks. He was informed that the 115mm U-5TS smoothbore was in testing but had suffered some problems as installed in the Obiekt-166 tank, which the NIIBT reported as having sheared a road-wheel mounting arm when the gun was fired. He apparently exploded in fury: 'Are you trying to smack me over the head with some sort of an excuse about a road wheel arm? You can play bad jokes on me, but *get me that gun!*' He amplified his demand with claiming he wanted it now even if it had to be strapped on the back of a pig!

Suitably humbled, the NTK GBTU representatives then asked Kartsev if he could quickly get Obiekt-166 into series production in short order. At first Kartsev refused, citing the fact that in the background UVZ had been working on Obiekt-167, an even more improved tank design. While GBTU refused to consider that, the VPK (the military production committee) at the direction of Deputy Chairman of the Council of Ministers of the Soviet Union (SM SSSR) Dmitry F. Ustinov, came to an agreement in July 1961 with I. V. Okunev to begin production of Obiekt-166 as soon as possible. As a result, on 12 August 1961, the SM SSSR passed Resolution No. 729-305, 'On the Acceptance for Service of the T-62 Medium Tank'. Thus the new tank received its formal service designation and right to existence.

However, at the same time so did Obiekt-165, which was accepted for service as the T-62A. The respective new tank guns were standardized as the 100mm U-8TS and the 115mm U-5TS (GAU designators 2A24 and 2A20 respectively). Testing was continuing on both guns in their new mounts, but testing on the U-8TS showed it was inferior to the U-5TS. Its armour-piercing projectile had a muzzle velocity of only 1,070m/s versus 1,615m/s for the APFSDS projectile of the U-5TS; and the direct fire range was 1,200m versus 1,800m. Its complete round was 34.6kg (over 76 pounds) versus 20.7kg (45.6 pounds). Armour penetration against plate set at 60 degrees from the vertical was 85mm versus 135mm at 2,000m, and was 235mm at a more typical 1,000m engagement range.

This was due to the fact it had to use an obsolescent blunt-nose armour-piercing projectile that had to be much heavier (mass x velocity – slow and heavy versus fast and light) to provide the kinetic energy needed for penetration. When the British Chieftain appeared, it was judged to be the greatest threat to Soviet Army tanks; however, only the 115mm U-5TS was assessed as being able to defeat its armour protection. This was confirmed during the Iran-Iraq War when Iraqi T-62 tank guns were able to penetrate even the frontal armour of Iranian Chieftains, after which the 'Stillbrew' armour increment was developed in the mid 1980s.

Immediately upon acceptance an establishment lot of 25 T-62 tanks were ordered into production. These tanks were built in the autumn of 1961 and sent to the Carpathian Military District for service trials in a tank unit.

While this was taking place, analysis of American tanks convinced the Soviets to again consider the option of an automatic transmission. As a result, on 25 October 1961, per Resolution No. 972-416, Plant No. 174 in Omsk was tasked with developing a T-62 tank with an automatic transmission which was then designated Obiekt-612. They did so, and offered it with options for fully automatic,

The T-62 made its maiden display to the public during the 9 May 1965 parade but it was not until the 1967 'Dnepr' exercises that the West got to see the tank in action. This tank was photographed during a Soviet parade in East Germany.

semi-automatic, and manual control of the gears; however, long-term testing proved that the design was not sufficiently durable for service, and the project was terminated in late 1965.

On 1 January 1962, UVZ shut down production for six months in order to retool for series production of the T-62 tank. One unresolved minor design detail regarding the T-62 – now again officially a 'tank' rather than a 'tank destroyer' – was whether or not it should mount the fixed 7.62mm bow machine gun as in the T-54 and T-55. But falling back on its primary 'political' if not altogether 'operational' function as a tank destroyer, the Ministry of Defence published an Order on 6 June 1962, stating the T-62 should not mount a bow machine gun. As with the then-current T-55, it was also not felt useful at the time to mount an anti-aircraft machine gun due to the use of jet-engine fighter-bombers by both NATO and the Warsaw Pact, so the tank was originally built with no provision for a tourelle-type ring mount.

Meanwhile back in Nizhny Tagil, UVZ was directionally still at a bit of a loss about the T-62 versus T-62A production order. The SM SSSR reinforced its decision of 12 August 1961 with Resolution No. 1096-460 dated 22 October 1962, which stated that both tanks would be built in parallel. That instruction was again abruptly changed on 27 December when the same Council of Ministers ordered production of all medium tanks to convert over to produce the Kharkov-designed Obiekt-432 tank.

The Obiekt-432, better known as the early series production T-64, was the pet project of Deputy Defence Minister Ustinov. While Kartsev and his team had been working on the T-62, Morozov and his team had taken the unsuccessful Obiekt-430 and redesigned it with new components and concepts. The new design, Obiekt-432, included many changes – it added a cross-turret rangefinder, a better-designed 5TDF two-stroke diesel engine that promised to produce 700hp, composite armour on the glacis, a similar 115mm

2A21 tank gun to that of the Obiekt-166, but also introducing a radical new concept – a turret-mounted 30-rounds-capacity autoloader allowing elimination of one crew member, namely the loader. The autoloader used separate loading ammunition with partially combustible propellant charges.

In parallel with the work on the T-62, Kartsev, Nabutovsky and Venediktov had disassembled and rebuilt the Obiekt-140 tank as a test mule for testing new running gear variations. The tank was subsequently redesigned by UVZ and offered to the Soviet Ministry of Defence as Obiekt-167.

The new tank was a significantly modified design, and all it kept from the previous tank was its six-road-wheel/three-return-roller running gear and slanted engine layout. The turret was directly taken from the T-62. The Obiekt-167 design involved reducing the armour protection down to minimal acceptable level. For example, the loader's hatch armour thickness was reduced to 20mm, while the hull rear armour plate was only 30mm – vulnerable to even 14.5mm calibre armour-piercing ammunition.

The provision of 'podboy' radiation lining within the fighting compartment improved potential NBC battlefield survivability, but it significantly reduced visibility from within the tank, by 22 per cent for commander, 16 per cent for the driver-mechanic, and most significantly 64 per cent for the gunner, and 77 per cent for the loader. Testing in 1962 showed the Obiekt-167 and its new components to be worthy of further development. Among other developments UVZ later added an autoloader of their own design dubbed 'Zhelud' (actually the name of the design theme rather than the autoloader itself, though Kartsev referred to the autoloader by this name) and adapted the tank to use it with the same 115mm 2A21 gun then fitted to Obiekt-432 (as the Obiekt-167M) This device used 21 below-the-floor two-chamber cassettes holding projectiles on the bottom and propellant on the top, protected under the turret floor. The 30-round device in the Kharkov tank stowed all of the propellant charges in an open ring around the inside of the turret, which Kartsev looked at as being exceedingly dangerous. The Obiekt-167M conceptual design was ultimately rejected by GKOT in May 1964 as being a 'poor man's' T-64.

The non-autoloader version of the Obiekt-167 tank meantime underwent competitive testing with an Obiekt-432 prototype, and even GKOT had to admit it was superior to both the existing T-55 and the new T-62. It was also more in line with what the military wanted. Alas, it was not what Ustinov wanted, and he still remembered Kartsev's earlier withdrawing of the Obiekt-140 as not suitable. This was in spite of the Obiekt-430 proving to be no better, even though he (Ustinov) had given the latter his blessing. After much politicking, Ustinov won out with the aforementioned December

The T-62 had all the fittings of the late production T-55, including the TDA thermal smoke generator system, which directed fuel straight into the exhaust system

resolution to have all tank plants produce the Kharkov-designed Obiekt-432 and the fate of the Obiekt-167 appeared sealed.

Obiekt-432 was, however, still in a very raw state – suffering what the Russians call 'detskye bolezny' (children's illnesses) or teething troubles, so none of the power brokers wanted to bank everything on its imminent success, which was in any event not the Soviet norm. The older T-55 and new T-62 both continued in series production. As regards the choice of development direction of the T-62 versus the T-62A, that was solved by two SM SSSR resolutions: No. 2235rs* on 28 October 1963 confirmed the T-62 would be the only variant built; No. 2238rs the next day terminated production of the T-62A. In the end only five production models of the latter tank were ever built.

While Ustinov and the Army still argued over the protracted Obiekt-432 programme, Kartsev and his design team at UVZ continued to work on both the T-62 and Obiekt-167. On 26 February 1964, the NTK GKOT approved a proposal to upgrade Obiekt-167 with the newly proposed 125mm D-81T gun and also to use the 'Zhelud' autoloader and a 780hp engine. Now dubbed Obiekt-167M, this tank was considered to be the prospective T-62B tank if approved. Ustinov rejected the proposal in May 1964 as described above.

*   RS – classification for secret; SS is sovershenno sekrentno or most secret/top secret.

There followed a proposal to install the new 700hp GTD-3T tank turbine engine in both the T-62 and Obiekt-167. This was based on a Ka-25 helicopter engine, and the Obiekt-167T, so-fitted, began trials on 18 January 1965. But the designers at Nizhny Tagil did not consider there was a future in this concept due to excessive fuel consumption, and Kartsev was personally against it. Development efforts on the Obiekt-167T ended on 10 February 1965.

The next proposition was the Obiekt-166M, a combination of standard T-62 components such as the hull and turret and elements of the Obiekt-167 suspension, the V-36 version of the V-2 diesel engine, and including the new RMSh rubber-bushed tracks, which provided a significantly longer lifespan. Testing in January 1966 showed this design to have superior mobility to the production T-62, but once again Ustinov gave it a thumbs down, albeit as he still wanted to use a turbine engine installation, the GTD-3T unit was modified and refitted as the GTD-3TU engine and once again underwent testing. This variant was also ultimately rejected.

In September 1966 the UVZ proposed building the T-62 with the 115mm 2A21 gun and the 'Zhelud' theme autoloader. This proposal was subsequently altered to instead use the 125mm D-81T (GAU index 2A26) tank gun, and upon receipt of a prototype gun a prototype T-62 with those systems was assembled. On 5 November 1967, this tank was demonstrated to the Minister of Transport Machinery S. V. Zverev. He was initially furious that Nizhny Tagil had developed a new autoloader and had not used the one proposed for the next Kharkov tank, Obiekt-434 (the future T-64A). The new design was now a 28-round open 'cabin'-type (to the Russians – as it was around the circumference of the turret floor with shells sticking up like palisades) autoloader that replaced the 30-round one with the 115mm gun in the Obiekt-432 (later T-64) tank. But when demonstrated for the minister the functioning of the 'Zhelud' autoloader was so quick and smooth that instead he recommended Kharkov adopt the Nizhny Tagil design for Obiekt-434. Kharkov turned this kind suggestion down for two reasons: namely that it only held 19 rounds versus 28, and, perhaps ultimately more significant, the typical engineering rejection – NIH – 'not invented here', in this case by Kharkov.

Although the Obiekt-167 prototypes investigated a range of potential design improvements compared with the T-62, the Obiekt-167 had reduced armour protection, an element of restricted anti-radiation protection, lower firing accuracy, lack of rangefinder (or the ability to install it), and a significantly lower number of rounds, albeit in an autoloader carousel. For the larger Obiekt-167 to have armour protection improved up to the level of the Obiekt-432 (T-64), the tank would have a combat weight in excess of 40

RIGHT A rebuilt early model T-62 in a museum with the later three-section snorkel and RMSh tracks. These items were added to the T-62 soon after they were approved.

BELOW An interim production T-62 Model 1967 tank with the new engine deck and covers for the radiator grilles at a museum site. These changes meant the tank crew could prepare it for wading or fording with only their own labour.

metric tonnes. The largest Soviet transport aircraft of the day, the An-22, had an 80-metric-tonne load capacity, and the weight restriction was in part to enable the transport of two Obiekt-167 tanks in a single aircraft.

Meantime, as myriad T-62 variants and potential improvements were developed and tested, the T-62 itself remained relatively enigmatic. Though the existence of the T-62 was known abroad, not least during its excursion into Czechoslovakia in 1968, the tank was proving more elusive to foreign observation than most Soviet tanks. There were few photographs of the tank in service during the 1960s, even though the tank had debuted on Red Square on 9 May 1965.

In 1969 the Soviet Ministry of Defence revisited the concept of an anti-aircraft machine gun on medium tanks. The reason was simple to understand: while such weapons still could not effectively engage jet-engine aircraft, the new threat came from attack helicopters armed with rockets or anti-tank guided missiles that could destroy tanks from a low hover. The first Soviet tanks to receive anti-aircraft machine guns were new production T-55 and T-55A types – with a retrofit kit available for some users – but the T-62 did not receive this feature until 1972. This was because the T-62 used a single-piece cast turret, and so a new turret had to be designed and new moulds produced and the result tested, rather than simply modifying the T-54 and T-55 type turret with welded-in turret roof sections. The turret design featured a ring mount on the loader's hatch for a 12.7mm DShKM heavy machine gun.

Production of the T-62 tank continued until 1973 when the production plant closed down to retool for their next new tank – Obiekt-172M, which became the production T-72. The Obiekt-172M owed much of its design to the shelved Obiekt-167 and Obiekt-167M, and it could be argued with good reason that the Obiekt-167M tank, armed with its 125mm gun and 'Zhelud' theme autoloader, and its six-road-wheel suspension with three return rollers and RMSh tracks, was actually the functional prototype of the T-72.

A total of 19,019 series production T-62 tanks were built over the tank's 11-year production run in the Soviet Union. (The Chinese WZ-122 and Korean Ch'onma tanks were later developments and will be covered in Chapter 4 on derivative vehicles and variants.)

The T-62 was from an economic standpoint a particularly viable tank to manufacture – it took 5,855 hours to build a T-62 Model 1961 and cost only 62,000 Roubles – just under 25 per cent of the time needed for an Obiekt-432 (T-64) tank (22,564 hours) and 33 per cent of the latter tank's cost (194,000 Roubles). From an operational perspective, a complete ammunition reload operation took 518 individual tasks by a four-man crew as opposed to 852 by the three-man crew of the Kharkov machine, albeit the former involved unitary rounds and the latter separate loading of projectile and charge cartridges.

The T-62 was a popular tank with Russian tank crews, relatively easy to operate and maintain, and reliable in service. But by the late 1970s and early 1980s the T-62 had served its time as a first-line Soviet main battle tank, and was now being replaced by the T-64A (and T-64B), the T-72A (and T-72B), and the T-80B tanks. Initially in the forward area, they were cascaded down to second-line Soviet formations such as divisions or to forward area independent tank regiments. These were formations of around 148–150 tanks that were basically replacement battalions for tanks lost during initial combat by first-line divisions. As more of the new tanks flowed forward, they were brought back and given to lower and lower readiness classification units. The T-62 would, however, experience a new lease of life due to combat experience in Afghanistan.

A Resolution of the SM SSSR dated 25 July 1981, one and a half years into the Afghan war, directed that the T-55/T-55A and T-62 tanks be

A late production T-62 Model 1972 with the new 12.7mm AA MG mount in the US 7th Army Opposing Forces (OPFOR) training detachment at Grafenwohr, Germany. It was used as it was a 'runner' and is fitted with Velcro straps for MILES laser simulation fire training equipment.

upgraded with a number of improvements and modernizations to make them more suited to modern combat. These included new fire controls, a laser rangefinder, supplemental passive armour (the so-called BDD package) for the hull and turret, more powerful engines, steel reinforced rubberized fabric side skirts, more dynamic suspension, and the addition of a through-the-bore anti-tank missile capability. Initially 785 T-62 tanks were to be modified to this standard over five years, becoming the T-62M when fitted with the ATGM (anti-tank guided missile) capability and T-62M-1 without it. There were several 'M' configurations, similarly numbered with the detail right down to where the hyphens were placed, as follows:

- T-62M – full set of improvements, V-55U engine
- T-62M1 – additional armour package, V-55U engine, etc. but no ATGM complex
- T-62M-1 – same with V-46M-5 engine (distinguished by the external air filter on right side)
- T-62M1-1 – M1 with V-46M-5 engine
- T-62M1-2 – M1 without additional armour package including additional floor armour
- T-62M1-2-1 – M1-2 with V-46M-5 engine

The rather complex set of variants and sub-variants was as a result of the cost of installing the ATGM system (as later also happened with the T-72B and T-72B1), hence the differentiation for tanks not so-fitted, while the other sub-variants were added due to differing technical capabilities of different tank repair plants, and the availability of components, etc.

In 1983 it was proposed to fit the T-62 with the 'Drozd' anti-tank defence projectile active protection, consisting of radar, a ballistic computer, and eight launcher tubes for anti-projectile munitions. While this system was reportedly fitted to some 700 T-55 and T-55A tanks, to date there is no definitive information on how many T-62s were fitted with it, though the number would appear to have been minimal. T-62M tanks fitted with the 'Drozd' system were designated T-62MD and MD-1.

Finally, in 1985 some T-62M tanks were upgraded with the new 'Kontakt-1' explosive reactive armour (ERA) on their hulls, turrets and side skirts. During the war in Afghanistan, some T-62 tanks were fitted with 'reshetka' grille armour, which was fitted more commonly for defence in combat in built-up areas during the war in Chechnya in the following decade.

The T-62 was officially removed from service with the Russian Army in 2013 by order of the Russian Ministry of Defence, having served reliably in the Soviet and latterly in the Russian Army for five decades. At that time, there remained approximately 2,500 T-62 tanks in strategic storage, which was reduced to 900 due to the balance present in the Russian Federation being cut up for scrap. The Russian MVD (Interior Ministry) had also continued to use a small number of T-62 tanks but these are now also out of service. This leaves some of the former Soviet republics, as well as 31 different

TOP LEFT A T-62M series tank on a flatcar for movement showing its new hull floor, glacis and turret armour protection. It has the laser rangefinder but since the sight cannot be seen it is not known if it is an M1 with the ATGM (anti-tank guided missile) or an M1 without it.

LEFT A T-62MV, the ultimate Soviet model of the tank, sporting its set of 'Kontakt-1' explosive reactive armour 'bricks'. This tank, a Ukrainian rebuild, also has the 1K13-41 sight for the 'Sheksna' missile and fire control system.

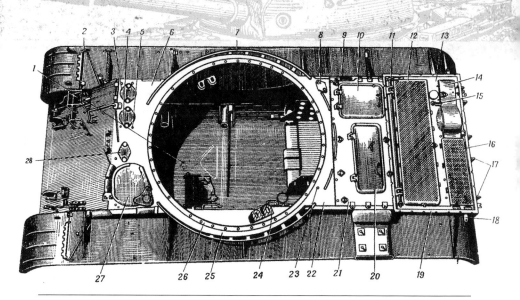

ABOVE The manual illustration of a T-62 Model 1961 with the turret removed. This clearly shows the early tanks were essentially a 'long body' version of the T-55.
BELOW The hull of the T-62, showing that it copied the same road-wheel arrangement of the T-55 (four trailing arms, one leading arm) but with new spacing.

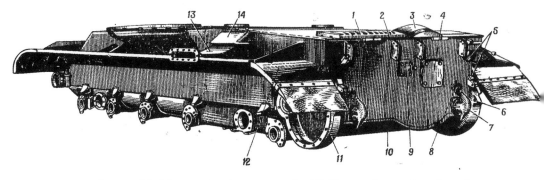

countries worldwide continuing to use the T-62, nearly six decades after it entered production – not a bad record for a tank with an initially maligned reputation from a NATO perspective.

Meanwhile, the 900 Russian T-62 tanks that had remained in strategic storage and not been subject to the cutting blowtorch were recently resurrected, as Russian concepts with regard to obsolescent tanks – and potential threats – again changed in the 21st century. A large number of T-62 tanks of various modifications have been removed from storage, rebuilt, and are to be used for reserve driver-mechanic training. A consignment of rebuilt T-62M and MV tanks were sent to the Syrian Arab Army in summer 2019. And in the Russian Federation the mounting of a current generation ATGM system on the T-62 chassis is being considered to extend the tank's viability. At the end of the second decade of the 21st century, at a time when politicians worldwide have not let a 'good crisis' go to waste, the Russian

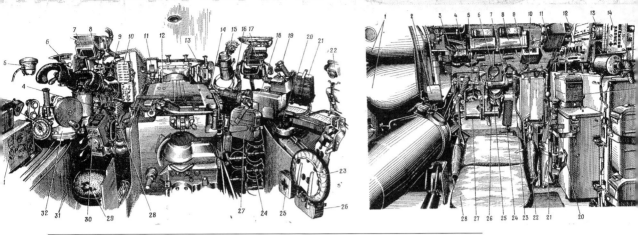

ABOVE LEFT The gunner's position in the T-62 Model 1961. This was the first Soviet tank to get 'Cadillac' controls for the operation of the gun and firing controls. This tank apparently does have the later modified guard around the breech to prevent injury from the automatic casing ejector system.
ABOVE RIGHT The driver/mechanic's compartment in the T-62. It is nearly identical to the T-55 but no longer has the machine gun and ammunition mount to his right nor the guard protecting him from the cycling bolt on the gun. Note that the seat goes up and down but does not have front-to-rear traverse; it does fold flat so the driver can exit the tank via the turret or emergency hatch.

Federation has adopted the same principle and not let a 'good tank' go to waste. The T-62 is a design 'survivor', the service record of which equates to that of a British Mk V first used in 1916 still operating around the world in 1976 … not bad for a tank that was often maligned when first encountered en-masse abroad in 1973, and then in non-Soviet hands, based on which use many assumptions were made as to the tank's true capability. By 2020, the T-62 had long outlived its original reputation (and some of its successors) and had taken its rightful place in Soviet tank development history as the last of the 'simple' Soviet medium/main battle tanks.

Longitudinal cross-section of a T-62 Model 1961 showing the layout of the tank. Thanks to the longer hull and larger turret ring, more ammunition could be stowed up against the firewall than in the T-55.

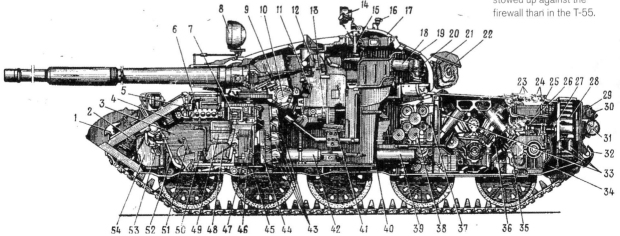

CHAPTER THREE

DESCRIPTION OF THE T-62 MAIN BATTLE TANK AND ITS VARIANTS

OBIEKT-142 (OBIEKT-165 PROTOTYPE)

The initial effort from the UVZ that yielded the T-62 Medium Tank was centred on the Obiekt-142 prototype. This tank used standard T-55 components but changed over to a new hull that was 386mm longer than the T-55. It was fitted with the much wider turret from Obiekt-140 in order to mount the 100mm D-54TS gun and support it; the turret race was expanded from 1,816mm in diameter to 2,245mm. As a result the hull, like that of Obiekt-140, bulged out above the fender line to provide hull fillets to support the new turret. This feature precluded the use of a full set of fender fuel tanks as found in the T-54 and T-55 as well as the standard spare parts/tools/equipment (ZIP) bins from those tanks. It also retained the 12.7mm DShKM heavy machine gun mount over the loader's hatch.

The hull was similar in design to that of the T-55 but had the five road-wheel stations rearranged to better distribute the weight of the new turret and gun. When the T-62 was first seen by Western observers along with the rarely spotted SU-122-54, many thought that the latter was a self-propelled 130mm gun based on the T-62 chassis and not a T-54-based vehicle as they had similar road-wheel positions. This misconception was erroneously carried by several Western military intelligence manuals for many years. The new tank had four blade-type rotary shock absorbers, one at each corner of the suspension on road-wheel stations 1 and 5. There were no return rollers, but standard T-55 idlers and 13-tooth drive sprockets were used, as were OMSh tracks. Due to the longer hull the tank now used a total of 97 links per side versus the 90 of the T-55.

The only major change to the hull profile of the new tank as compared with the T-55 was at the rear of the hull. The longer engine deck now slanted downward at an angle of 4 degrees from the horizontal and joined its stern plate at a 90-degree angle; the result was that the rear plate also had a 4-degree rearward angle from the vertical. The resulting plate was shorter than that of the T-55, and due to other changes the seminal bulge to accommodate the cooling fan had to be added to the lower rear plate as well.

The turret replicated the engineering used on the Obiekt-140 in that it was completely cast. There was a flattened area at the

rear for the commander's and loader's hatches, and also a massive ventilator fan at the rear due to problems with propellant gases from the D-54TS gun. It did introduce the ejector hatch for the 100mm casings.

Total fuel capacity for the vehicle was 1,000 litres. The tank also mounted the TDA thermal smoke generator device from the T-55 in its exhaust system as well as fittings to permit it to drive across underwater obstacles, but not the standard fittings found in the OPVT-54B system then in use by the T-54B and the T-55. Provision was made to fit the infrared searchlights and sights for night combat then in use on those tanks but only the sight and headlight seem to have been fitted to the prototype. Although the Obiekt-142 project was cancelled, the concepts and developments considered in the design were reworked by the factory to become the Obiekt-165 prototype.

T-62A MAIN BATTLE TANK (OBIEKT-165)

The final prototype in the development of the T-62 medium/main battle tank was the Obiekt-165 (T-62A), which was developed to prototype stage in 1958. The Obiekt-165 was armed with the 100mm D-54TS tank gun with its distinctive multi-baffle muzzle brake from the earlier Obiekt-140 in a modified turret and mounted on a reworked hull.

There were in fact two main Obiekt-165 prototypes, the M-1958 and the M-1959 and several specialized derivatives. The original M-1958 prototype mounted the turret from the Obiekt-140 and a hull similar to the Obiekt-150. Armament consisted of a 100mm D-54TS (2A24) gun with 'Kometa' (Comet) stabilizer system, and two 7.62mm SGMTs, one coaxial in the turret and the other one in the glacis. TSh2A day and TPN-1 night sights were fitted, as was a PAZ overpressure system. Power was provided by a standard V-55 engine developing 580hp. The tank had a crew of four. The later M-1959 prototype had a new cast turret as per the series production T-62, and L2 'Luna' infrared projector, TPKUB day sight, TKN-2 combination vision device with OU-3, and a Mk 4 vision device set for the loader. The modified prototype also had a pneumatic system to clean the driver-mechanic's vision devices, a TPU-120 intercom and a GPK-48 land navigation system. A PPO fire-fighting system was fitted. The tanks were otherwise identical as described below.

The modified Obiekt-142 hull was, as used on the Obiekt-165, now much closer in design to the T-55 in that it only needed armour fillets in the area of the turret race to support the wider turret instead of a completely bulged upper hull. This meant it could now use standard T-55 fittings on its fenders.

The major difference between the Obiekt-165 and the earlier Obiekt-142 was a completely new cast turret (on the later M-1959 prototype) with an upward slope from the front to the rear and smoothly cast-in mounts for the commander's cupola and loader's hatch. Based on then-current belief that an anti-aircraft machine gun (AAMG) was no longer useful, it was eliminated, resulting in a smooth curve on the right side of the turret. It had a slight forward bulge of thickened armour at the front of the turret around the gunner's telescopic sight and the coaxial machine gun aperture. It mounted the complete T-54B/T-55 infrared sighting suite with the commander's and gunner's searchlights and sights, with the gunner's L-2 searchlight using the articulated platform mount then being fielded on current production T-55 tanks.

The OPVT (Oborudovanie Podvodnogo Vozhdeniya Tankov) underwater driving equipment now matched the OPVT-155 equipment then in use on new production T-55s, which used a small combing around the radiator air intake and exhaust grilles vice the brackets used on the OPVT-54B system. It carried mounts at the rear of the hull for the standard brackets for 200-litre auxiliary fuel tanks as well as stowing the two-section snorkel and also an unditching log.

The interior of the tank was rearranged to accommodate the new gun and its ammunition. The forward 'stellazh' fuel tank/ammo racks were modified to hold only eight rounds each (16 total), and the new firewall and extended fighting compartment permitted 20 rounds to be stored against the firewall in fast-open clips. Two more were mounted on the right side of the fighting compartment and two were stowed at the rear of the turret for a total of 40 rounds. But unlike the T-55 only 1,000 rounds of 7.62mm ammunition were carried for the single SGMT machine gun.

The 100mm D-54TS (2A24) tank gun was a 100mm rifled gun with a 58.4-calibre long-barrel fitted with both a long bore evacuator and a three-baffle muzzle brake. It used the two-axis 'Meteor' stabilizer system and was provided with a TSh-2-41 direct fire sight. Communications consisted of an R-113 VHF FM transceiver and the R-120 tank intercom device (TPU).

With the exception of the armament, the Obiekt-165 was identical in almost all respects to the Obiekt-166, which became the production T-62. The Obiekt-165 tank prototype weighed 36.8 metric tonnes.

After a long and protracted development history, it was ultimately determined that the 100mm D-54TS (service designation U-8TS or GAU 2A24) was a development 'tupik' or dead end and would not be developed further as a viable gun for use on the battlefield. Also, with the 115mm U-5TS-armed Obiekt-166 (T-62) having been accepted for series production, it eclipsed the 'rival' Obiekt-165 (T-62A) developed in parallel. In

The prototype Obiekt-166 with the 115mm U-5TS gun was accepted as the T-62 'tank destroyer' due to problems with the Obiekt-432 (T-64) tank.

Obiekt-166M – one of the proposed variants of an improved T-62 Model. It used a modified Obiekt-167 running gear with other improvements from the Obiekt-167 but was not accepted for series production.

consequence only a pre-series batch of five T-62A tanks were built before production was terminated. Another reason that the Obiekt-165 (T-62A) was terminated was that at the time the rival Obiekt-430 (which would, via the Obiekt-432, become the T-64 main battle tank) was very much expected at the time to eclipse both the Obiekt-165 (T-62A) and Obiekt-166 (T-62) designs in production and service.

As mentioned, the Obiekt-165 was a family of prototypes and experimental developments rather than a single tank prototype. Other variants developed included the Obiekt-165 command variant developed in 1960, and the Obiekt-165P with an improved PAZ nuclear protection overpressure system. The Obiekt-165M was developed to prototype stage in 1965, long after the Obiekt-165 had been abandoned in favour of the Obiekt-166 as the series production T-62, with a modified Obiekt-167 chassis with only five road wheels, a V-36 engine developing 580hp and a new OPVT system.

T-62 MODEL 1961 MAIN BATTLE TANK (OBIEKT-166)

The T-62 Model 1961 initial production tanks were virtually identical to the T-62A with the exception of the replacement of its 100mm U-8TS rifled gun with the 115mm U-5TS (GAU 2A20) smoothbore gun. The new smoothbore 115mm U-5TS gun was at the heart of the new design, with the combination of gun and new armour-piercing fin-stabilized discarding sabot (APFSDS) ammunition providing a higher muzzle velocity with less wear than a conventional rifled tank gun.

Ammunition stowage was the same with a nominal breakdown of ammunition as follows: 16 high explosive-fragmentation rounds, 8 high explosive anti-tank rounds, and 16 armour-piercing fin-stabilized discarding sabot rounds, total carried 40 rounds. The originally specified SMGT machine gun now received 2,500 rounds of ammunition. It also carried a folding AK-47 rifle with 120 rounds and ten F-1 hand grenades.

RIGHT The Obiekt-142 (see page 37) was one of the first development steps between the T-55 and production T-62, with a lengthened hull, rearranged road-wheel stations, and a new turret closely resembling that used on the later production T-62, armed with a 100mm D-54TS gun.

BELOW RIGHT The turbine powered Obiekt-167 variant. From this angle the only way to tell it from the Obiekt-167 version is the lack of an exhaust outlet on the left rear fender.

The U-5TS, nicknamed 'Molot' (hammer), had a 52.6-calibre-long barrel fitted with a bore evacuator but no muzzle brake; it was assigned ballistic table 41. Its direct fire telescopic sight was the TSh2B-41 (later the improved TSh2B-41A) and its periscopic sight was the TPN-1-41-11. Indirect fire was possible with a lateral angle indicator and an azimuth table inside the turret. Direct fire range was 4,000 metres (effective range was 2,100 metres) and indirect fire range, limited by elevation, was 5,800 metres. It was fitted with the 2Eh15 'Meteor' two-axis gun stabilizer.

In order to clear the turret of the particularly long 115mm spent shell cases, and prevent the need for the gunner to handle them, the T-62, as with the T-62A, was fitted with an automatic shell casing ejector for the main armament. This device automatically grabbed the expended casing and simultaneously opened a sprung hatch in the rear of the turret, violently ejecting the casing. The gun stabilizer system then automatically moved the gun into the loading position angle (2 degrees 30 minutes to 4 degrees 30 minutes elevation to receive a new round). When the loader chambered the round and closed the breech, the gun went back to its last firing elevation.

The commander received the new TKN-2 (TKN-3 from 1963) commander's viewer/sight. His cupola was identical to the one used on the T-55 tank.

(1) This composite walk-around of three different T-62 Model 1961 tanks provides the best overall coverage of the tank design.

(2) This tank is serial number 305Vxxxx which was a May 1963 production tank. It is missing its auxiliary fuel tanks, mounts and the snorkel.

(3) Proper tension of the tracks locates them about 80mm above the centre road wheel. This tank has been updated with the later three-section snorkel.

(4) This tank has similar tension but has been 'spruced up' with white paint. The mounting for the OPVT flapper valve on the exhaust is highlighted.

(5) Three-quarters rear view showing the rear of the fenders and mud flaps; the T-62 had a flat rear to the fender with wraparound rubber mud flaps, which was unique to it. T-62s nearly all mounted four stowage bins on the left, with the third one housing bore cleaning supplies for the main gun and the last one the main searchlight when dismounted.

(6) Close-up of the exhaust outlet. The bolt holes and studs were for the reserve oil tank.

(7) Stern plate with all elements missing. This tank has tubing welded to it at the top which was normally used to shield wires running to auxiliary equipment such as smoke canisters and mine-trawl path markers.

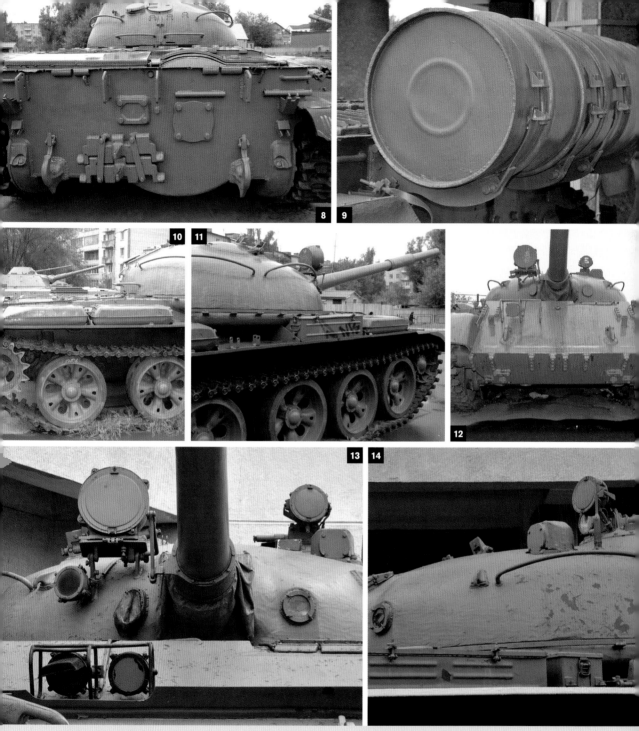

(8) Another T-62 stern plate, showing the mounting for the RMSh spare tracks as well. The bulge for the tilted fan mount is clearly seen.

(9) The twin 200-litre auxiliary fuel tanks are shown in place. The unditching log mounts are present but the log is not.

(10) The two rear 95-litre external tanks were in the same place as on the T-55 and plumbed into the fuel system in the same way.

(11) Some tanks also had two smaller bars fitted to support the canvas used for garrison storage of the tank. T-62s mounted one L-shaped stowage bin and another 95-litre tank forward on their right fenders. The idlers on all T-62s were the later T-55 'fluted' design with extensions to provide better support for the tracks.

(12) The glacis was a straight weld with lower glacis overlapping the upper one. This tank is missing its splash board but does mount the fittings for attaching mine trawls or a bulldozer blade.

(13) This tank has both glacis-mounted lights in place with the light positions reversed.

(14) A slightly different arrangement can be seen on this tank, with a small bin and two spare track links on the fender vice the first stowage bin. Also visible are the brackets and strip used to protect the turret race from shell fragments.

(15) Rear view of the turret showing its ventilator and the ejector door for shell casings. This one also has all of the tie-down brackets in place for the storage tarpaulin. T-62s had only three lifting lugs for removal of the turret – one on each 'cheek' and one right in the middle at the rear. Also visible is the position light directly above the ejector door.

(16) Right-side shell fragment guard and the connectors for holding the front and rear tow cables in place when mounted.

(17) T-62s had a round main gun sight aperture, which often had the fording cover (clear glass) fixed in place. This one has been plated over.

(18) In addition to his day and night sights, the gunner also had a standard TPN-165 viewer for his use.

(19) Like the late T-55 cupolas, the T-62 commander's cupola did away with the rear-facing prismatic viewer. It did retain the flare pistol or flag port.

(20) The front marker lights for night use faced forward and also to the rear at a 45-degree angle for short-range visibility of the tank's position.

(21) The cable heads were usually attached to the tow hooks with a snap-lock device to keep them from slipping out.

(22) Left-hand tow hook installation and the splash board.
(23) Left forward and midships stowage bins.
(24) Left rear stowage bins.
(25) Searchlight stowage bin showing its locking clasps.
(26) The right side showing the tow cables fixed to their mounts and the hatch cover for the radiator fan. The fuel lines from the three 95-litre tanks feed into the hull near the vent for the 'guitara' on the front right side of the engine compartment.

(27) An oil pump was part of the basic issue items for the tank, but in most cases was stored inside one of the larger bins. Here an early one is a 'stand-alone' on the right fender.
(28) This tank has had its radiator intake and exhaust grilles permanently sealed with sheet steel, but the large number of lifting rings and bolts used to attach the engine deck and radiator deck are easily seen as well as the OPVT framework.

(29) The cooling vent for the 'guitara' transfer case is seen here, but the fuel lines have been removed. The two openings where they entered the hull are visible.

(30) The driver's hatch is identical to that of the T-55. The hose running to the front of the two viewers is a washer device to clean them when covered with mud or dust.

(31) Rear view showing a tank with the radiator grille mesh still in place. The slot visible at the centre on the left side of the turret to the right of the shell fragment guard is where the bilge pump exits the hull just under the rear edge of the turret.

(32) Just visible here under the edge of the turret is the bilge pump exit.

(33) The ejector door here is welded shut, but this shows its rectangular shape.

(34) The location of the marker light assembly is clearly seen here.

(35) The loader's hatch is very simple with only a port for using the opening wrench on its outer surface. He is also provided with an MK-4 viewer in front of his hatch.

(36) The muzzle of the 115mm gun is thickened for protection but does not have a collar. The details on the bore evacuator are also visible.

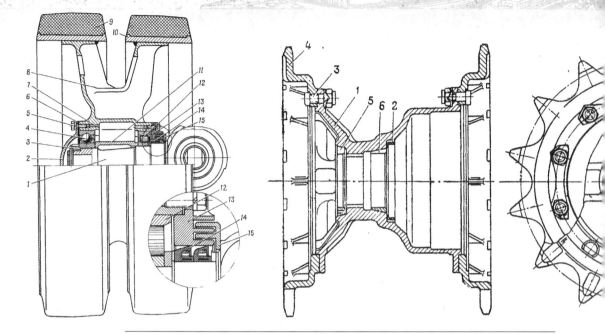

ABOVE LEFT The 'starfish' wheel sets used on the T-62 were similar to those used on the T-55 in that they were cast in one piece, but the first and fifth wheel stations had larger bearings similar to the later first and last road-wheel stations on the T-55.
ABOVE RIGHT The early OMSh tracks used a 13-tooth drive wheel, but when the tank adopted the RMSh rubber-bushed tracks they changed to a 14-tooth driver as shown here.
BELOW LEFT The OMSh tracks on an early production T-62.
BELOW RIGHT The RMSh tracks on the driver showing the pin mounts engaging the drive teeth.

The hull armour thickness was similar to that of the T-55; with a 100mm upper glacis set at 60 degrees from the vertical and a lower glacis of the same thickness set at 50 degrees from the vertical. As it was cast, the thickness of the turret varied from 191mm at the front to 183mm at the lower sides and 65mm at the rear. Side armour was 80mm except in the areas of the turret race bulge, but as that was sloped it was probably close to the same equivalent thickness.

Running gear was taken from the T-55 with slightly improved shock absorbers and a track run, like that of the T-62A, seven OMSh links longer at 97 links per side.

The tank was also fitted with the OPVT-155 underwater driving system consisting of covers over the radiator air intakes and exhaust, a flapper for the engine exhaust, seals for openings in the hull and between the turret and hull, a bilge pump, and a two-section snorkel carried under the auxiliary fuel tanks at the rear of the hull.

The tank was provided with three headlights – an FG-100 with infrared lens and an FG-102 white light with blackout mask, another fixed light on the main searchlight bracket, a rear-facing marker light with red lens and masks, an L-2 main searchlight with infrared lens, and an OU-3 commander's infrared searchlight. Marker lights were provided at the front of the hull with translucent white lenses and at the rear of the hull and rear of the turret with translucent red lenses. The electrical system was 24–26 volts using either storage batteries or a 6.5-kilowatt generator.

A number of T-62 tanks produced were fitted with the glacis mounts (four upper and eight lower) for fitting either the KMT-4M or KMT-5M mine trawls for mine clearing, as well as the BTU-55 bulldozer blade assembly. (They could also fit newer devices such as the later KMT-7.)

As with all Soviet tanks, the T-62 continued to evolve over its production life.

T-62 Model 1962: Starting in March a collar was added around the commander's cupola to protect it from shell fragments and bullet splash. The ring was 10mm thick and 20mm high. In November the TDA smoke-generating apparatus was given a sealed pump to ensure better smoke production. Also, a special rubber buffer with a steel cover was added over the torsion bar/road wheel arm joints to protect them from bullets and shrapnel. Side facing marker lights were also added to the existing set of marker lights on the tank.

T-62 Model 1963: To ensure more reliable operation of the shell casing ejector, a fixed limiter with reinforcing ribs was added and the gun protective guards were reinforced. The lower part of the mantlet was increased in armour thickness from 17mm to 25mm to more reliably protect the gun opening. To provide for better cooling of the engine when using the OPVT system, additional plates were added along the bottom of the rubber-impregnated canvas cover to give stand-off space for air circulation. New fuel filler nozzle access covers were added to make refuelling easier. Three track deflectors were added under the fenders on the sides of the hull to reduce damage from track slap and movement at higher speeds. Two support brackets were added to the rear of the turret to help support the tank covering tarpaulin when not in use. The supercharger was fitted with rubber-bushed mounts for it and its connection tubing. The coaxial machine gun was fitted with a spring compensator and a flash hider at the muzzle. The stowage inside the tank was also rearranged. The tank received many improved assemblies and apparatus such as a stronger main clutch. And, the pre-heater system for cold weather starting was improved.

T-62 Model 1964: A new control system for the engine radiator louvres was introduced to the tank. The searchlights were replaced with improved L-2G and OU-3GK models with better all-weather sealing. The commander's cupola was fitted with four detents: TKN-2 forward, left periscope forward, right periscope forward, and TKN-2 to the rear. Road wheels received better bearings. The MK-4 viewers had their upper prisms reset for better vision. New grousers were designed to fit on the OMSh track links with one every ten links being the approved allocation. The 'Meteor' stabilizer (now 'Meteor-M') underwent some changes to ensure that loading speed and ease could be improved. In order to fit two tanks on one railway flatcar a new gun-lock that held the gun barrel at an elevation of 12 degrees off the tank centre-axis was added. In June the R-113 and R-120 were replaced with the improved R-123 VHF FM radio set and the R-124 tank intercom system, and the commander's TKN-2 was replaced by the TKN-3. In August the SGMT was replaced by the new 7.62mm PKT machine gun. The FG-125 and FG-127 replaced the FG-100 and FG-102 in service for better night illumination. A new mechanism was installed to permit the manual elevation control to reach its highest elevation and lowest depression angles. Safety springs were added to the 'stellazh' shell nests to ensure rounds would not pop out when moving over rough terrain. External ZIP stowage was rearranged and new track pin knockers were added.

T-62 Model 1965: The engine exhaust manifolds were improved. A stronger gearbox with better 3rd and 4th gear meshing was added with new gear angles as well as improved final drives. Both of these were interchangeable with earlier production items. The TPN-1 night sight received an armoured front cover plate to replace the sheet steel cover of the earlier models. DV-3 rubber-bladed fans were added for the driver, gunner and loader at their positions. A new rubber-impregnated canvas cover was added to the OPVT equipment that had hatches over the radiator air intakes and radiator air exhaust (left side) for better engine cooling prior to entering the water. The new 115mm 3BM6 APFSDS round was introduced with the muzzle velocity increased 45m/s over that of the original round. And at the end of the year the new RMSh tracks were introduced along with a 14-tooth drive sprocket replacing the earlier

13-tooth design (the original tracks lasted only 2,000–3,000km before needing replacement). Combat weight rose to 37.5 metric tonnes. The TPN-1-41-11 sight with night vision capability was added in 1965.

T-62 Model 1966: The only major change to the tank in this year was the replacement of the GPK-48 gyrocompass with the improved GPK-59.

T-62K COMMANDER'S TANK (OBIEKT-166K/OBIEKT-166KN)

The T-62K followed the T-62 as the T-55K had followed the T-55 in previous production cycles. It was produced in small numbers each year. The T-62K was accepted for service in 1964.

Most of the components and capabilities of the T-62K were identical to those of the line tank. The main differences from the line tank were the addition of an R-112 HF AM command set, a TNA-2 land navigation device, and an AB-1-P/30U petrol generator set. The interior of the tank was rearranged with the result that it carried four fewer main gun rounds (36 versus 40) and 750 fewer 7.62mm rounds (1,750 versus 2,500). The tank also had to carry an 11-metre telescopic antenna mast for use in fixed positions when using the R-112 for long-range communications.

The R-112 was located at the rear of the turret next to the R-113 radio set, and the AB-1-P/30 was nestled to the right side of the driver, replacing three 7.62mm ammunition canisters of 250 rounds each. The TNA-2 had its components located about the fighting compartment with the directional indicator next to the commander. The vehicle also carried a PAB-2A artillery compass plotting table for the commander's use. The ammunition complement was reduced to 36 and 1,750 rounds for the main and secondary armament respectively.

In 1964 the tanks received the R-123 radio and R-124 intercom, and later in their life the R-112 was replaced by the R-130 and then R-134 HF AM set. ZIP stowage was also rearranged.

Between 1963 and 1965 160 T-62K tanks were built at Nizhny Tagil, but final production numbers were around 627 built over the entire production run of the T-62 tank.

T-62 MODEL 1967 MAIN BATTLE TANK

As noted the T-62 was refined and evolved from year to year. One major area of focus was on simplifying the use of OPVT equipment and ensuring all of

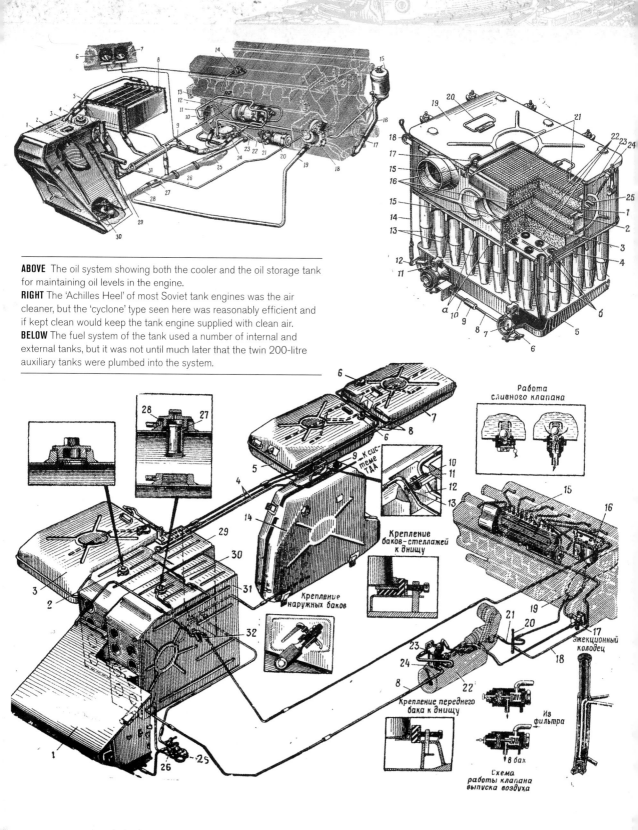

ABOVE The oil system showing both the cooler and the oil storage tank for maintaining oil levels in the engine.

RIGHT The 'Achilles Heel' of most Soviet tank engines was the air cleaner, but the 'cyclone' type seen here was reasonably efficient and if kept clean would keep the tank engine supplied with clean air.

BELOW The fuel system of the tank used a number of internal and external tanks, but it was not until much later that the twin 200-litre auxiliary tanks were plumbed into the system.

Работа
сливного клапана

К систе-
ме ТДА

Крепление
баков-стеллажей
к днищу

Крепление
наружных баков

Крепление переднего
бака к днищу

Из
фильтра

В бак

Эжекционный
колодец

Схема
работы клапана
выпуска воздуха

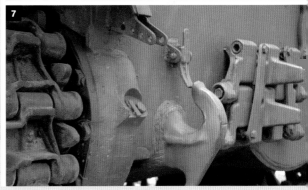

(1) At the Muzei Tekhniki near Moscow is this Model 1967 tank, partial serial number 905VXXXX. It was built in May 1969. The tank is more complete than some of the other museum examples, which is helpful when giving detailed explanations of its design features. It has a wooden splash guard (one of three types used), which on this tank is installed backwards!

(2) Once again the tank has been rebuilt and features RMSh tracks with 14-tooth drive sprockets. The occasional red-painted bolt heads indicate lubrication points.

(3) These tracks are in 'factory fresh' shape. A different kind of stowage bin can be seen in the second position and the tank has a small stowage bin placed over the exhaust outlet instead of the auxiliary oil tank.

(4) Like most of the other tanks at this display the auxiliary fuel tanks and their brackets have been removed.

(5) As with other T-62 models this has 'wraparound' mud flaps on the rear fenders. The U-shaped bracket is for the tow cable when carried.

(6) The RMSh tracks are in good shape, showing light wear.

(7) There are two spare RMSh links carried on the stern plate.

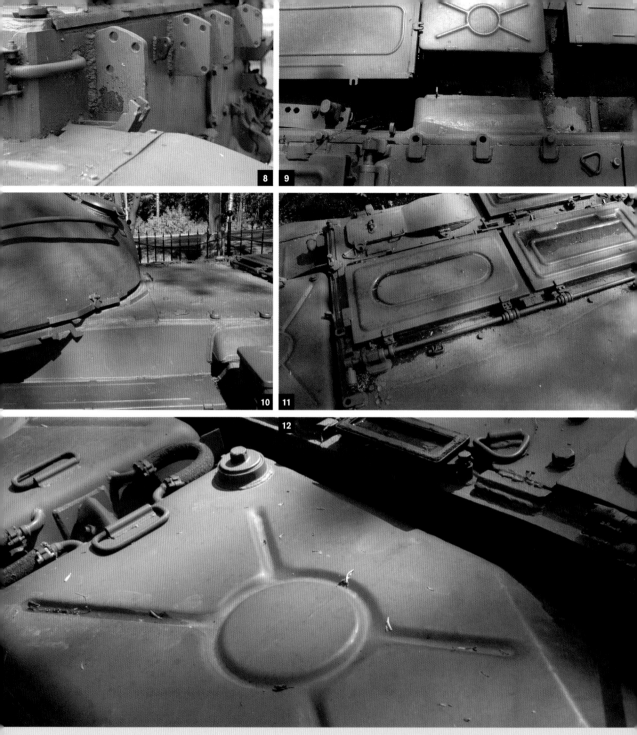

(8) All bracket bases are in place for the auxiliary fuel tanks and also for the unditching log.

(9) Top view of the rear three bins on the left fender (the rear one is the searchlight stowage bin). Note the drain holes in the fender to prevent water from pooling and rusting the components.

(10) This tank has a small bracket on the turret rear roughly above the exit for the bilge pump.

(11) The new engine deck arrangement on the Model 1967 is seen here. The fording covers are in place over the radiator intakes and radiator exhaust as well as the cover being bolted down over the fan shroud. Note that the protective cover for the fording covers when not in use is missing, and that there are two different designs pressed into the radiator intake covers; it is likely that the one on the left is a replacement as the one on the right mirrors the radiator exhaust exit at the left rear.

(12) The tank still carries the mid-production T-55/T-62 external fuel tanks; early ones were welded up from four parts; later ones with two but only one chamfer, and final ones had dual chamfers at one end.

(13) The fuel tanks are bolted to the fender stiffeners at both ends of the tanks.

(14) Some damage is visible to the RMSh links as seen here directly above the centre road wheel. While still functional this link would most likely be replaced at some point.

(15) The tow hooks still have their snap-lock features in place.

(16) From the front the Model 1967 is identical to the Model 1961 with the same features. This tank has a white headlight fitted to the searchlight mount. Both of the driver's daytime periscopes are erected and not painted over.

(17) Both lights are present but the shielded light is bent. As can be seen, having the splash board reversed is no help!

(18) Two rail transport locks in place on the left front fender. They clip down to the edges of a flatcar and the tank then drives onto them, with the resulting effect of preventing sliding when the train is in motion. Also visible is the lock for holding the front mud guard in place when moved back for inspection and track tensioning.

(19) Close-up of the left marker light assembly, the fittings for the transport lock and the mud guard spring lock. Like other tanks the marker lights point forward and at an angle to the rear from the front of the fenders.

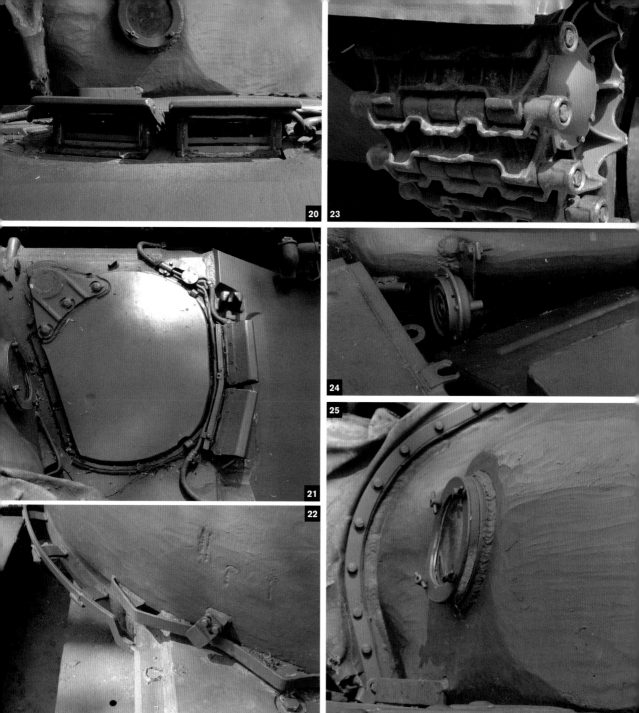

(20) The two periscopes in the raised position. The washer lines have been cut off on the left side of the driver's periscopes.

(21) The driver's hatch from above showing the power cables to the marker lights and the hose for the washer assembly.

(22) Close-up of the left rear turret bracket. It may have something to do with the snorkel (this tank used the three-section one usually carried at this side of the turret).

(23) The Model 1967 used the same idler assembly as the Model 1961.

(24) Wedged into the midst of all of the left-side bins is the small horn. It is unclear how loud it was or if the bins muffled its sound.

(25) The thickest protection on the turret was on its front 60-degree arc, and due to the fact there is a hole in the turret to accommodate the gunner's sight it is thickened over this aperture. The Model 1967 features the same shell fragment guard around the turret race as the Model 1961.

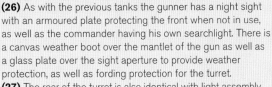

(26) As with the previous tanks the gunner has a night sight with an armoured plate protecting the front when not in use, as well as the commander having his own searchlight. There is a canvas weather boot over the mantlet of the gun as well as a glass plate over the sight aperture to provide weather protection, as well as fording protection for the turret.

(27) The rear of the turret is also identical with light assembly, ventilator, ejector door, NBC vent, and lifting lug (missing here).

(28) The weather cover over the machine gun has been pushed back into the turret here. Also the fixed nature of the auxiliary headlight is obvious. As before, the loader also retains his MK-4 periscope. This periscope mount is also used to attach the snorkel when fording.

(29) The bracket for elevation of the searchlight is missing and it is not bolted in place on its mount (the holes can be seen where it is supposed to go). It is just 'stuck on' via its power feed and rear bracket.

(30) There is a pressed steel plate that connects the rear of the mantlet cover to the turret and also moves in conjunction with the mantlet.

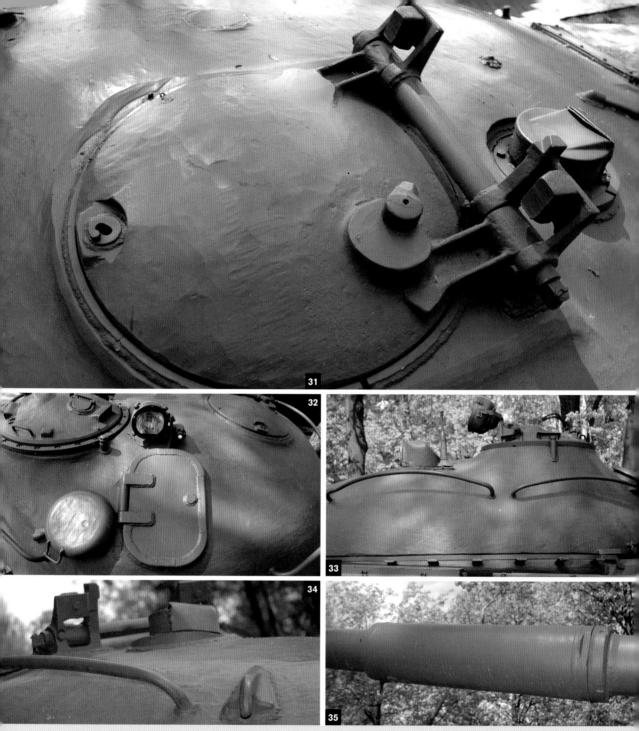

(31) The loader's hatch which here has a locking mechanism visible (there is a lever for unlocking on the inside) and the oval port for the locking wrench at the rear of the hatch.

(32) The ejector door is identical to that of the Model 1961. There is a small 'footman's loop' on the ventilator for securing the vehicle's storage tarpaulin when carried.

(33) As previously noted, the 'desant' rails are sharply curved.

(34) The front lifting lugs are still present on the tank; this is the right-hand one.

(35) The bore evacuator is made up of several components; here marks can be seen on the rear attachment ring to determine if the can section has rotated.

it could be stowed on the tank so that no support vehicles were needed to prepare the tanks for wading.

The main area of redesign was the complete forward part of the engine deck. Previously it had been like that of the T-55 with a large access hatch for the engine and a smaller access hatch for the cassette type air cleaner. In the new model this was now a solid armour plate that could be hinged up to the rear for access. At the rear of this plate were two permanently attached hermetically sealing hatches that covered the two radiator air intakes on the engine deck. These were stowed under a corrugated steel cover to protect them from damage. At the rear of the engine deck were two more covers hinged at the rear; a flat cover with a slight forward rise covered the radiator air exhaust grille on the left and the previous cover with a domed centre on the right covered the fan grille. At the same time, a new, more compact three-section snorkel was provided that stowed at the right front of the turret (later moved to the left rear).

All of these changes meant that, with just the labour of the four-man crew, the T-62 could now be prepared for wading in 11 minutes instead of 21 minutes as required before, and without requiring any external assistance or support.

T-62 MODEL 1972 MAIN BATTLE TANK

In the late 1960s the Soviet Army began to consider that while jet aircraft were not likely to be successfully engaged by tank-mounted anti-aircraft machine guns, the same was not true against a new threat – attack helicopters fitted with either anti-tank guided missiles or rockets. The US tested a Bell UH-1 'Iroquois' utility helicopter (colloquially known as the 'Huey') with SS-11 anti-tank missiles and offered an armament kit mounting six of them for use against tanks. Also the new Bell AH-1 'Cobra' then appearing in Vietnam was designed to carry the then-new TOW anti-tank missile. European helicopters were at the time also being fitted for Milan or HOT anti-tank missiles.

The result was that the Soviet Army once again asked for tanks to be fitted with anti-aircraft machine guns, now to deal with the new helicopter threat. As helicopters had to be within line of sight of the target with the early generations of missiles, and could only fire from a stationary hover position, the anti-aircraft machine guns once again gave Soviet tanks a defence within 2,000 metres of the enemy.

The T-55 was first to re-adopt the machine gun as a simple cast mount could easily be fitted or even retrofitted to earlier production tanks. This

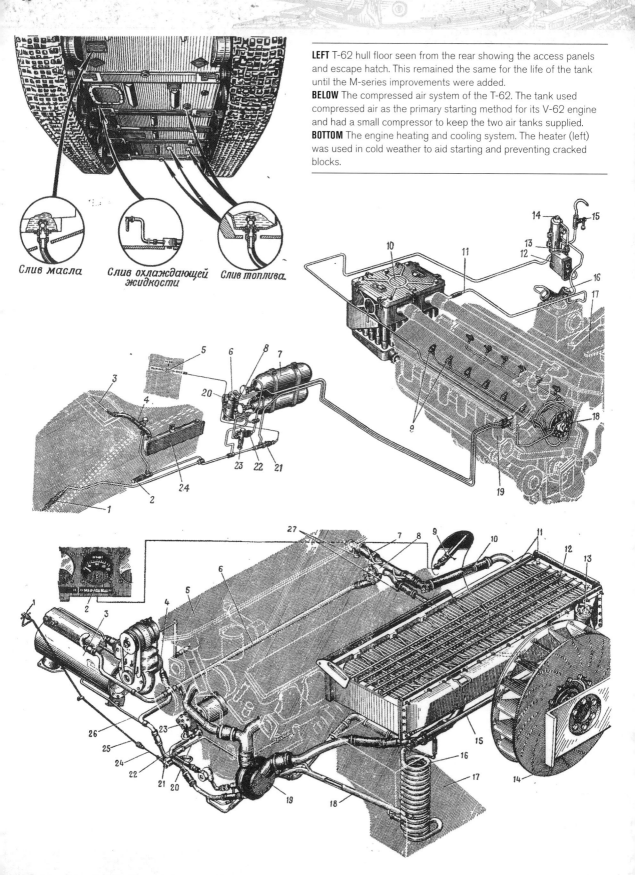

Слив масла

Слив охлаждающей
жидкости

Слив топлива

LEFT T-62 hull floor seen from the rear showing the access panels and escape hatch. This remained the same for the life of the tank until the M-series improvements were added.
BELOW The compressed air system of the T-62. The tank used compressed air as the primary starting method for its V-62 engine and had a small compressor to keep the two air tanks supplied.
BOTTOM The engine heating and cooling system. The heater (left) was used in cold weather to aid starting and preventing cracked blocks.

(1) Most of these photos are from the Partizanskaya Museum near Bryansk. This Model 1972 T-62 tank is serial number M04VT5765 built in April 1972. (Photos 1–21 Alexander Morzhitsky)

(2) The tank carries all of the fittings for either KMT type mine trawls or bulldozer blade attachment and has also been fitted with the RMSh tracks, which may be original, as they were created for the Obiekt-167 and at that time were fitted to the Obiekt-172M T-72 prototypes.

(3) Hull fittings matched the previous two variants and it carries the two railroad platform locks on the front of the left fender.

(4) The bin for the bore cleaning equipment is present. The rod on the side of the engine compartment is for releasing the fording covers upon exit of the water.

(5) This particular tank still has the auxiliary oil tank fitted to the top of the exhaust outlet. It uses the same pattern of pressed stiffeners as the external fuel tanks. The searchlight stowage bin can be seen to its right.

(6) Likewise, it also uses the wraparound mud flap on the rear of the fender. The rear marker light/taillight has been knocked out of alignment.

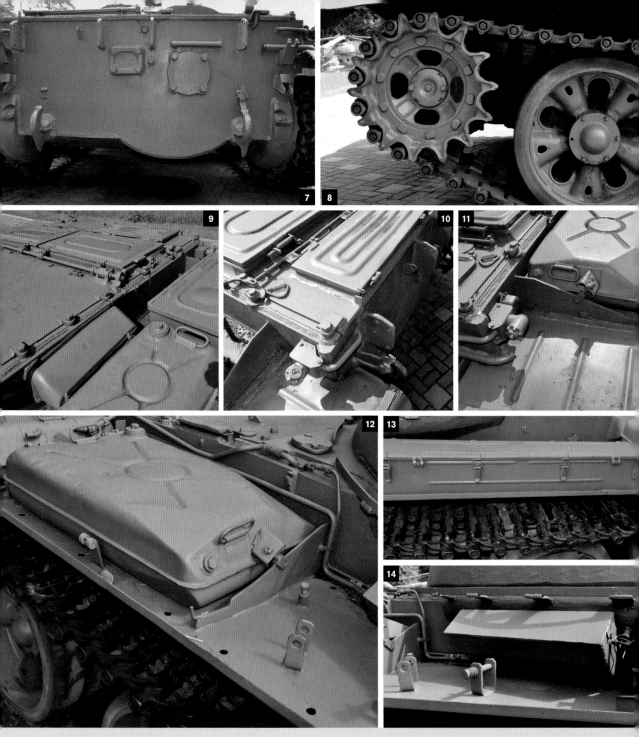

(7) The stern plate is the same as the previous tank's. This one is missing all of the fuel tank brackets and strapping for the unditching log, as well as the left-hand tow hook snap-lock.

(8) It has 14-tooth drive sprockets for the RMSh tracks.

(9) This tank has matching radiator intake covers and a similar radiator exhaust cover to the Model 1967.

(10) The two radiator covers are spring loaded with torsion bar springing. The bell crank and rodding on the left let the radiator covers pop open by means of a lever inside the fighting compartment.

(11) This tank has the late model external fuel tanks with dual bevels at the front of the tank.

(12) The tow cable brackets and drain holes in the fender are visible here. While slightly bent, all of the external fuel lines are in place. This tank is also fitted with external guards and support brackets for the rear tow cable when installed.

(13) This tank has straight stowage bins on its left fender and the previous L-shaped one appears to have been dropped.

(14) Another small bin present on some T-62s. From its size it may be where the electric fuel pump for the auxiliary fuel tanks is stored when not in use.

(15) As with all T-62s it retains the shell fragment guard around the turret race.

(16) This tank still retains the L-shaped bin on its right fender.

(17) Once again, the tank uses the fluted idler wheels for extra support for the tracks. This is mainly to reduce the chance of a thrown track.

(18) All of the previous frontal fittings on the turret, fender and hull are present. It also has the machine gun weather cover.

(19) The searchlight linkage is present and in good order.

(20) The museum has displayed their T-62 Model 1972 next to the tank which was supposed to be the winner of the competition, the T-64. This one is an upgraded T-64A.

(21) Both tow hooks and their snap-locks are present. Once again the tank is missing its splash guard board across the centre of the glacis.

(22) Here is another veteran T-62 Model 1972 with all parts present. This one has the most common ribbed steel splash guard board in place. (John Ham)

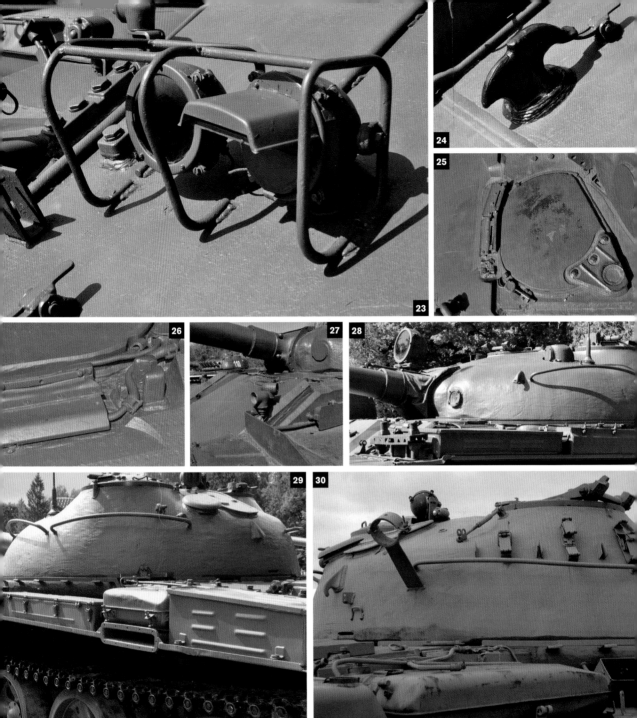

(23) Whereas this tank has no splashboard. The headlight cluster is identical to previous models.

(24) A clear shot of the snap-lock for the tow hook; this is to keep the tow cable from slipping off if slack is encountered when in use. The hold-down spring for the mud guard and its lock when folded up are visible, as well as the tube for the controls for the bulldozer blade when fitted.

(25) The driver-mechanic's hatch, again the same as previous variants. It is also missing the hoses for the periscope washing system.

(26) Close-up of another tank showing the hose as fitted to clear the viewers.

(27) The damaged marker lights of the same tank.

(28) The left side of the turret of the Model 1972 is identical to the previous variants. As with most T-62s the protective glass cover for the primary sight is always left in place.

(29) The footman's loops and brackets for the snorkel have been removed from the turret.

(30) The right-hand side now includes all sorts of additional items. Here there are three racks for 50-round 12.7mm ammunition canisters as well as mounts for storing the AAMG when travelling.

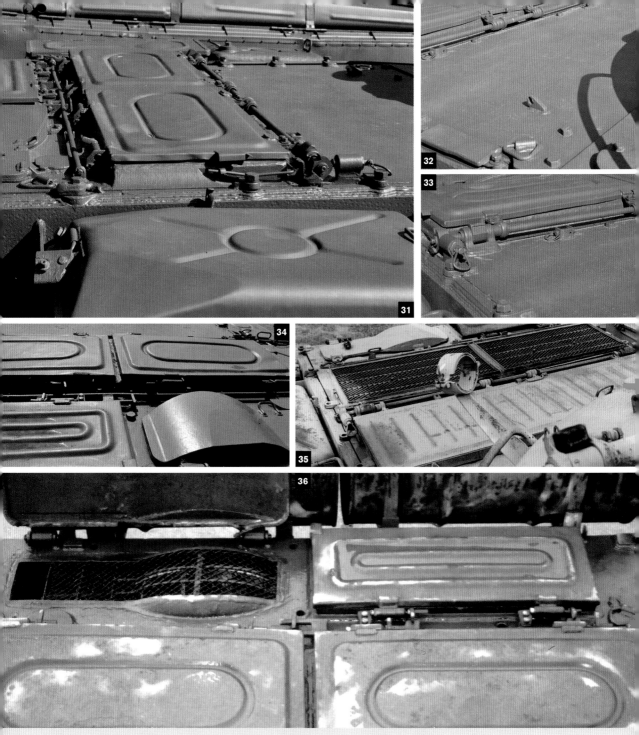

(31) A view of the rear of the engine deck showing the rodding for releasing the radiator covers. The fan shroud cover has a spring-loaded lock and a bracket to hold it open when not in use. These covers are bolted down for fording and only opened manually by the crew after fording is complete.

(32) When unbolted the engine deck (flat plate in the foreground) swings up and to the rear on hinges.

(33) The right-side engine deck hinge and the locking pin for the protective cover when in place.

(34) The radiator exhaust cover has no lifting spring; when released it is opened up by air pressure created by the fan drawing air in through the radiator air intakes. The rodding and trips for the radiator air intake covers are just visible in the centre of the photo.

(35) Here is the engine deck area of the APG Museum T-62. This one still has the protective cover, but the locking bracket for the fan shroud cover is missing.

(36) The rear of the engine deck on the 7th Army OPFOR Detachment T-62. There are two styles of covers for the fan shroud, a thick plate and this cast hollow one.

(37) Another T-62, this one having the DShKM machine gun mounted as well as the 200-litre auxiliary fuel tanks. Note that this one has a cut-out behind the turret bracket over the exit port for the bilge pump. (John Ham)

(38) The mantlet weather cover is present and in much better shape than on some other preserved tanks.

(39) Once again the same rear fittings are present on the turret.

(40) The loader's hatch mount is blended into the turret to maintain ballistic integrity. While the T-55 could have a mount simply welded or bolted in place, the turret required extensive redesign to accept the tourelle mounting.

(41) This preserved T-62 is something of a mess, but the base plate for the L-2G searchlight is visible here rotated forward on its mounting.

(42) This L-2G is intact and in place, but its power cable is missing. Once again a spare white headlight is fitted to the fixed bracket.

(43) Front of the 7th Army OPFOR tank. The Velcro strip around the turret is a US fitting to carry the MILES laser combat simulation system.

(44) The gun and bore evacuator assembly on the Muzei tank.

(45) Another preserved Model 1972, but this one has the protective covers on both the L-2G and OU-3 searchlights. (John Ham)

(46) The AAMG in place. This one appears to be a DShK and not a DShKM as it has the original 'tulip'-shaped muzzle brake. The latter usually has a twin-plate circular one. (John Ham)

(47) The 7th Army OPFOR tank with its DShKM machine gun in place.

(48) The rear of that weapon. Both its AA sight and its left-hand control lever and swing brake are missing.

(49) Rear of the APG loader's hatch showing the lock and 'lever-operated' ever-operated release on the top of the hatch cover.

(50) American thinking: why use a locking wrench when a key-operated brass lock will do the same job?

(51) Overview of the complete loader's hatch. The port at the front is for the locking wrench.

(52) Once again, the loader has his TNP-165 viewer, also used to mount the snorkel when fording.

(53) The commander's cupola remains the same as well.

(54) The gunner's fixed TNP-165 viewer is visible just in front of the commander's cupola.

(55) The brackets remain in place for the rear marker light and identification light, but the lights themselves are missing.

(56) The gunner's night sight and the radio antenna port are unchanged from the earlier variants.

(57) The 'pig's snout' mantlet without its cover. Other than a thicker lower edge added early in its production life, all T-62 gun mantlets are identical in shape and attachment. It retains the metal panel above the mantlet cover. This one is completely missing its searchlight but the two mounts are visible.

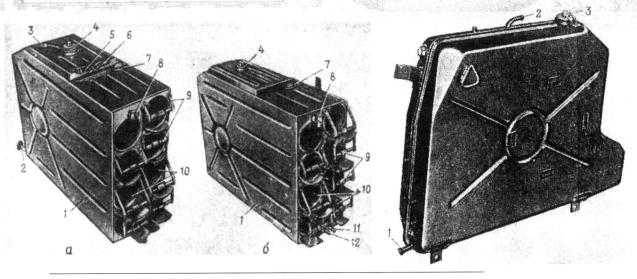

ABOVE LEFT The two 'stellazh' ammo racks and fuel tanks to the right of the driver each held eight rounds of ammunition.
ABOVE RIGHT The main fuel tank – showing the traditional Soviet method of stiffening the steel casing – was mounted to the right rear corner of the combat compartment (it was called 'middle tank' in the manual).
BELOW By the time the T-62 entered service, the auxiliary fuel tank pump had changed over from manual crank type to electrical run off vehicle power. It still required a crewman to attach it to the external tank and feed the hose into whichever tank they wanted to fill up.

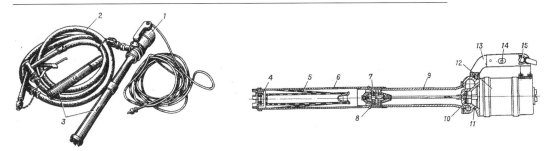

only needed to be welded in place on the flat panel on the right side of the turret roof. After approval in 1969, the T-55s soon began sporting this feature as the older T-54 had done before them.

But due to the wholly cast turret design of the T-62, this was not possible if the integrity of the armour protection was to be retained. As a result, research and development, most likely involving NII-48 and VNII-100 (now VNIITransMash), was required. A new turret design with a blended mount for the tourelle-type ring used on the T-55 was created and entered production in 1972. The 12.7mm DShKM machine gun had an effective rate of fire of 150 rounds/minute and an effective range of 1,500m against slow-moving aircraft and 800m against lightly armoured ground targets, the weapon being able to penetrate 10mm of armour at standard engagement ranges. The weapon was provided with 300 rounds of ammunition, carried in six 50-round canisters in snap-lock mounts on the outside right rear of the turret. The T-62 M-1972 continued in production until the T-62 tank series was removed from production in favour of the new T-72. The T-62 M-1972 was provided with an improved TSh-41U day sight, with a KTD-2 laser rangefinder added to some tanks before it became standardized from 1975. A small batch of T-62K command tanks were also built on the T-62 M-1972 chassis.

T-62 MODEL 1974 (T-62 MODEL 1975) MAIN BATTLE TANK

The T-62 M-1972, when fitted with the KTD-2 laser rangefinder but no other upgrades, was designated T-62 M-1974, or more commonly T-62 M-1975 according to conflated sources.

T-62M SERIES MEDIUM TANKS

As time passed and the T-62 began to fall behind newer Western designs, few efforts were made during the 1970s to keep up with changing capabilities. The only external change was seen in 1975 when T-62s began to be fitted with the new KTD-1 laser rangefinder over the gun barrel on top of the mantlet as mentioned above.

But in 1981, after the initial results of combat operations in Afghanistan as well as analysis of any prospective war with NATO, a number of new changes were made to both the T-55 and the T-62 (the T-54 series was by then considered no longer viable in front line combat and did not receive as many upgrades).

A company of mixed variant T-62M tanks; however, these now have been fitted with the Type 902B eight-tube smoke grenade launchers. The same unit can be seen as number 28 on page 87.

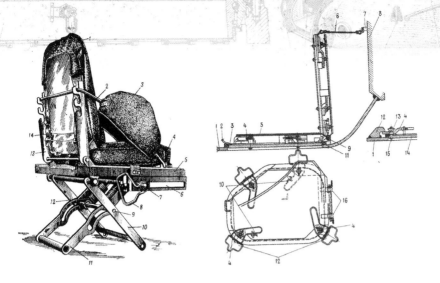

FAR LEFT The original driver's seat. It was not adjustable in fore-and-aft directions but did move up and down. It was later replaced in the M series by one attached to a pillar in order to prevent direct shock against the driver when mines were struck.

LEFT The escape hatch located behind the driver.

T-62M MAIN BATTLE TANK (T-62 M-1983) (OBIEKT-166M6)

On 25 July 1981 a Resolution of the SM SSSR was adopted concerning the upgrade of T-55, T-55A and T-62 main battle tanks to bring their combat capability up to the level of the newer T-64A and early T-72 main battle tanks. With regard to the T-62, a prototype was developed as the Obiekt-166M6, with the T-62 upgrade being accepted for service with the Soviet Army in 1983 as the T-62M. The T-62M upgrades were done in batches, starting with a handful being done in 1981 and 1982, and with the majority being undertaken from 1985 in accordance with drawings approved on 1 December 1985.

The T-62M received many of the same upgrades as applied to the T-55 but tailored specifically for the T-62 tank. These included the following items:

- Installation of a completely new fire control system encompassing the 1K13-1 combination sight and missile guidance system, a BV-62 ballistic computer, a TShSM-41U telescopic sight, always the newer KTD-2 laser rangefinder, and the improved 'Meteor-M1' (2Eh15M-1) two-axis stabilizer system;
- Provision to carry and use the 9K116-1 'Sheksna' SUO* or fire control system and which incorporated the new ZUBK10-2 round with its 9M116-2 through-the-bore guided missile system that used laser beam following guidance. This was nearly identical to the 9M116-1 'Bastion' missile in the T-55M series but was modified to fit the 115mm gun barrel;

---

*   SUO – sistema upravleniya ognyom.

- A thermal sleeve for the 115mm gun barrel to prevent distortion due to variable weather, as the 2A20 barrel was longer and the wall thickness thinner than the 100mm tank guns;
- The BDD appliqué armour package to provide better protection from HEAT munitions that included the following elements:
- A stand-off appliqué array for the glacis with an outside plate of 30mm armour plate and an interior space filled with spaced 5mm armour plates cast in a Penopolyurethane matrix;
- Two turret 'brow' modules constructed in the same manner and mounted on the front left and right sides of the turret, called 'Ilyich's Eyebrows' after the flyaway eyebrows of then Premier Leonid Brezhnev;
- Reinforced rubber-fabric side skirts 10mm thick running the entire length of the fenders on both sides of the tank providing protection from RPG-type and cumulative rounds;
- A reinforced box made of 20mm armour plate and providing about 80mm of stand-off under the hull floor of the tank from the lower glacis to just in front of the second road-wheel pair. This was to prevent mine damage and concussion injury or death of the driver-mechanic;
- A strut between the belly and roof of the hull to which the driver's seat was connected to reduce the chance of injury from a mine or IED (improvised explosive device) explosion;
- A modified emergency escape hatch in the belly of the tank with a jettisonable armoured cover to ensure protection by the belly plate in the area of the hatch.
- Anti-radiation vests for the crew if it was felt the tank would have to operate in areas with radiation hazards (recall that although originally planned for the T-62M, the T-62 had no radiation 'podboy' liner nor a 'nadboy' external one) though a small number of tanks would appear to have been fitted with 'nadboy' external turret lining;
- Upgrading of the radio suite from the R-123/R-124 to the R-173 VHF FM solid-state transceiver and the R-173P receiver as well as the R-174 intercom system. Command tanks also received an R-134 HF AM command set to replace the R-112 or R-130 sets;
- The Type 902B 'Tucha' eight-barrel smoke grenade launcher system to provide smoke screens to the front of the tank in an emergency (the TDA was retained but only left smoke from the exhaust opening);
- The engine was replaced by either the V-55U engine of 620hp or the V-46M-5 engine of 690hp;

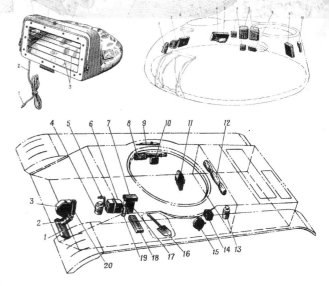

- New 'electroslag' steel alloy torsion bars to increase the dynamic travel of the suspension as well as fitting a shock absorber to road-wheel station two on each side;
- Retrofitting RMSh to any tanks not previously upgraded and adding a deflector disc to the middle of the drive wheels to reduce thrown tracks.

The T-62M upgrades undertaken from 1985 included the 1K13-1 combination sight and missile guidance system, the 9K116-1 ATGM system, a KTD-1-1 or KTD-2 laser rangefinder, 'Volna' fire control, the aforementioned TShSM-41U telescopic sight, 'Meteor-M1' (2Eh15M-1) gun stabilizer and BV-62 computer. Armour improvements included the BDD 'brow' armour as standard, and radiation lining, with the engine options as noted above. The T-62M had a combat weight of 41.5–42.0 metric tonnes.

Originally 785 T-62s were slated for upgrading to 'T-62M' standard. Ten T-62 tanks were upgraded to T-62M standard in 1981, followed by a further 25 in 1982 – probably the pre-production test lot. The T-62M upgrade was accepted for service in March 1983, following which rebuild gradually increased exponentially – with 50 tanks being built in 1983, 100 in 1984 and 600 in 1985. More tanks were upgraded between 1986 and 1990 in accordance with modified upgrade drawings approved on 1 December 1985, but no figures for exact production are available. The tanks were upgrades at BTRZ depots not at the main UVZ production plant. In November 1990 a total of 1,001 T-62M models of all types were present in Soviet forces west of the Ural Mountains.

TOP LEFT For foul weather driving a canvas hood with fixed glass windshield was provided. The windshield had a built-in defroster for use in winter.

TOP RIGHT Storage of equipment inside the turret – 6 is flares and 10 is the flare pistol.

ABOVE Internal storage of spare parts and tools. 2, 4 and 13 are water bottles; an entrenching tool is stowed on top of the escape hatch.

T-62M1, T-62M-1, T-62M-1-1, T-62M-1-2 AND T-62M1-2, T-62M2 MAIN BATTLE TANKS

Considering that the 'M' series upgrades were carried out over a nine-year period with different base models, there was a complex list of base variants and what was included:

- T-62M – full set of improvements, V-55U engine
- T-62M1 – additional armour package, V-55U engine, etc. but no ATGM complex

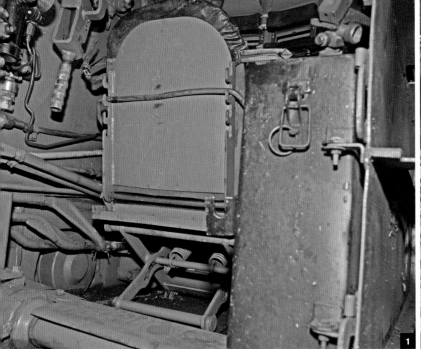
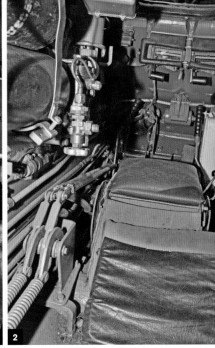

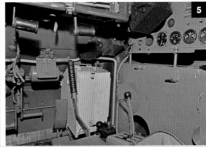

(1) Driver-mechanic's seat from the rear. The back folds down to permit the driver to exit through the turret. This is the original design; the M-series seat is attached to a pillar to prevent shock from a mine injuring the driver. (All images in this interior photographs section courtesy of Andrey Aksenov)

(2) Seat back down with the massive control rods on the left side of the position. The twin compressed air tanks for starting are on the upper left.

(3) Driver's foot pedals – accelerator on the right, service brake to the left and clutch on the far left. Mount in the centre is for the GPK-59 gyrocompass when fitted.

(4) Driver's viewers with the adjustment handles visible under the periscopes. The dial on the left is the speedometer in kph. This tank has 52.9km on it since rebuilding.

(5) Right side of the compartment. The red items are fire suppression system controls.

(6) Driver's main instrument panel. Dials are (l to r) tachometer, oil pressure gauge, oil temperature gauge, water temperature gauge, and ammeter. The circuit breaker panel is above the gauges.

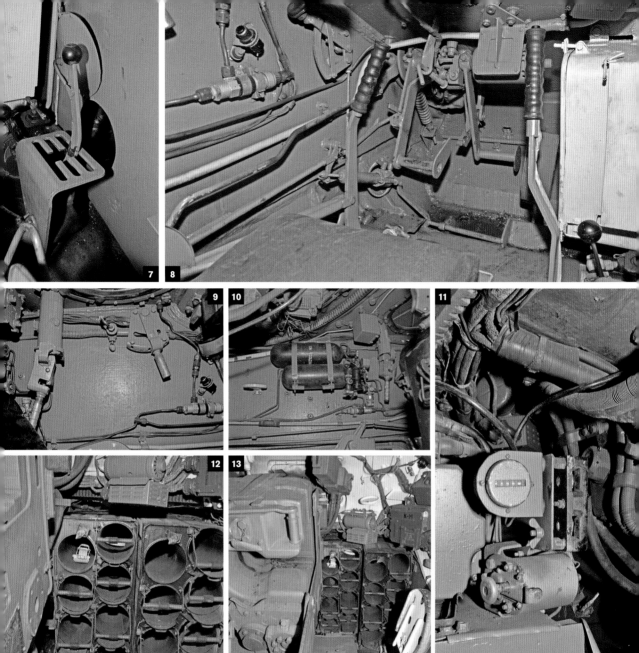

(7) Gear selector and shift gate. Shift pattern is 2-3-R-1-4-5.
(8) Left side showing various lines and controls. Grey ones are control rods, blue are air lines, and yellow fuel lines. The lever is the louvre control for the engine deck.
(9) The cylinder on the left is the mount for the driver's hatch with its lift and turn mechanism. The button on the far right is for the signal or horn. The gauge at the left is air pressure in the tanks.
(10) The air tank assembly. There is a small compressor in the engine bay that feeds them when the tank is running. Primary start for this tank is by air pressure with electrical starter motor backup.

(11) The engine hour gauge covering running time for the engine. This one has 215 hours shown after rebuilding.
(12) The twin forward 'stellazh' fuel tanks and ammo racks. Each holds eight rounds. The brown-coloured item above the racks is the fuse box for some of the turret circuitry, mounted just above the turret race.
(13) There is little space between the gun and the side of the turret and hull. The flip-down seat is for the loader when moving and his hatch is closed.

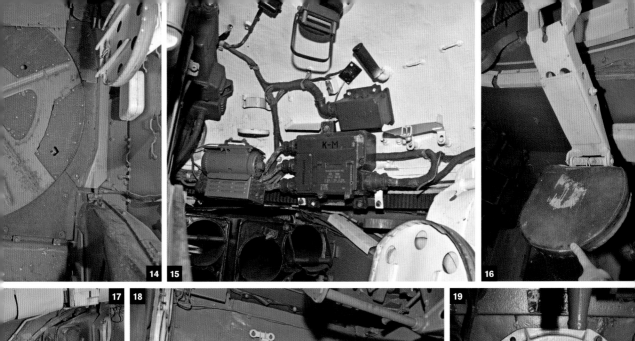

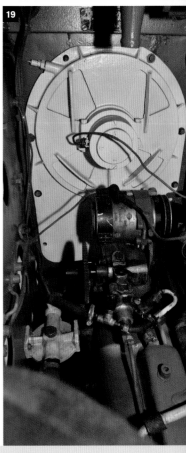

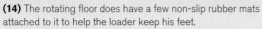

(14) The rotating floor does have a few non-slip rubber mats attached to it to help the loader keep his feet.

(15) The loader's position showing his seat, MK-4 viewer, and a grab handle to help him avoid injury on rough terrain.

(16) Loader's seat folded down for use.

(17) The midships fuel tank with the mounts for ammo stowage on its inner face.

(18) Firewall ammo stowage. A total of 20 rounds are stowed here in an alternating manner with their primer ends fitted into the rings and a large strapping device holding them in place until needed. Only the remains of the latter are visible.

(19) The engine pre-heater assembly for cold weather at the left rear of the fighting compartment. This device is similar to the one in the T-54/55 which was the first assembly created by chief designer Leonid Kartsev.

(20) The engine pre-heater control panel at the top. The number of bare wires is a bit unsettling!

(21) The commander's TKN-3 observation and sighting scope. The handles let him tilt it up or down as needed.

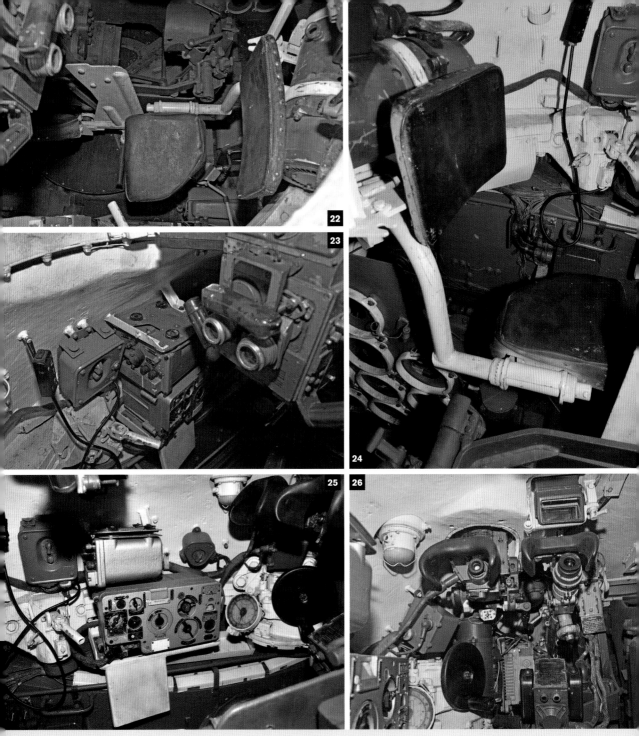

(22) The commander's seat on the rear side of the turret. He has a few guards to protect him from the actions of the gun when moving and ejecting the cartridge casing.

(23) Commander's position showing left to right his radio control box for his headset and microphone, intercom/radio selector panel, R-123 radio and amplifier, and the commander's sight. The handle is for the turret lock.

(24) Another view of the commander's seat. The pad may be lifted up to permit the gunner easier access to his seat.

(25) The complete R-123 radio installation. The commander's control box is on the left and the gunner's intercom control is on the right. The large gauge is the turret azimuth indicator dial.

(26) The gunner's sighting complex. At the top is his TPN-165 viewer; under that is the telescopic sight and to the left the persicopic/night sight; the controls for the gun (American term 'Cadillacs') are under the telescopic sight. Manual turret traverse control is on the left.

(27) The 'Cadillac' control box with instructions. The button on the left-hand grip fires the machine gun; that on the right fires the cannon. The left grip controls traverse, right elevation.

(28) Close-up of the turret azimuth indicator. The turret-shaped arrow shows the turret position and the other one is input from the commander directing the gunner to a specific azimuth.

(29) Complete overview of the gunner's position. Switches and circuit breakers are on the right with a warning to remove the turret brake before engaging the traverse control.

(30) The breech end of the U5-TS gun. To the lower left is an adjustment to bring the gun to a true elevation bearing. The twin 'ear' brackets at the rear of the breech are for a typical Soviet gun travel lock. They use a small bar which clips to the breech of the gun and the roof of the turret to hold the gun steady when moving.

(31) Top view of the casing ejector assembly. When activated it will throw the casing out of the ejector hatch to a distance several metres behind the tank.

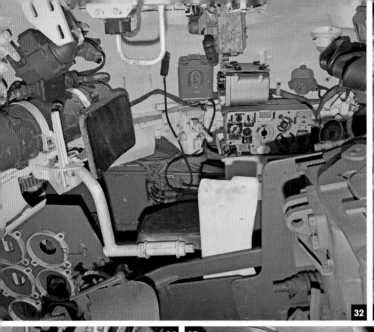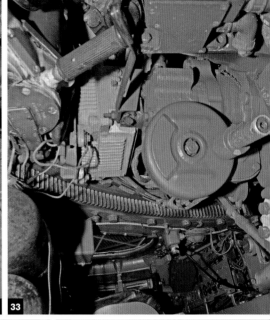

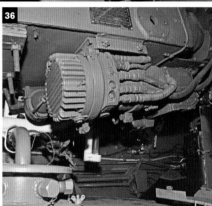

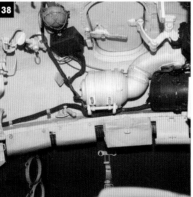

(32) Cross-turret view showing how cramped the commander and gunner positions are in relation to each other.

(33) The gunner's manual elevation control is mounted beneath his sighting complex.

(34) The gunner also has a flip-down foot rest at the front of his seat mount.

(35) This tank has been 'de-milled' with the breechblock cut through with a torch making it acceptable to be a museum piece. Also the coaxial machine gun mounts have been removed along with the machine gun itself. Stops can be seen mounted above the gun breech to prevent it slamming into the turret roof and cracking it in a mishap.

(36) Part of the gun's vertical stabilizer system mounted under the barrel.

(37) Right-side view of the casing ejector mechanism.

(38) View of the turret rear and the ventilation motor and exhaust duct. This serves to help clear propellant gases from the turret. The ejector hatch with its locking handle is just above it.

(39) Turret ready rack for two rounds. The tank carries 16 in the 'stellazh' racks, 20 in the firewall rack, two rounds here and two others elsewhere in the tank.

80

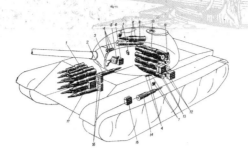

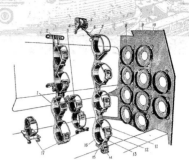

RIGHT Original disposition of ammo stowage inside a Model 1961 T-62 tank.

FAR RIGHT The left-side rack for ammunition stowed against the firewall. In some cases this was increased to 20 rounds.

- T-62M-1 – same as T-62M1 but with V-46M-5 engine (added with external air filter on right side)
- T-62M1-1 – M1 with V-46M-5 engine
- T-62M1-2 – M1 without additional armour package including hull floor armour. 40.5 metric tonnes
- T-62M1-2-1 – M1-2 with V-46M-5 engine

T-62M tanks without the 'Sheksna' system or the 1K13 sight were designated as T-62M1 (with the V-46-5M they became the T-62M1-1); without the BDD armour package they became the T-62M-1-2 and with the V-46-5M the T-62M1-2. The T-62M1 and later designations also included upgrades including the KTD-1 (KTD-2) laser rangefinder, a 902B 'Tucha' smoke grenade launcher rack and a new armoured filter box on the track guard. Some tanks were also fitted with mine trawl mountings.

The T-62M2 (known as T-62M1-2 in some sources) was the designation when without additional glacis and hull floor armour, also known as 'VLD'.

The T-62M and T-62M1 were first observed in service with the Soviet Army during the decade-long Soviet war in Afghanistan. In Western intelligence circles the modified version with distinctive turret brow armour was originally designated 'T-62D' on the basis that the up-armoured BMP-2D was similarly designated. As would be later understood, in Soviet terminology the updated tank as first seen in Afghanistan was the T-62M, with the designation T-62D referring to the variant modified with the 'Drozd' active defence system. Some T-62M tanks operating in the Far East Military District (Khabarovsk) have been observed fitted with a thermal gun barrel sleeve and the 12.7mm NSVT anti-aircraft machine gun installation.

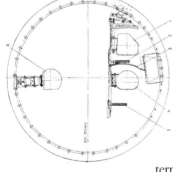

Turret seating with the bottom of the sketch being forward. The loader has a relatively larger amount of movement, but the seat was relocated with the Model 1972 so he could man the AAMG.

T-62MK COMMANDER'S TANK

A commander's tank version of the T-62M was produced, with the standard T-62M upgrades plus the same commander's upgrades as the T-62K, but with the TNA-2 land navigation system of the earlier tank replaced by a TNA-3 type.

T-62M WITH 'RESHETKA' ARMOUR

During the Soviet war in Afghanistan, the Soviet Army modified a number of T-62 tanks with the installation of 'reshetka' or 'grille armour', which provided considerable protection against RPG rocket fire which was a major threat to tanks operating in mountainous terrain. The modification is not understood to have been common, but some years later, as a result of particularly vicious combat experience in Chechnya in 1994–95, the Russians began to refit their T-62M series tanks with a standardized set of such 'reshetka' protective devices – armour segments along the sides and around the turret. Formed of thin strips of steel plate roughly 50mm wide and 5mm thick and spaced approximately 70mm apart, they were designed to stop the major threat to tanks in combat in cities and built-up areas – RPGs and ATGMs using HEAT warheads. The main army unit in the Second Chechen War, the 42nd Guards Motorized Rifle Division, was primarily equipped with T-62 tanks mounting 'reshetka' panels on them for that reason. Most appear to have also kept their hull floor and upper glacis armour. T-62M tanks with 'reshetka' armour were used by the Russian Army in Chechnya and Georgia having been initially used by the Soviet Army in Afghanistan.

T-62D MAIN BATTLE TANK WITH 'DROZD' ACTIVE PROTECTION SYSTEM (OBIEKT-166D 'DROZD')

In 1983 the Soviet Army started fitting the T-55 with a new system they referred to as 'Kompleks Aktivnoy Zashchity' (KAZ) – or 'complex of active protection' against incoming ATGMs or RPGs. This was the Type 1030 'Drozd' (thrush) system that consisted of a set of motion-sensing radar antennas to detect incoming ATGMs, a fire control computer, and eight launchers in four two-round sets splayed to cover the frontal 60-degree arc of the tank.

Developed between 1977 and 1982, the T2A2 'Drozd' KAZ system was designed to detect incoming anti-tank missiles (PTURs in Russian) and then fire a 107mm ZUOF14 round (basically a gigantic shotgun shell firing ball bearings) at the incoming weapon to destroy it; engagement was when the projectile reached about 130 metres from the tank with destruction taking place around 6.6 metres in front of the tank. Targets with incoming velocities of 70 to 700m/s were to be engaged when they were considered inside the destructive range of the round. To ensure a kill, two rounds from the same module would be fired at once.

The radars were mounted on the front left and right top edges of the turret and the computer was located in an armoured housing on the rear of the turret. The two launcher-modules, mounted either side of the turret front, each had four launch tubes arranged two above and two below, with the upper and lower pair of launch tubes being set at different angles. No reload rounds were noted as carried by the tank but that was never verified.

These tanks entered into service as the T-55D or T-55AD depending on the model. Since the same equipment would also fit on the T-62, a near-identical T-62D variant was developed and approved for service in 1983 concurrently with the T-55 installation. The full T-62 T2A2 'Drozd' upgrade in addition to the 'Drozd' active protection system included additional armour on the hull and BDD 'brow' armour on the turret and combination armour side skirts as mounted on the T-62M series. The T-62D retained the standard armament with a TShSM-41U sight and TPN-1 night sight, 'Meteor' gun stabilization system and a full complement of 42 rounds of 115mm ammunition. When fitted with the V-46-5M engine, the tank was designated T-62D-1.

It is unknown how many T-62 'Drozd' tanks were converted, but the expense of the system apparently outweighed the cost of the base tank, and the project was cancelled after a small number of tanks had been produced for long-term service evaluation trials. The tank was regularly seen during open days at the Kantemirovskaya Tank Division base at Naro-Fominsk in the mid to late 1990s. While the 1990 Conventional Forces in Europe Treaty (CFE) noted around 700 T-55s of all models with 'Drozd' equipment in service, no T-62D models were noted as present in active service units west of the Urals.

Beyond the cost implications, another reason the 'Drozd' system quickly fell out of favour with the Soviet Army was that, during manoeuvres, motorized rifle troops discovered that the 'Drozd'-equipped tank would protect itself no matter what – even if they were deployed in front of it! No commander wanted his troops shot in the back by their own side no matter what that meant. As a result, tactics for the technically ingenious but operationally nuanced 'Drozd' system were constantly undergoing revision. The system was apparently later sold to China.

T-62MD MAIN BATTLE TANK WITH 'DROZD' ACTIVE PROTECTION SYSTEM

The 'Drozd' active protection system was also transferred to the later T-62M series in 1985. The installation was modified to accommodate installation around the 'brow' armour fitted on the T-62M. Whether a significant number of T-62M tanks were so-modified is unknown.

(1) A T-62D with the equipment removed in the Kubinka 'back yard'. While some tanks were fitted with this system, none were apparently ever operationally deployed. This tank appears to have only mounted the launchers and brackets for testing as none of the radar or control systems appear to have ever been installed.

(2) Another prototype with more fittings still in place such as the rear-mounted control elements. (Andrey Aksenov)

(3) This vehicle still has the two twin launcher tubes in place. (Andrey Aksenov)

(4) Rear view of the same tank showing some of the bracketing in place. (Andrey Aksenov)

(5) A preserved T-55 'Drozd' with the intact control assembly in place on the rear of the turret. This processed the incoming data from the radars and selected the correct ammunition to fire at the incoming threat.

(6) Right-side assembly with the launchers and radar in position.

(7) Left-side assembly on the same T-55, showing the rear of the launchers. Munitions are loaded from the rear through the simple breech assembly seen here.

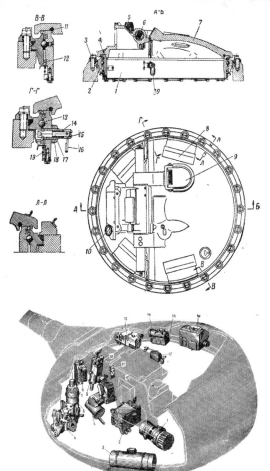

TOP The commander's cupola remained unchanged for the life of the tank but did have its sights replaced as they were improved.

ABOVE Layout of the fire controls and stabilizer elements for the two-axis stabilizer for the armament. The gunner's controls for this design were little different than for the T-55.

T-62MV MAIN BATTLE TANK VARIANTS

When the Israelis invaded Lebanon in Operation *Peace for Galilee* in 1982, one of the surprises to Soviet observers operating with Syrian forces was the use of 'Blazer' explosive reactive armour (ERA) protection mounted on Israeli M48 and M60 tanks. Blazer armour had been developed for the Israeli Defence Forces (IDF) in collaboration with the German engineer Dr Manfred Held.

A captured M48 was sent back to Moscow for evaluation and the result was a number of Soviet experts pointing out that, while they had recommended such armour since as far back as 1949 at the Scientific Research Institute of Steel (NII Stali), with work in the 1950s having resulted in early prototypes in the 1960s and the system being ready for service in the early 1970s, the technology had not at the time been adopted by the Soviet Army due to 'psychological unpreparedness' in the military powers that be.

As a result, the same NII Stali and other institutes returned to the previously shelved subject and created the first generation of explosive reactive armour for Soviet tanks; the T-62, like the T-55, T-64 and T-80, was among the first recipients of this new technology. The 'new' technology was created in record time, with less than a year passing from specification to design, build, test and approval, much helped by the two decades of previously shelved development.

The first generation of KDZ* was dubbed 'Kontakt-1' and consisted of a heavy steel weather-proof container that mounted two 'sandwiches' with each made of two steel plates with a thin layer of explosives between them. The plates were dubbed 'flyers', and the idea was that when the casing was penetrated by the molten jet of a HEAT round it would detonate the explosive; the top flyer plate would then disrupt the jet and

---

* KDZ – Komplekt Dopolnitelnoy Zaschiti (additional armour set). DZ is also referred to more specifically as Dynamicheskaya Zashita (dynamic protection).

(1) Here is a typical M-series upgraded T-62 tank at the Leningrad Breakthrough Museum at Nevsky Pyatachok, Leningrad, now St Petersburg. This one is serial number 806V2179, a T-62 Model 1967 built in June 1968. All three variants of the T-62 were given the upgrade packages. The tanks were all fitted with additional armour consisting of a hull floor pack, a glacis package and the two circular packages on the front of the turret.

(2) Interestingly this tank has both the KTD-2 laser rangefinder and the 1K13 combination sight fitted. The array does not cover the gunner's sight area and leaves a large port for the sight to view through it.

(3) The glacis armour was modified to permit use of the engineer equipment fittings when required such as KMT mine trawls. Part of the upgrade includes the RMSh tracks for those tanks not refitted with them.

(4) The KTD-2 has an armoured door that can be opened from inside the tank to go into operation.

(5) Likewise, a similar type of door is part of the 1K13 armoured sight head mount.

(6) Due to the presence of the BDD sections the forward 'desant' hand rails have been removed from the tank. Two lifting lugs were part of each turret armour array to permit them to be mounted by a crane.

(7) There is a small circular ring present where the front 'desant' rail was removed.

(8) All turret fittings other than the rails are still present, but now the fixed auxiliary headlight is mounted on the right BDD armour section.

(9) A notch is provided at the front edge of the right BDD section to permit unhindered fire from the coaxial machine gun. Searchlight linkage remains as before; the auxiliary light is properly aligned with the zero angle of the turret and parallel to the main gun.

(10) The power cable for the auxiliary headlight runs through the BDD armour section.

(11) The L-2G searchlight has its protective cover fitted on this tank.

(12) The searchlight linkage on all T-62s is connected to a ring bolted to the front of the bulge at the base of the gun.

(13) The lower glacis armour has some small openings in it but has a removable section located underneath the tank's emergency exit hatch that can be dropped when the hatch is used. The tubes for controls for either a mine trawl or bulldozer blade also were ported through the glacis and can be seen on either side of the glacis package.

(14) The tow hooks have been moved to the top of the glacis BDD panels. The angled braces are for use to protect the tank, when using a mine trawl, from having it bounce too high.

(15) The mud guard locks are still used on this tank as well. They hold the mud guards out of the way when adjusting track tension.

(16) Although not quite visible in this photo the serial number is also inscribed on the outer casing of the glacis BDD armour where the shadow of the gun barrel falls on the centre of the glacis.

(17) Because of their bulky and projecting nature, the two turret BDD sections were colloquially nicknamed 'Brovi' (eyebrows) or 'Ilyich's Eyebrows' after those of Leonid Brezhnev by tank troops.

(18) Surprisingly no thermal jacket was provided in the upgrade package for this T-62 at the Muzei Tekhniki at Arkhangelskoe, Krasnogorsk, near Moscow.

(19) Here is a newly refurbished T-62M Model 1972. It does not appear to be using the normal travel locks on the tracks. The rail car says it is 1954 construction but apparently is a dedicated delivery car and not a more common transport car.

(20) This tank now mounts the three-section snorkel at the rear of the turret and only has mounts for three ammo canisters for the 12.7mm machine gun. As can be seen here the brow armour sections stand-off about 30cm from the surface of the turret.

(21) This transport car seems to load 'circus style' from one to the other and has extra bracing materials and inter-car ramps stowed at the front. Note that the covers for this material fold down to let the tank pass.

(22) Another T-62M Model 1972 (at the Kantemirovskaya Tank Division base at Naro-Fominsk near Moscow) with the upgraded skirting and also with a splash guard in place in the centre of the glacis package.

(23) It is possible that these latter photos of the T-62M Model 1972 could be the same tank in different paint schemes; in recent years tanks offered for sale abroad are often repainted between shows.

(24) A T-62 Model 1972 being shown with only the laser rangefinder and 1K13 sight upgrades. This particular T-62 belonged to the KBP Design Bureau, Tula, and was used for testing ATGM systems and sights. (Andrey Aksenov)

(25) A T-62M Model 1972 at another arms show thoughtfully labelled to tell you what it is! (Andrey Aksenov)

(26) A company of T-62Ms on exercise; the front one is a Model 1972 with the AAMG dismounted and the rest are either Model 1961 or 1967 tanks.

(27) Another view of the same company showing the different variants.

(28) Another unit coming down a mountain road.

the bottom one would bounce off the armour of the vehicle to finish negating its penetration capability. However, it only had a marginal effect on APFSDS rounds. State trials with 'Kontakt' (later Kontakt-1) KDZ were conducted for potential series fitment on the T-55, T-62, T-64B, T-72A and T-80B in 1982.

The first ERA elements were, however, only 250mm in length, and not as effective as Western ones of up to 500mm. Also it took up to 200 elements to fully protect a T-62 on its glacis, turret and front third of the side skirts. The fittings for the ERA elements (studs to receive bolts that held them in place) had to be installed by a depot or tank repair factory, but the installation of the element flyer plates and explosives could be done by unit and crew level labour. The armament, fire control system and ammunition complement of the T-62MV was unchanged from the T-62M.

In addition to the 'Kontakt-1' KDZ armour package, the modified T-62MV tanks (as designated when fitted with the V-55U diesel engine) and T-62MV-1 tanks (when fitted with the V-46-5 diesel engine) usually had all of the other M-series modifications, including the additional hull floor and glacis armour, the 'Volna' fire control system, KTD-2 laser rangefinder, BV-62 ballistic computer and a thermal sleeve for the gun barrel. The T-62MV was accepted for service with the Soviet Army in 1985. A T-62MV with a full set of ERA blocks had a combat weight of 38.4 metric tonnes. Some T-62MV tanks had KDZ blocks mounted on the side skirts.

T-62 M-1996 MAIN BATTLE TANK (TULA-OKB PROJECT)

In 1996, the Tula-OKB based in the famous arms-producing city created an upgraded version of the T-62 tank with a modified fire control system and optics package. The tank was tested for service but as far as is known no further development was undertaken.

T-62M (T-62 M-2001) KBTM OMSK

Following the collapse of the Soviet Union, the KBTM design bureau and the Omsk Machine Building Plant, as with all military enterprises, struggled for new work and to maintain any ongoing series production. In addition to developing new designs such as the ultimately cancelled

Obiekt-640 'Chorny Oryol' (Black Eagle), the design bureau and plant also worked on the modernization of older Soviet-era tanks, concentrating on the T-55 due to its wide export distribution. In the first decade of the 21st century the plant also, however, designed an upgrade for the long-serving T-62 tank that was first seen at the 'VTTV Omsk-2001' military exhibition held in Omsk in June 2001.

The new T-62M (technically T-62 M-2001 based on the year of its development) – but not officially so-designated – featured a new 1K13D fire control system, new sighting for the gunner and a new TKN-3M commander's sight, a thermal sleeve for the armament, the 'Meteor' twin axis gun stabilization system and a new 12.7mm NSVT heavy anti-aircraft machine gun. Armour protection was upgraded by the installation of first-generation 'Kontakt-1' ERA blocks on the hull and modified integral second-generation 'Kontakt-5' additional armour on the turret, side skirts for the running gear protecting from HEAT rounds, and new smoke grenade launchers. The driver-mechanic was provided with a TVK-3 day/night vision device, while the tank was provided with new communications, and central fire extinguisher system. Power was now provided by a V-46-5MS diesel engine developing 690hp, giving the tank a maximum speed of 50km/h and an improved road range of 610km. There were also upgrades to the running gear. The 'T-62M' tank was built and tested for service and for potential export, but did not progress beyond prototype stage. Timing is everything as they say, and with the Omsk facility now incorporated into UVZ the plant produces the T-72B3 upgrade of the also not-so-young T-72 as an alternative to the production T-90A, which originally replaced the T-72 series in production. Had the financing been available a few years earlier, perhaps the T-62 would also have had a second life in post-Soviet, Russian Army service.

CAPITAL REBUILDS

The T-62 underwent a series of major standardized upgrades during its service life as detailed above. T-62 tanks were rarely scrapped, but in the process of capital rebuild there was inevitably some mixing of components, such that for instance an upgraded T-62M might have been rebuilt based on an early M-1968 production hull, but fitted with the later M-1972 turret, and then later upgraded to T-62M standard. There are therefore some anomalies in specification reflecting the wide usage, and modifications, of the tank series over six decades of service.

CONCLUSION

Officially the Soviet Union built a total of 19,019 T-62 tanks, including 627 T-62K command tanks, and an additional pre-series batch of five T-62A tanks when production at the UVZ ceased in October 1973, after 11 years of series production. The tank had proven an excellent replacement (or rather supplement) for the T-54 and T-55 in Soviet Army service, retaining the best and proven elements of the earlier tank designs including the general layout, engine, transmission and running gear, but with a radical and significantly more powerful main armament, increased engine power output and improved range.

Overall the T-62 proved to be a rugged and generally reliable design, with a relatively high-assessed durability rate per 100km driven. The main items likely to fail according to Soviet records were in the engine and main armament groups, mostly due to the much more powerful gun than the D-10TS in the T-54 and T-55. Guaranteed running between capital rebuilding was 7,000km. After newer tanks replaced it in the Soviet Army, many T-62s were sold or given to other countries and went on to serve in their militaries until the present day. Large numbers of T-62s were scrapped in the early 1990s in accordance with Conventional Forces Europe (CFE) treaty limitations, with T-62 tanks quietly rusting away in open scrapyards at Strelnya near St. Petersburg and Stepnoy near Omsk in the early 1990s. There were also significant numbers of T-62 tanks inherited by now independent former Soviet republics, in particular Kazakhstan, Ukraine and Uzbekistan, some of which were scrapped. Small numbers of T-62 'Jubilee'* tanks remained in service with the Russian Federation into the 21st century, however, with the T-62 being officially removed from Russian Army service in accordance with a Russian Ministry of Defence directive only in February 2013, after five full decades of service.

With the T-62 still serving with the modern Russian Army in small numbers today, a service life of more than 55 years is rather impressive for any tank in this day and age, which is testament to the sound principles of the original design, greatly contested as it was within Soviet design bureau inner politics at the time of its difficult birth.

---

* The T-62 was occasionally referred to as the 'Jubilee' tank, on the basis that its debut appearance was at the 9 May 1965 Victory Parade on the 20th anniversary of the end of World War II in Europe in May 1945. Development of the tank had, however, begun in 1957, the 40th anniversary of the Russian Revolution, and it is often referred to as having had its public debut on Red Square on 7 November 1965, the 50th anniversary of the Russian Revolution, so the tank spans several different jubilees.

(1) A T-62M Model 1967 upgraded with 'Kontakt-1' reactive armour replacing the brow armour package. However, all of the covers have been removed for its use as a preserved tank.
(2) The same tank showing the 1K13 sight on the left side of the turret.
(3) From the rear this tank shows no difference from an unmodified tank.
(4) A fully kitted out T-62MV Model 1961 or 1967 in transport at the Muzei Tekhniki, Arkhangelskoe, near Moscow. The flyer plates for the reactive armour are not present unless the tank is going into combat, but the protective covers ('bricks') are in place. A full set of reactive armour units is over 200 blocks or

elements and covers the front 60-degree arc of the tank. This one has the full side set including elements mounted on the auxiliary upper skirting.
(5) A full side set is 44 elements arranged as shown.
(6) The reactive armour protects the hull sides between the road wheels and the fenders and upper hull. Due to the bolts used for mounting, the elements cannot cover the hinges between skirt panels.
(7) The elements are stacked on the turret in this manner – usually a column of three – to provide as much cover as possible.

(8) The rear of the tank is left to its own devices in this fitting.

(9) Given most angles of engagement – and the Soviets did a lot of work on this during the Great Patriotic War – it was felt that nothing coming at the tank from the front would cause much damage after this length of the side so these are the last elements needed.

(10) Close-up of the T-62MV Model 1972 in a tank graveyard. This has a slightly different fit for the side elements.

(11) More T-62s in the Strelnya plant scrapyard in 1994. (Andrey Aksenov)

(12) In 2005 KB Transmash (Omsk) offered an upgraded version of the T-62M, now fitted with 'Kontakt-5' reactive armour and a new set of containers on the turret. The 'Kontakt-5' panels were interchangeable with 'Kontakt-1' so the hull elements were retained. (Andrey Aksenov)

(13) This tank is a Model 1967 but Omsk has now added a pintle mount for the AAMG behind the loader's hatch as well as one forward and to the left of the hatch. (Andrey Aksenov)

(14) Side view showing the two pintle mounts as well as the ammo canisters, smoke grenade launchers and the new reactive armour containers. (Andrey Aksenov)

(15) The skirts are drilled to accept the side reactive armour elements but not installed; maybe it was easier to advertise this way! (Andrey Aksenov)

(16) There are four of the new containers on each side of the turret; this tank now also sports a Type 902B smoke grenade launcher set on each side of the turret (16 tubes). (Andrey Aksenov)

(17) There is a slightly different arrangement of the reactive armour containers on the glacis as well. (Andrey Aksenov)

(18) Close-up of the new machine gun mount on the front pinion. This appears to be for a newer weapon like either the 12.7mm NSVT or 'Kord' machine guns. (Andrey Aksenov)

(19) Close-up of the mounting of the reactive armour containers on the turret. Each one holds multiple flyer plate elements. (Andrey Aksenov)

(20) A new bin with an armoured cover has been installed on the right fender for the V-46M-5 external air filter. (Andrey Aksenov)

(21) The modified tank is put through its paces at an arms display. (Andrey Aksenov)

(22) The changes do make the tank look impressive! (Andrey Aksenov)

CHAPTER FOUR
DERIVATIVE VEHICLES AND FOREIGN COPIES

INTRODUCTION

Unlike the T-54 and T-55, there were no directly manufactured derivative tanks or vehicles built on the T-62 chassis that were adopted for service. It did have one 'half brother' in the IT-1 missile-armed tank destroyer favoured by Soviet Premier N. S. Khrushchev as well as the prototypes of experimental armed and armoured vehicles and the stillborn Obiekt-167, which could have become the T-62B.

While no country was fully licensed to build the T-62, the Democratic People's Republic of Korea did have partial rights and used them to develop two tanks on its own, the Ch'onma and the Pokpo'ong. The Ch'onma was sold in limited numbers as the 'Korean T-62' to those countries that sought them. The People's Liberation Army of China (PLA) captured a Soviet T-62 tank in 1969, relatively early in its Soviet career, and reverse-engineered it to become their WZ-122, but after testing did not accept it for service.

Worn-out T-62s were converted into either recovery vehicles like the BTS-2 and BTS-4 (Bronirovanniy Tyagach Sredny or Sredny Tankovy Tyagach meaning medium tank tractor) or into various prototype fire-fighting vehicles such as the 'Impulse-2'.

T-62 DERIVATIVES AND PROTOTYPES

IT-1 ARMOURED 2K4 MISSILE SYSTEM ARMED TANK DESTROYER (OBIEKT-150)

As anti-tank guided missiles began to appear as viable battlefield systems in the mid 1950s, the Soviets began to carry out research on both the missiles and their guidance systems and on methods to carry them for use on the battlefield. This received an official blessing from the SM SSSR on 28 May 1955, when research was authorized into this area. V. A. Malyshev, who was then the Minister of Transport Machinery Construction, called a meeting on this topic in August 1956. After two days to consider the idea, all parties (Leningrad, Kharkov and Nizhny Tagil) presented their ideas.

Initially the Leningrad 'Kirov' Factory under Zhosef Kotin eagerly accepted the task, but Kartsev also offered the services of the UVZ to investigate the problem. He initially proposed using first the defunct Obiekt-140 chassis and then a T-54B chassis for the missile carrier, but later changed it over to the new Obiekt-165/Obiekt-166 chassis. They submitted a draft proposal for the carrier vehicle and it was approved by the NTK GBTU on 31 December 1957 (this was after Malyshev's death but clearly he was the one who had drafted it).

As was the norm in the Soviet Union, development work on main battle tanks armed with 'PTRK' anti-tank guided missiles (ATGMs) was undertaken in competition at several design institutes. Work on mountings for the T-62 tank was undertaken by Plant No. 183 in Nizhny Tagil, and at the VNII-100 institute. Development work on such systems was authorized in accordance with a Resolution of the SM SSSR dated 8 May 1957, with the future IT-1 (Obiekt-150) developed at Nizhny Tagil in accordance with 'Thematic No. 2' of the aforesaid resolution relating to purpose-built tank destroyers on a tank chassis.

Kartsev and his team at UVZ in Nizhny Tagil initially worked with OKB-16 (later TsKB-14, and then KBTochMash) – led by A. Eh. Nudelman – on development of the 3M7 missile for the new vehicle, with the work later headed by a group led by A. A. Raspletin, along with institutes including KB-1 (controls), TsNII-173 (stabilization) and TsKB-373 (sighting).

The original design drawings completed in 1958 at Plant No. 183 envisaged work being initiated on a T-54 chassis for trials purposes, and indeed UVZ duly provided a T-54 tank chassis for the 2K4 'Drakon', but as protracted development work continued the switch was made to the Obiekt-166 chassis. The specific design chassis for the 2K4 'Drakon' system became Obiekt-150 on the Obiekt-166 (T-62) platform and was to mount the 2K4 ATGM system firing the 3M7 'Drakon' missile. This missile was selected to be the new ATGM for mobile armoured chassis deployment on 18 December 1958, when it received approval from the Main Artillery Directorate – GAU (soon to become the Main Missile and Artillery Directorate or GRAU, reflecting its changing and widened role).

The first system was installed in a T-54B chassis in April 1959, this vehicle duly arriving at the NIIBT at Kubinka on 7 September 1959. It was demonstrated to the Politburo on 22 July 1960, and caught the imagination of Soviet Premier Nikita Khrushchev. Kartsev presented the prototype to the First Secretary; however, after climbing inside a helicopter at the same exhibition he began cursing. He then asked Colonel I. K. Kobrakov, deputy chief of the NIIBT, if the 'Drakon' missiles opened up in flight. When told, no, he directed the developers to look at work that Vladimir Chelomey (chief of OKB-52) had done with missiles. Khrushchev then turned to

Kartsev and asked him if Obiekt-150 carried its missiles in a drum loader. Kartsev told the First Secretary, no, it did not. Khrushchev was adamant that it should have a drum, but was then pointedly told by Kartsev that if it did then it would have no place for the crew in the turret; anyway, the rectangular ammunition stowage worked well enough. The rumour later started (as an anecdote from Kartsev but apparently apocryphal) that Kartsev had apparently grabbed Khrushchev by the lapels to get his point across and some joked that the First Secretary was afraid of him! As it was, Khrushchev thanked him and work progressed on Obiekt-150.

In June 1963 tests at the NIIBT, with the system now on the T-62 chassis, were quite promising as the vehicle managed seven hits out of ten missiles; one was a clear miss and two others failed; 70 per cent accuracy was considered outstanding. On 14 September 1964, a firing demonstration was held for Khrushchev. He had some comments about it, later stating no more tanks were needed but just anti-tank guided missiles. Six weeks later he was removed as First Secretary by Leonid Brezhnev, and the Obiekt-150, as well as all of the tank projects, continued to develop.

With the particularly protracted development of the IT-1 with its complex 2K4 'Drakon' missile system and semi-active command line of sight (SACLOS) radio guidance finally completed, the Council of Ministers of the USSR (SM SSSR) finally accepted Obiekt-150 for service on 3 September 1968 as the IT-1 tank destroyer (Istribitel Tankov – tank destroyer) under Resolution No. 703-261 and confirmed by Order of the Soviet Ministry of Defence No. 0269 dated 6 November 1968.

The IT-1 was issued on a limited scale of one battalion with the Belorussian Military District (BVO) and another with the Transcarpathian Military District (PrikVO), with IT-1 'Drakon' vehicles being rotated out of storage and the crews training for the most part on standard T-62 tanks. The IT-1 'Drakon' was 'series' produced from 1968 to 1970; it is the only tank armed exclusively with missile armament to ever achieve production and service in the Soviet Union, albeit in modest (by Soviet standards …) numbers.

The IT-1, armed with the 2K4 'Drakon' missile system and the radio command SACLOS-guided 3M7 missile was at the time of its introduction a technological marvel. The IT-1 could engage enemy armour at a range of up to 3,300m in daytime and up to 600m at night, and the 3M7 missile could penetrate 250mm of armour sloped at 60 degrees or up to 500mm of vertical armour plate. The radio command SACLOS guidance had variable channel settings and was relatively immune from interference jamming. It also featured a particularly high hit probability at range, claimed as 96.7 per cent. So why was it rapidly withdrawn from service? The reasons were multiple.

As with the T-10M, T-55 and Obiekt-167, the T-62 was also experimentally fitted with a triple 9M14 'Malyutka' ATGM launcher (see page 104). While good in theory it failed in practice. This tank was officially described as 'Obiekt-166 PTUR' during trials.

The IT-1 system had been developed as one of several 'themes' related to alternative and competitive ATGM development dating from an SM SSSR resolution of 28 May 1955. The development of the IT-1 had been undertaken at Plant No. 183 at Nizhny Tagil as 'Theme No. 2'.

Not least, the IT-1 development programme, specifically the missile command system, had taken far longer than anticipated to perfect, as a result of which the IT-1 entered service 7–8 years behind schedule. However, the parallel 'themes' included similar if less complex ATGM systems mounted on lightly armoured and even unarmoured vehicles. The first-generation 3M6 'Schmel' (NATO: AT-1 Snapper) ATGM mounted on the GAZ-69 and BRDM armoured car chassis had been joined by the 3M11 'Fleyta' (NATO: AT-2 Swatter) and the 9M14M 'Malyutka' (NATO: AT-3 Sagger) on the same chassis all in the time the 'Drakon' had been in development. Further, as all such vehicles were long-range ATGM systems operating beyond the accurate range of their tank-gunned opponents, the need for a relatively heavily armoured launch vehicle for such a role was superfluous. The IT-1 was in part a victim of its own development complexity and the rapidly changing operational deployment of alternative ATGM systems that could perform the role the IT-1 was envisaged for. In summary, the IT-1 had, by the time it entered service, already been overtaken by other, less expensive and complex, solutions taken into service while it had been in development. The vehicle was removed from service in the early 1970s, having had one of the shortest service records of any Soviet armoured vehicle – then years in development followed by only three years in active service. Some redundant vehicles were for several years used for driver training, with a large percentage later converted to BTS-4V armoured recovery vehicles. Decommissioned IT-1 vehicles could still be seen in the storage yard of the LTRZ in Lvov as late as 1984.

However, the 3M7 'Drakon' concept would live on, being further developed into the 9M112 'Kobra' through-barrel ATGM as initially installed on the T-64B accepted for service in 1973 and subsequently used by other Soviet tanks.

With regard to the description of the IT-1, the vehicle was basically a standard T-62 chassis with a low cast turret. The commander sat on the left of the turret, provided with a 7.62mm SGMT machine gun, with the missile operator on the

ABOVE LEFT A handful of T-62 chassis, or more often as here IT-1 chassis, were rebuilt as BTS-4V tank recovery vehicles (see page 103). Other than being on the T-62 type chassis it was not any different than the T-54/T-55 based vehicles.

LEFT Another view of the standard BTS-4 vehicle on a T-54/55 chassis. All of the equipment between the BTS-4 and BTS-4V was identical other than the base chassis.

Like the T-55 and T-10M tanks, the T-62 was also trialled with the ZEhT-1 'Zontik' expanding mesh anti-ATGM/RPG screen (see page 104). It was considered too fragile and vulnerable to snagging and damage to be viable.

right; they were separated by the 2K4 launcher and two six-round containers stowing 12 missiles in the autoloader. Three 'reserve' missiles were stored at the rear of the fighting compartment for a total of 15 missiles carried within the hull. The missiles were loaded onto a stabilized launcher that elevated them about 60cm above the turret for firing. The driver-mechanic sat in the usual 'T-62' location. The vehicle had a combat weight of 34.5 metric tonnes.

The 2K4 'Drakon' was typical of ATGM missiles of that period in that it was large (180mm in diameter and 54kg in weight) and relatively slow with a maximum flight speed of about 215 metres per second. It used SACLOS radio guidance as detailed above, so the gunner had to see the missile to guide it to the target, with daylight and night ranges of approximately 3,300 and 600 metres as also detailed above. Video on the Internet shows test shots against captured World-War-II German armour demonstrating that a single missile could obliterate a medium tank like a Pz.Kpfw III.

Firing was accomplished either from the halt or moving at cross-country speeds. When the missile was extended, a hatch opened and the launcher popped up. The missile was held in light square-shaped shipping guards, which then broke free and allowed the main wings at the rear to extend and the protective guard over the warhead to drop away. When the operator acquired a target, he pressed fire and then kept the missile in his sight all the way to the target. A reload operation took just a few seconds, but the operator could only control one missile at a time. The missile used a choice of seven different radio frequencies and two different code settings to avoid interference from other launchers or jamming.

OBIEKT-150 WITH 73MM 2A28 'GROM'

In 1968, the year the Obiekt-150 was taken into production as the IT-1 tank destroyer, a version was developed mounting the same armament as the BMP-1 MICV. Details are not currently known.

BTS-4V ARV

In the mid 1970s, approximately 100 IT-1 vehicles were converted at the Lvovskiy Tankoremontny Zavod (Lvov Tank Repair Plant – BTRZ) as the BTS-4V armoured recovery vehicle. The BTS-4V was an almost identical conversion – with the same set of recovery equipment – as the standard BTS-2/4.

T-62-BASED EXPERIMENTAL VEHICLES

T-62 WITH ZEHT-1 'ZONTIK' TANK APPLIQUÉ ARMOUR

As with the T-55 that preceded it, the T-62 was in 1964 trialled with unique folding screen armour protection. Designed by VNII-100 and referred to collectively as *Protivokumulyativnaya Ehkrannaya Zaschita* or anti-cumulative round appliqué protection, it was also called 'Setchataya Ehkrannaya Zaschita' (SEhZ), or screen (net) armour shielding. The additional appliqué armour was intended to provide extra frontal protection against cumulative rounds and RPG-type rockets by means of the 'Zontik', with six duraluminium shields providing additional stand-off protection for the sides of the tank.

Two types of particularly novel screen 'Ehkrannaya Zaschita' or appliqué armour were developed, designated respectively 'Zontik' (umbrella) and 'Shater' (tent). The 'Zontik' system, as the name suggested, consisted of a large five-section unfolding wire mesh umbrella stowed on (around) the gun barrel, which unfolded forward to form a 360-degree forward-facing 'umbrella', giving the base tank stand-off protection over its frontal aspects. The 'Zontik' system took 15 minutes to install around the gun barrel, and thereafter 2–3 minutes to deploy as required, providing a mesh screen approximately 1.8 metres ahead of the hull armour. The 'Zontik' added a negligible 60kg to the combat weight of the tank.

The 'Shater' system was a similar but vertically mounted 'tent' or 'yurt' which provided 360-degree protection for the whole tank including its upper surfaces, long before the advent of indirect flight path guided munitions and attack helicopters. The 'Shater' kit weighed 200kg. The system also included the aforementioned shields, which sprung out at 30 degrees to protect the tank sides, and also concurrently tested duraluminium reinforced rubber skirts to protect the hull above the road wheels from ATGM and RPG projectiles.

The ЗЭТ-1 (ZEhT-1) or 'Zashita Ehkrannaya Tankovaya' (tank appliqué armour) was tested at the NIIBT polygon at Kubinka in 1964 for use with the T-62. The test results showed a considerable increase in overall protection; however, the 'Zontik' and 'Shater' systems were ultimately dropped, albeit the use of spring-out combination armour shields continued to be developed for the Obiekt-432A (T-64A) and T-72 main battle tanks. The use of side skirts featuring combination steel and rubber armour would later become standard on series production T-62M and T-62MV tanks.

T-62 WITH 9K11 'MALYUTKA' ANTI-TANK GUIDED MISSILE SYSTEM (OBIEKT-166ML)

As with the T-55 and T-10, the T-62 underwent trials in 1961–63 with a rear-mounted turret 'cage' mounting three 3M14 'Malyutka' missiles for the 9K11 ATGM system in accordance with a Russian Ministry of Defence order dated January 1961. The intent was to provide secondary long-range anti-tank capability over the range 2,500–3,000m.

All three mounts were developed by OKB-174 at Plant No. 174 from 1961 under the direction of A. A. Morov. Initially the fixed launcher mount was situated on the right rear of the turret. But it was found that when firing the missiles they had to clear the searchlight on the front of the turret, and setting them at that angle made them fly high, whereupon it was difficult for the gunner to acquire the missile so he could track it and guide it to the target.

They next tried a motor drive to elevate the missiles but that was considered too fragile, and eventually they simply fixed the mount at a small angle to clear the searchlight but low enough so the gunner could see and acquire it. Preparation time was about 30 seconds. The 9M14M missiles were directed towards their target via a 9V332 control point/ML-250 sight mounted within the turret and aimed via a TShB-22 TSh-2B-41 tank sight. The T62-based prototype was tested at NIIBT Kubinka in October–December 1964; however, although 30 systems were built on the T-62 MBT for long-term service evaluation purposes, the system was not taken into service, as the unarmoured launcher rack was considered vulnerable and the inability to fire on the move was a major drawback. Development of the 'Malyutka' secondary anti-tank system continued on the T-62 but was ultimately not standardized on any Soviet tank.

T-62 WITH 125MM D-81T GUN AND 'ZHELUD' AUTOLOADER

After trials with the Obiekt-167 tank (see below) the final effort that Kartsev made to upgrade the T-62 to better deal with new threats was to fit the 125mm D-81T (2A26) gun and the 'Zhelud' autoloader to the tank in 1967. While it worked well – and showed that later other countries like Iraq and the DPRK could make the same swap – it found no favour with the Soviet government and was cancelled.

T-62P (OBIEKT 166P) WITH POV-50 RADIATION LINER

Two T-62P (Obiekt-166P) prototypes were built at Plant No. 183 in Nizhny Tagil under the direction of Kartsev in December 1962, and tested at the NIIBT polygon at Kubinka from 20 February until 20 March 1963. The vehicles were fitted with a combination of POV-50 anti-radiation material, with (Podboya and Nadboya) screening on the hull and turret. The hull was fitted with 30mm-thick 'nadboy' panels on the upper armour surfaces, with the turret fitted with 55mm 'nadboy' armour. The armour was designated podboya (nadboya) 'POV-50'. The modification was not carried out on series production tanks.

T-62 PST-63 'PLAVSREDSTV' SYSTEM (OBIEKT-619B)

The PST-63 (Obiekt-619) 'Plavsredstva' ('amphibious device') was developed at the KB (*Konstruktorskoye Byuro* or design bureau) of the Omsk Transport Machine Building Plant (OZTM). The PST-63 was a modification the earlier PST-54 system developed at Kharkov from 1953 for operation with the then-current T-54 tank. The overall purpose of the system in its various modifications was intended to provide forced-crossing capability over short stretches of open water.

The PST-63 system locked a T-62 tank between left and right pontoon sections, which were discarded when the tank reached shore or soon

A conventional attempt at an amphibious tank landing system was the PST-63 pontoon assembly, which also clipped onto the tank.

thereafter. The advantage of the system was that the tank (at least theoretically) could fire its main armament while afloat. The T-62 tanks attached to the PST-63 were standard production tanks, but fitted with front and rear location points welded to the hull immediately above the track fenders. In official documents the system was referred to as the PST-63, but during plant trials as the PS-3. The T-62 tank was modified for use with the PST-63 pontoon set as the Obiekt-619B.

The system could operate within a maximum sea state of Storm Force Five, at a speed of 12km/h, and with a range of 80–100km. The original PST-54 was subsequently modified as the PST-U, the PST-63 and latterly the PST-64M. The PST-63 was developed for use with T-55, T-62 and T-64 tanks as the Obiekt-619A, Obiekt-619B and Obiekt-619V respectively. The original prototype underwent trials from 1968 and was accepted for service with the Soviet Army by an Order of the Soviet Ministry of Defence dated 24 February 1969. A total of 162 PST-63 systems were built at OZTM in Omsk between 1969 and 1975. The majority of the systems used adapted T-55 tanks, with a smaller number of T-62 modifications being built as the Obiekt-619B.

LEFT The tank was used to power the assembly with the pontoons providing buoyancy. But even with their bulk they were offset by the weight of the tank.

BELOW LEFT The tank had sufficient room to rotate its turret in the forward hemisphere of the assembly.

CENTRE LEFT However, like all such assemblies, it required very gentle approaches to water to avoid either damaging the pontoons or pranging them on the bottom.

BELOW As can be seen the entire assembly had very low freeboard. A large trunk around the engine air intake and exhaust grilles was necessary to avoid flooding the engine bay.

FAR LEFT This looks like fire, but is more likely the splash when launching the assembly from another vessel at sea.

LEFT An overview of the PST-63, in this instance mounting a T-55 tank.

OBIEKT-80 (OBIEKT-626B) T-62 TANKODESANTNOYE PLAVSREDSTVO HYDROFOIL ASSAULT LANDING SYSTEM

One of the most fascinating military machines of all time to actually make it into metal incorporated the T-62 as the 'transport load'. The system, designated the Obiekt-80 'Tankodesantnoye Plavsredstvo' (tank-desant-assault swimming), was an even more extravagant means of crossing water than the PST-63 as already described, with the difference being in the speed of travel.

The Obiekt-80 was developed in 1964 at the SKB (spetsial'noye konstruktorskoye byuro, or special design bureau) of the Navashinsky Shipbuilding Plant, also known as the 'Oka' plant, located in the Gorky region. The Obiekt-80 was described as a high-speed tank-desant 'plavsredstva', basically a high-speed assault craft for delivering tanks across large areas of enclosed sea or inland open water. So fascinating was the idea itself that not only were several prototypes of this strange but amazing system built and tested, but moreover the system was put into limited production and service.

The T-62 tank integral to the Obiekt-80 design was modified as the Obiekt-626B under the direction of A. A. Morov. As with the 'slow boat' PST-63, the 'express' transport version of the T-62 was a standard line fitted with welded cross-section mounting points for attachment to the Obiekt-80 pontoon sections.

The original Obiekt-80 was tested from December 1964 until February 1965 using a T-55 built at Plant No. 174 in Omsk duly modified as the Obiekt-626A for use with the Obiekt-80 'plavsredstvo'. The tank was mounted between the two large pontoons, which were effectively high-speed motor launches, constructed of V48-4T grade aluminium. Each launch was powered by a naval M50 F-3 diesel engine developing 1,200hp and driving a 670mm-diameter three-bladed propeller via a long prop-shaft. Steering was by means of an electrically controlled rudder. In comparison with the earlier and similar looking 'PST' means of delivering tanks across water, and the tracked GSP pontoon ferry, which served the same purpose, the Obiekt-80 added the dimension of speed. Once waterborne, the Obiekt-80 launches built up speed, and then hydrofoil 'wings' were hydraulically lowered under the front and rear of each pontoon launch section and the engines opened up to full power, lifting the hulls and tank straddled between them clear of the water.

The 16.3m-long and 10.7m-wide Obiekt-80 weighed 22 metric tonnes without the tank suspended by the aluminium pontoons. Each Obiekt-80 pontoon launch had its own control cabin with a driver – or more accurately pilot – and a mechanic. The launches could also carry a small number of infantry to directly support the tank on landing.

Mounting the tank to the Obiekt-80 pontoon sections required 45 minutes, the tank being located via four welded attachment beams mounted above the track fenders and by steel cables. As the Obiekt-80 reached shore, the hydrofoils were raised, the pontoons dropped back into the water and the tank could eject the pontoons in shallow water or once on dry land. The maximum beach slope the system could overcome was 15 degrees.

In addition to moving T-62 tanks, the pontoons were also able to individually ferry loads of up to 7,000kg or to be joined together to transport up to 40,000kg including secondary tracked and wheeled vehicles – effectively operating as a high-speed GSP ferry. The Obiekt-80 could operate at up to 60km/h in Force 3 sea conditions in hydrofoil mode, with a range of 400km, or as a 'conventional' powered pontoon system with the hydrofoils stowed and the pontoons in the water in a sea state of up to Force 6. Without the hydrofoils lowered or with the engines cranked to full throttle, the Obiekt-80 could conduct the above roles at a more leisurely 16km/h. The tank could fire its armament from water, doubtless with significantly varying accuracy depending on sea conditions. The use of the hydrofoil system versus pottering along at 16km/h (a typical cargo shipping speed) would have been dictated partly by operational requirements and partly by the weather. It is difficult to describe the Obiekt-80, as it could operate as a high-speed hydrofoil pontoon system, a launch or as a conventional 'low-speed' ferry as required.

ABOVE The tank rode high on the pontoons and in theory could use its gun to suppress beach fire.

LEFT CENTRE As can be seen here, the pontoons used retractable front and rear hydrofoil blades to lift the craft clear of the water at speed. The solution turned out to be the 'Aist' class of LCAC air cushion vehicles which could each carry one tank.

LEFT Another view of the beached hydrofoil pontoons in place on the tank.

ABOVE One of the pontoons has also been preserved. Here it sits in the Kubinka scrapyard in the 1990s. Note the control cabin at the front of the pontoon.
LEFT The prototype 626B tank remained for several years at Kubinka. Note the fittings to attach the tank to the pontoons. Other than those fittings, the T-62 is a standard line tank.
BELOW LEFT One of the moveable locating arms that locked onto the T-62 hull. The pontoon has suffered damage, most likely while being moved around the yard.
BELOW Rear view of the surviving pontoon showing the engine bay (empty) and the missing elements at the rear of its hull.

The highly secret system employed the same method of mounting a T-62 tank straddled between two left and right Obiekt-80 hydrofoil launches as for the PST-63. The early experiments with the T-55 (Obiekt-626A) were followed by the same experiments using the T-62 (Obiekt-626B) and also the T-64 (Obiekt-626V) modifications, using the same Obiekt-80 'plavsredstvo' launches.

Fascinating though the technology was, the purpose of the Obiekt-80 was just as interesting. The system was not designed for short river crossings but for high-speed assault crossings of enclosed seas, specifically the Baltic and the Bosphorous, or, as once humorously pointed out to one of the authors by a Russian officer while on an official visit to Kubinka 'for crossing the English Channel'. The Obiekt-80 was accepted for service in 1971, in all tank-borne variants, but with the two battalions formed in Sevastopol, Crimea, and in the Baltic (presumably Kaliningrad) being equipped with modified T-55 rather than T-62 tanks. The systems were apparently deployed for any required armoured assault operations in the Baltics or the Bosphorous. Considering the (now NATO) Baltics and the question of Crimea and keeping the Bosphorous open relative to recent events in Syria and Turkey, the forward planning from a Soviet viewpoint seems quite prophetic.

T-62 WITH UB-32 MULTIPLE ROCKET LAUNCHER POD

One of the most unusual field modifications to the T-62 was the mounting of UB-32B 57mm rocket pods on the turret roof of T-62 tanks during the decade-long Soviet war in Afghanistan. Three rocket pods, as used on the Mi-8MT helicopter, were mounted on a frame welded directly to the front of the turret roof, and used as an ad hoc weapon in mountainous terrain. It is not clear how many of these Soviet Army field modifications were undertaken.

IMPULSE-2M FIRE-FIGHTING VEHICLE

The Impulse-2M tracked fire-fighting vehicle was developed at the Konstruktorsko-Tekhnologichesky Tsentr (KTs) in Kiev in the Ukrainian Soviet Socialist Republic at the very end of the Cold War, as the Soviet Union was considering alternative uses for armoured vehicles. The Impulse-2M mounted a 50-barrel 'multiple rocket launcher' on the T-62 chassis. The turntable-mounted launcher fired special capsules filled with dry powder, which could be launched at the centre of an inferno. The vehicle was designed for industrial applications such as oil-well blowout fires in the oil industry. Although designed at KTs in Kiev, production was undertaken at the Lvov tank repair plant (BTRZ) in Ukraine, with ten vehicles being built in total. The majority of Impulse-2M vehicles were later scrapped.

OBIEKT-167 MEDIUM TANK SERIES

OBIEKT-167 – BASE MODEL

As noted in Chapter Two, Leonid Kartsev and his two classmates, I. A. Nabutovskiy* and V. N. Venediktov, and with the backing of I. V. Okunev, the plant manager, worked on an initiative development of a better version of the T-62. In 1961 they decided – as with all of the evolutionary projects – to keep what worked and change what would make it better. As a result, they switched to the V-26 supercharged version of the V-2 engine. This engine produced 700hp versus the 580hp of the V-55 engine in the T-62. This was provided with a new radiator and tilted fan assembly that permitted a lower engine deck, better access to the final drives, and provided room to carry more fuel under armour – 745–760 litres. The transmission and 'guitara' were taken straight from the T-62.

The suspension was changed over to a new design of cast aluminium road wheel 750mm in diameter and 170mm wide. Six of these pairs were installed on each side, with limiters on stations 1, 2, 5 and 6. Dynamic travel was 242mm and the road-wheel arms were shortened to 230mm. Three return roller pairs were installed on each side with the wheels being 250mm in diameter. Initially the prototypes mounted OMSh tracks, but these were soon switched to the new and improved RMSh type rubber-bushed tracks. With the latter and 14-tooth driver sprockets replacing the T-55 style 13-tooth drive sprockets, overall track life was significantly increased together with an improvement in general mobility. Maximum speed went up from 50km/h to 60km/h and range from 450–500km to 550–600km.

Two prototypes were built at Plant No. 183 in parallel with the T-62 entering series production. The first prototype, factory serial number 110V001P, was built in October 1961 and the second one, 112V002P, in December of that year. Testing began in April 1962 and showed it to be superior to the T-62 and other tanks then in production. Against the prototypes of Kharkov's vaunted Obiekt-432 it demonstrated at least equal mobility and higher reliability. It was noted that it could replace the T-62 in production in 1963 without additional capital outlay as it used many standard T-62 elements.

While it was recommended for service with the Soviet Army, as noted, political shenanigans intervened and it was rejected. The main reason was

---

*   I. A. Nabutovskiy was a classmate and close friend of Kartsev during their work at Nizhny Tagil. His older brother, M. A. Nabutovskiy, was also there at the UVZ, but he was a 'Kharkovian' who hated it and finally managed to get a transfer back to Kharkov to work with Morozov.

that D. F. Ustinov and S. N. Makhonin saw it as a threat to Kharkov's Obiekt-432 tank, a vehicle that Ustinov found particularly fascinating. After it was finally terminated, Marshal Chuikov later told Kartsev he liked the tank and would have approved it, but accepted that it was not within his purview. Had it gone into service it would soon have given the Soviet Red Army a tank with the basic capabilities that were later found in the T-72 – and ten years earlier.

OBIEKT-167 WITH 9K11 'MALYUTKA' ANTI-TANK GUIDED MISSILE SYSTEM

As with the T-62, Obiekt-167 was trialled with the 9K11 ATGM system, mounting a triple 9M14 'Malyutka' launcher mounted in a 'pod' on the rear of the turret. The prototype suffered the same problems as the T-62-based prototype. In addition to the 9K11 system, the prototype also featured RMSh tracks and drive sprockets, and a modified engine deck. One of the test models is now preserved in the NIIBT Museum at Kubinka.

OBIEKT-167ZH WITH 'ZHELUD' AUTOLOADER

In July 1962 Kartsev decided to use the prototype Obiekt-167 tanks as test mules for various projects, and the first one was his new 'Zhelud' (theme) autoloader. This required the tank to mount the 115mm D-68 (2A21) separate ammunition loading version of the 115mm U-5TS gun versus the unitary loading 2A20 model in the T-62.

Having seen the 'cabin'-type autoloader Kharkov was proposing for their Obiekt-430 tank, his team designed a 'cassette'-type autoloader that was far safer for the crew and the tank. This used a cassette carrier that held separate loading ammunition with the projectile on the bottom and the propellant charge on top. The autoloader consisted of an elevator mechanism and a chain-driven rammer. In operation, the cassette of the selected round came out of a hatch on the turret floor, ran up to where the projectile was in line with the breech of the gun and was rammed; the cassette then dropped down, rammed the propellant, and the cassette dropped back into the floor and the hatch closed, all within about three seconds. These cassettes carried 19 rounds. When fired, the stub casing of the semi-combustible propellant was grabbed and ejected from the tank via the T-62 casing ejection hatch, leaving the breech open for the next selected round.

Since operation was so fast, a rate of fire of up to eight rounds a minute was possible with the autoloader. MTrM minister S. A. Zverev came out to see it and at first berated Kartsev for not using the Kharkov 'cabin' design, but when he observed it in operation recommended Kharkov use it instead of their own design. But 'NIH' – 'not invented here' – and the Soviet Army's desire for 28 rounds versus 19 rounds (22 in the later version developed for the T-72) meant that it did not happen.

Ultimately, when used with discretion (half of the ammunition was stowed unprotected inside the fighting compartment on the tanks with the 'Zhelud' autoloader), it was found that if only the autoloader was used and the tank's fighting compartment penetrated by a HEAT round the tanks with this device were less likely to explode. The autoloader developed during these early experiments was later used in the T-72 and T-90 tanks, reducing the crew to three.

OBIEKT-167 WITH 'DESANT' (DISMOUNT TEAM) COMPARTMENT

In the late 1960s the Soviet Army came up with a proposal to create dismount scout team accommodations in medium (later main battle) tanks. Each of the major factories worked on this proposal and presented design studies to Glavtank for analysis.

The UVZ study was based on their proposed Obiekt-167 tank design, and simply added a section to the hull 345mm long in front of the firewall and behind the turret. In place of the stowage for 12 rounds of ammunition, three transverse seats were provided for a three-man dismounted scout team. No provision for hatches was included in the base study, which was primarily to determine if the team could be accommodated inside the hull.

Eventually the Soviet Army command decided that the expense of specialized tank models for what amounted to the tank reconnaissance platoon (three tanks) of a tank or motorized rifle division was not worth the effort and dropped the idea.

OBIEKT-167M WITH 125MM D-81T GUN

At the same time that Obiekt-167Zh was being built and tested, plans were underway to upgrade from the 115mm gun to the new 125mm D-81T tank gun (initially the 2A26 model was to be used). Dubbed the Obiekt-167M in this configuration, one proposal was that Kartsev offer it to the Soviet Army with the proposed designation T-62B. Once again, it was refused.

OBIEKT-167P WITH 'PODBOY' RADIATION LINER

At the same meeting where the 'Zhelud' and 125mm recommendations were made, it was also proffered to fit a 'podboy' radiation liner into Obiekt-167. This was done, but it had the same drawbacks as the one installed in the T-62 and was not seen as a viable option.

OBIEKT-167 WITH 3M7 'DRAKON' ATGM (IT-1 PROTOTYPE)

When the idea of developing an armoured tank-based chassis as a launch platform for a new generation of ATGMs was conceived, several chassis in varying stages of development were considered. The Obiekt-150, mounting the 3M7 'Drakon' ATGM on a modified T-62 chassis, was the only prototype to make it to series production. The same system was, however, considered for development based on the Obiekt-140, Obiekt-167 and Obiekt-432 chassis, none of which are known to have progressed beyond paper concept studies.

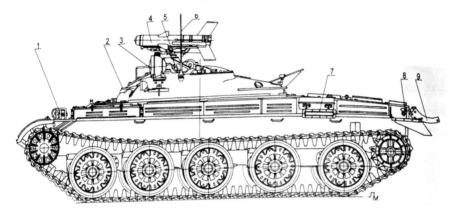

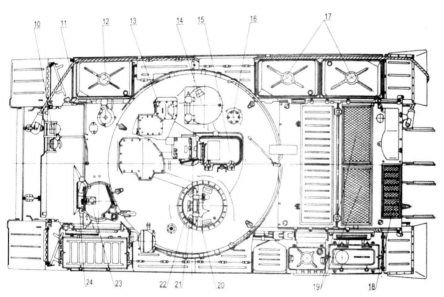

ТУРС 3M7 в транспортном состоянии

A drawing of the Obiekt-150 vehicle with the launcher erected and the 3M7 'Drakon' missile in firing position (see pages 98–100). The bottom sketch is of a missile in its transport carrier.

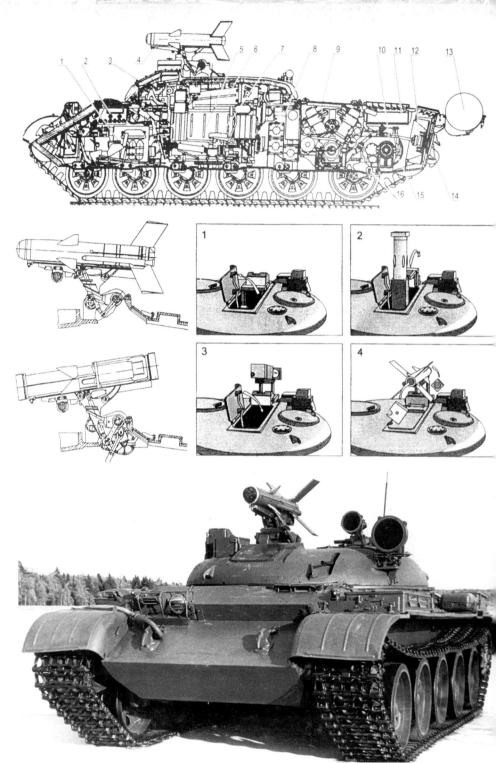

RIGHT Cross-section of the prototype Obiekt-167 (see page 118), showing the magazine for the missiles on the right side and spare missiles in their racks stowed against the firewall.

CENTRE LEFT The missile of an IT-1 (see pages 98–100) being erected; once all the way up the rack sections pop off and the fins (wings) unfold into firing position.

CENTRE RIGHT A series of drawings showing the erection and elevation sequence.

BOTTOM A production IT-1 tank destroyer with the 'Drakon' missile erected and in place. While not fast, it was so large that when it was accepted for service it was able to destroy nearly any enemy tank.

OBIEKT-167T WITH GTD-3 GAS-TURBINE

In the early 1950s the Soviets began to research the concept of putting a gas-turbine engine into a tank as its main power plant. These were lightweight, high-power engines capable of producing a great deal of speed and seemed to be a way to get faster tanks onto the battlefield. It was in 1960 that efforts were made by all three design bureaus to fit a turbine engine into a tank.

The GTD-3T gas-turbine (tank) engine was developed at the OKB-20 design bureau in Omsk based on a helicopter turbine developing 700-shaft horsepower. In May 1963, GTD-3T-03 (the third prototype engine) was installed in a T-54 tank for trials purposes, with development work continuing with the Obiekt-167T, Obiekt-166TM and Obiekt-003. After modifications and a 100-hour bench test, prototype engine GTD-3T-04 was sent to Nizhny Tagil in December 1963 for installation in the Obiekt-167 prototype as the Obiekt-167T.

Once again Kartsev called on Venediktov and Nabutovskiy to carry out the work on this project. They focused on their new star, Obiekt-167, and moved to create Obiekt-167T (turbine), installing the GTD-3T engine into the engine compartment along with all of its accoutrements and systems. Work on this was approved by Resolution 173ss of the SM SSSR dated 24 January 1961. The work was completed and the first test runs of the new vehicle took place at Plant No. 183 on 11 April 1964. Subsequent to plants trials, the Obiekt-167T was tested at the NIIBT polygon at Kubinka from 11 May to 16 July 1964, during which trials the engine failed and was returned to OKB-20 for rework. The engine was replaced with engine GTD-3T-05, which was tested between 6 September 1964 and 18 January 1965.

Obiekt-167T was the first gas-turbine-powered tank in the world,* and it was soon found to have a dichotomy that turned out to be insolvable to the Soviets. The tank, as advertised, was to be 50 per cent faster than a stock T-62 tank but had a range some 22 per cent lower, even with an extra 620 litres of fuel being carried.

On 14 September 1964, Obiekt-167T was placed in competition with the new Obiekt-432 fitted with the 5TDF diesel engine. While both engines produced around 700hp, the UVZ machine completely humiliated the Kharkov vehicle.

But as the Ministry of Defence considered the new tank, it soon came to the conclusion that it had no long-term future in the Soviet Army and cancelled it. Later one general noted he could not field such tanks unless he

---

*   It could be argued the Swedish Strv 103 'S Tank' could be first, but it used a hybrid system of a standard service diesel engine and an auxiliary turbine 'booster' engine for sprints on the battlefield.

had two to three times the number of fuel tankers (bowsers) to support them due to their voracious fuel demands. Another major drawback – which later came back to humiliate the Russian Army in Chechnya in 1994 – was that turbines burned nearly as much fuel at idle as they did at full power. Work on the GTD-3 gas-turbine engine, and the Obiekt-167T in which it had been installed for trials purposes, was finally curtailed by the SM SSSR on 10 February 1965.

The earlier decision to cancel development of gas-turbine engines in the mid 1960s did not deter Dmitri Ustinov, who later managed to get a turbine-powered tank into production and service when Nikolay Popov at Leningrad installed a modified GTD-3TU gas-turbine engine into a reworked T-64A tank to create Obiekt-219 – the T-80 tank.

OBIEKT-167 WITH 2K4 'DRAKON' ATGM SYSTEM

The Obiekt-167 was also considered as a suitable chassis for the 2K4 'Drakon' ATGM system and was developed to production stage on the Obiekt-150 chassis as the IT-1. The Obiekt-167-based project did not, however, progress beyond the initial project drawing stage.

OBIEKT-166M MAIN BATTLE TANK (T-62B)

Kartsev and his team did keep at the Obiekt-167 project, and finally decided to see if merging it with the production T-62 could bring part of its evolutionary design into being. The result was Obiekt-166M, which was a modernization of the T-62 developed to prototype stage at the SKB at Plant No. 183 at Nizhny Tagil from the spring of 1964 to the autumn of 1965. The Obiekt-166M combined parts of the Obiekt-167 running gear with the installation of a new V-36 multi-fuel diesel engine. The V-36 was the first multi-fuel engine to be placed in a tank, and later led to the V-45 and famous V-46 series engines. It only produced 580hp, the same as a standard V-55 engine, but the fuel options alone made it a more flexible engine. The V-36 could run on TS-1 and TS-2 aviation fuel and A-72 (i.e. low octane) petrol. Ten prototype V-36 engines were built in 1964–65 and installed in T-55 and T-62 tanks for trials purposes.

The Obiekt-166M featured modified running gear with modified wheel spacing. The tank used the road wheels, return rollers, 14-tooth drive sprockets and RMSh tracks, of the Obiekt-167, but only had five relatively widely spaced road-wheel stations. Combined with new more dynamic torsion bars, it now had a dynamic travel of 232mm on each

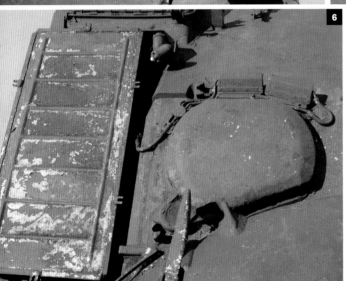

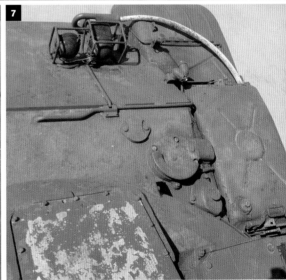

(1) An IT-1 (see pages 98–100) in service and on exercise.

(2) Another IT-1 on exercise. A video of one shows it firing the 'Drakon' at a captured Pz.Kpfw. III from the war and the missile blowing it to bits on impact.

(3) A preserved IT-1 at the Patriot Park display. The vehicle is relatively complete and shows the launcher in the erected position. Standard T-55/T-62 turret fittings were used on the flattened IT-1 turret. (images 3 to 36 Andrey Aksenov.)

(4) The only major difference is that the coaxial machine gun is now located in front of the commander and fired by him and not the gunner.

(5) The commander has the same cupola and searchlight assembly.

(6) The forward left stowage bin is the same as the T-62. However, unlike the T-62 the hatch of the IT-1 is thicker and appears to have radiation shielding added – the driver-mechanic's position still has the washer hoses in place.

(7) The fuel tanks and filler caps are different as there is no 'stellazh' rack needed for 115mm ammunition.

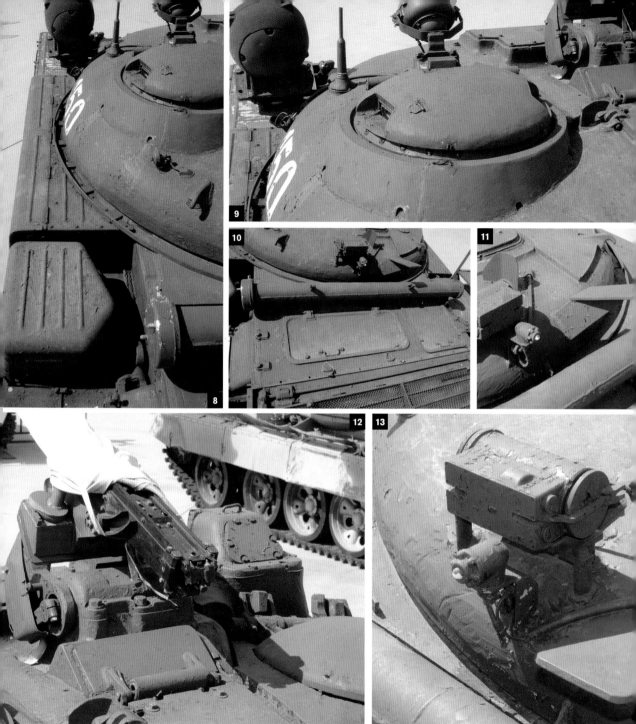

(8) The turret bulges out farther than the T-62 one; note that the access to the second fender bin is by a flip-up door and not a top cover. A small bin is also added behind it.

(9) The gunner's hatch is new and appears to also contain radiation shielding.

(10) The engine deck is identical to that of the T-55/T-62 tanks. This one has the older two-section snorkel now carried at the rear of the turret.

(11) Some different elements are now found on the turret. The plate at the right is a guard to keep the missile from damaging the snorkel during erection.

(12) The rear of the launcher. The missile clips onto the rail when loaded inside the turret and then flips over when the launcher is extended.

(13) This device is an early wind sensor – the doors on the side open and any breeze wafting through is measured and used to determine drift when the missile is in the air.

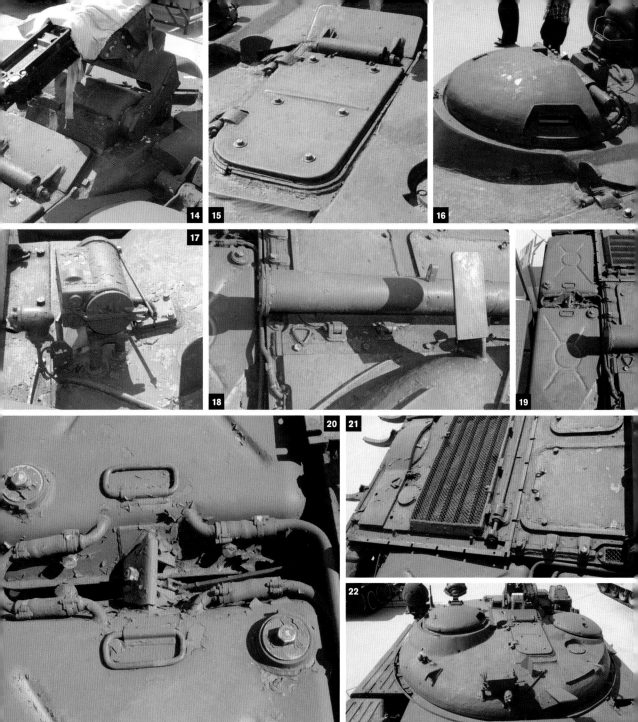

(14) Right-side view of the launcher rail.

(15) The small auxiliary flap on the main door helps to keep the length short.

(16) The radiation shielding is far more obvious on the commander's hatch and the base for it on the turret roof.

(17) A side view of the wind sensor showing the lock for keeping the doors closed in transit as well as the guard (blade device) and rear marker light.

(18) Snorkel and a view of the fuel line entry from the external tanks into the hull.

(19) The two rear fuel tanks. The object to the left is a set of access stairs to climb up on the vehicle.

(20) Close-up of the fuel tank connections and the attachment to the fenders.

(21) As previously noted, the engine deck is a standard T-55/T-62 arrangement. This one has the OPVT-54B frame for the sealing cover over the radiator intake and exhaust grilles.

(22) An overview of the rear of the turret.

(23) The curious little pentagonal case on the left rear fender.

(24) Cooling intake for the 'guitara' and the snorkel, showing it was not a drawn tube but welded up from sheet steel.

(25) Top view of the turret rear showing the shell fragment splash guards on the hull roof and engine deck.

(26) Close-up of the commander's hatch cover. The small flap covers the port for the access wrench.

(27) It appears this canvas cover may have been an actual basic issue item with the IT-1.

(28) Turret roof. As there is no MK-4 viewer for the gunner the small port with six bolts appears to be the mount base for the snorkel.

(29) Rear of the gunner's sight head. The vehicle could fire missiles on the move but at night range was limited to the range of the searchlight.

(30) Commander's hatch proximity to the missile launcher assembly.

(31) This plate appears to cover the drive motor used to flip the missile launcher assembly over from loading to launching positions.

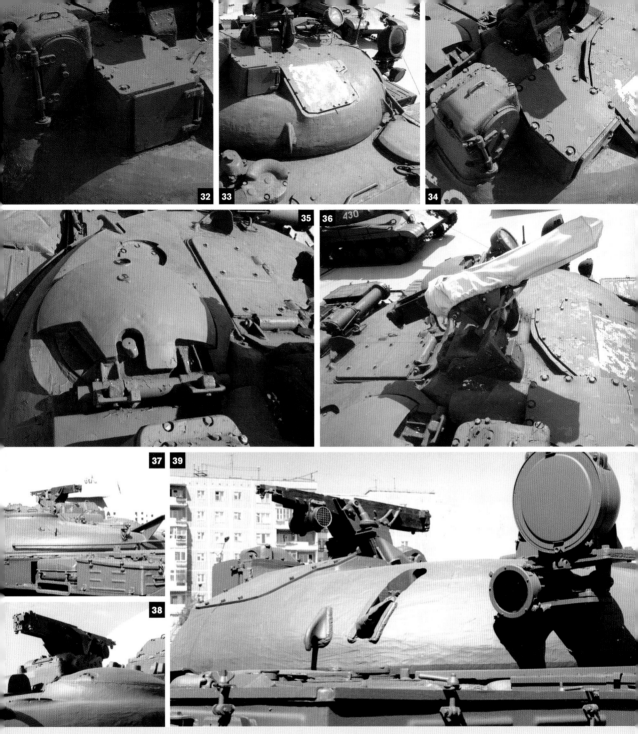

(32) Front view of the gunner's sights – the one on the left appears to be the infrared sight, the one on the right the day sight.

(33) There are four lifting lugs on the turret, two at the rear and two at the front; the T-62 only had three.

(34) Top view of the gunner's sights showing their shape.

(35) The gunner's hatch showing the lock (front, centred) and the access port for the access wrench (rear).

(36) Side view showing the compact length of the launcher rail assembly.

(37) Another IT-1 in preservation, this time with the rail uncovered. (Aleksandr Koshavtsev)

(38) Front view of the erected rail. (Aleksandr Koshavtsev)

(39) The motor assembly under the front of the rail activates discarding the travel protection elements and unfolding the fins and wings.

(40) Another view of the Patriot Park vehicle, here with its serial number visible on the glacis. It is 611V272 built in November 1966. (Andrey Aksenov).

(41) A three-quarters' 'beauty' shot of the same vehicle. (Andrey Aksenov)

(42) The preserved IT-1 at the UVZ Museum. A clear shot of the rail assembly.

(43) The vehicle is at the end of the row of T-62-related vehicles in its shed.

(44) A clear shot of the top of the rail assembly. The motor apparently pulls a shoe down the rail which trips the levers to discard the travel protection and pop open the wings and fins.

(45) The Kubinka Museum preserved IT-1. The tank to its left is the Obiekt-167 with 'Malyutka' launcher installation.

(46) Another 'beauty' shot of the second preserved IT-1. (Aleksandr Koshavtsev)

wheel and was 5km/h faster than a T-62 with better flotation over rough terrain. Five prototypes were built and tested; however, evaluation showed the tank to not offer enough of a change or advantage for it to be accepted for service, and the tank was consequently not accepted for series production.

OBIEKT-166TM GAS-TURBINE-POWERED MAIN BATTLE TANK

The Obiekt-166M tank was a modification of the Obiekt-166 that was also fitted with a GTD-3TU gas-turbine engine developing 800hp undertaken in parallel with work on the Obiekt-167T. The Obiekt-166TM was fitted with the transmission from the Obiekt-167, and featured numerous other design changes including new fuel tanks and track guards. The design was rejected for Soviet Army service, as was the Obiekt-167T, in part due to concerns with excessive fuel consumption. This tank was later used as a test mule mounting the 125mm D-81T (2A26) gun in a T-62 turret along with the 'Zhelud' autoloader with 22 of the total 36-round ammunition complement mounted in a carousel.

OBIEKT-166M-1 AND OBIEKT-166M-2 MAIN BATTLE TANKS

The Obiekt-166M-1 and Obiekt-166M-2 prototypes were developed concurrently from 1964. The Obiekt-166M-1 had Obiekt-167 wheels used on a standard, but modified, T-62 chassis and among other aspects tested a new gun stabilization system. The prototype was powered by a V-36 engine developing 580hp and had a combat weight of 36.8 metric tonnes. The Obiekt-166M-2 used the complete Obiekt-167 running gear (six wheel stations and return rollers) on a T-62 chassis, powered by a V-36F supercharged engine developing 640hp, and with an R-123 radio set and R-124 intercom system. The Obiekt-166M-2 had a combat weight of 36.5 metric tonnes.

Final comparative testing was carried out by UVZ with two more Obiekt-166M prototypes in October 1966, with the Obiekt-166M-2 proving to be the clear winner, but again no interest was shown by officials to use the new suspension arrangements on the by now series production T-62.

The Obiekt-166ML was an experimental version of the Obiekt-166M mounting the 9K11 'Malyutka' ATGM system on the turret.

(1) The UVZ Museum preserved Obiekt-167 with the V-26 diesel engine.

(2) The UVZ Museum preserved Obiekt-167T with the turbine engine.

(3) Another view of the Obiekt-167T. The tank to its right is the original Obiekt-140 tank, precursor of the Obiekt-167 series and the T-72.

(4) The Obiekt-167T in the Kubinka Museum.

(5) While this tank is missing the night sight, it shows that the Obiekt-167T used a stock T-62 turret.

(6) Another view of the Obiekt-167, this time moved outside into the 'boneyard' at Kubinka. The indicator is the '218' which is the exhibit number of the tank in the museum's collection. (The Obiekt-167T is exhibit 219, and the IT-1 is exhibit 220.)

7

8

9

10

11

12

(7) A view of the Obiekt-167 with 'Malyutka' launchers, outside at Kubinka. The vehicle to its right is a prototype of what eventually became the PT-76, the K-90. (Andrey Aksenov)

(8) Rear view showing the armoured 'basket' for the triple launcher assembly. (Andrey Aksenov)

(9) Obiekt-167 also appears to have been given a 'podboy' radiation liner. (Andrey Aksenov)

(10) Rear view of the launcher in its final configuration. It was originally to be fitted with a motor to raise and lower the launcher assembly into the confines of the armoured housing.

(11) Right side view – the simple rod welded in place is visible here as is the deep housing where the motor was originally mounted.

(12) Side view showing the hinge mounts at the front of the housing.

FOREIGN COPIES AND VARIANTS OF THE T-62 MAIN BATTLE TANK

TIRAN-6 (ISRAEL)

The first foreign modification of the T-62 was undertaken by Israel. During the Arab-Israeli 1973 'October' or 'Yom Kippur' War, Israel captured approximately 200 T-62 tanks in working order from Egypt and Syria. In contrast with the T-54 and T-55 the captured T-62s were not re-gunned with the American M68 variant of the British-developed 105mm L7 tank gun. This was because the original 115mm U-5TS gun was considered powerful and effective by the Israelis, albeit with the lack of ammunition compatibility with other tanks in Israeli service being an issue, as was the availability of 115mm ammunition.

Having inherited a considerable stock of T-62 tanks when the Soviet Union was dissolved, Ukraine modified its own version of the T-62M fitted with reactive armour, here apparently Soviet-origin 'Kontakt-1'.

Unlike Russian tanks, this tank has also been fitted with a thermal jacket for the 115mm U-5TS gun.

The T-62 tanks were, however, otherwise modified to conform with Israeli norms, including replacement of the radio communications equipment and the fitment of a new fire suppression system. Stowage and ZIP boxes were fitted on the turret and on the hull rear, with 0.50-calibre Browning machine guns also added for local defence. In the 1980s some T-62 tanks were also fitted with 'Blazer' ERA. The turret boxes also from a recognition perspective distinguished Israeli T-62 tanks from those of T-62 equipped potential enemy units on the battlefield.

Israel later sold a Tiran-6 to South Korea for familiarization purposes.

POST-SOVIET UKRAINIAN DERIVATIVES

T-62 with 125mm KBA-3 Tank Gun

After the break-up of the Soviet Union, Ukraine inherited a mix of Soviet-era tanks, including the Ukrainian-designed-and-built T-64 series and the diesel engine T-80UD version of the T-80 MBT also assembled in Kharkov, but in addition a number of older Soviet-era tank types including T-55 and T-62 tank models. For post-Soviet domestic purposes, Ukraine concentrated on upgrading the already old but 'domestic' T-64, and also on upgrading the Leningrad Kirov Plant-designed T-80 as the T-84. Ukraine also inherited a number of older Soviet tanks, however, including the T-55 and T-62, which were considered for upgrades for local use or export, or conversion to ARVs and other secondary applications. One such development was the experimental conversion of the T-62 fitted with the Ukrainian 125mm KBA-3 tank gun then in development as a replacement for the original Russian 2A81 tank gun mounted on the T-64.

T-62MV (Ukrainian Rebuild)

After the collapse of the Soviet Union, Ukraine in the 1990s modified a number of T-62 (T-62MV) tanks held in inventory with minor local modifications as a potential export tank.

When considering what to do with 'non indigenous' T-62 tanks post-1991 as they wore out, Ukraine also created a basic chassis for a T-62 recovery vehicle similar to the BREM but it was not adopted for service.

T-62BG

As mentioned, Ukraine inherited a number of T-62 tanks in service on Ukrainian territory when the Soviet Union collapsed and considered potential upgrades for export. One such tank was the T-72BG that was developed to prototype stage.

T-62-5TDF

The T-62-5TDF was developed from 2002 at the KMDB (the Kharkhov Morozov Design Bureau) at Kharkhov,* as a major modernization of the Soviet-era T-62 tank. Armament options included the 125mm KBA-3 tank gun or the 120mm NATO-calibre KBA-1 tank gun. The tank was protected by 'Nozh' ERA (a Ukrainian version of Russian 'Kontakt' ERA), and was powered by a Ukrainian-built 5TDF diesel engine developing 700hp. The original 12.7mm DShKM was replaced with a 12.7mm NSVT weapon. The project was undertaken as part of a proposal to upgrade Egypt's T-62 main battle tank park.

TOP This vehicle is essentially the T-62M but with Ukrainian fire controls and also fitted with the locally developed 'Nozh' reactive armour array.

CENTRE While it was rumoured to be upgraded with the Ukrainian 6TD engine the engine deck appears to show the original V-2 type engine in the tank was left in place.

ABOVE From this aspect the T-62BG appears to have borrowed some of the modifications from the Ukrainian-built T-80UD in regard to its appearance.

T-62 KTs (KhTV-62) Driver Training Tank

In the final years of the Soviet Union, in 1988–89, the No. 482 Konstruktorsko-Tekhnologichesky Tsentr (KTs) of the Soviet Ministry of Defence, located at Darnitse on the outskirts of Kiev, developed a programme to convert several older tank types as driver training vehicles, including the T-55, T-62 and T-72. As regards the T-62 conversion, seen designated as T-62KTs and also KhTV-62, a single prototype was built, but no series conversion of the T-62 tank was undertaken. The prototype consisted of a standard T-62 with the armament removed, a glass viewing panel mounted in the embrasure where the gun was removed, and the rear shell ejection hatch welded shut.

* Post 1991, Ukraine reverted to the Ukrainian spelling of Kharkhiv, replacing the Soviet Russian and widely used English spelling of Kharkhov.

ABOVE LEFT Some early T-62s were 'demobbed' for use as KTs-62 driver trainers by removing their main guns.

ABOVE A new position for the instructor was installed in the mantlet aperture with windscreen and wiper.

LEFT The KTs-62 tank remained a stock T-62 chassis with all capabilities and functions other than gunnery intact.

T-62 Dozer Vehicle

A simple ARV tractor modification of the T-62 chassis was developed in post-Soviet Ukraine. The turret was removed and plated over, and a BTU type dozer blade was added to the glacis.

THE WZ-122 MEDIUM TANK (CHINA)

As regards the Chinese relationship to the T-62, and indeed the combat debut of the tank – which was against the Chinese – this will be covered in Chapter Five. The overall situation as regards future Chinese developments involving the T-62 was, however, that relations between the Soviet Union and the People's Republic of China had throughout the 20th century constantly waxed and waned, and 1969 was one of the worst years of the 1960s. Sino-Soviet relations were soured by many events, including the ongoing proxy war in Vietnam with the Americans and their allies.

One major area of conflict was in contested border regions, including along the Ussuri River which formed the border between the Soviet Union and China in the area. The point of impact was Damansky Island, where on

22 January 1969, 25 People's Liberation Army (PLA) troops occupied the island, Soviet Border Guards fought back, causing some casualties on both sides, and the Chinese then withdrew. This was repeated on 23 February with similar results. But in March, as described in Chapter Five, more than 300 PLA troops from the 133rd and 73rd Infantry Divisions occupied the island and were initially engaged by 35 Border Guards in an incident that involved the first combat use of the new BTR-60PB armoured personnel carrier (one vehicle). By the end of the incident 32 Soviet Border Guards were killed and 17 more wounded. But while the Chinese pulled in more units from those two divisions, the Soviet Union moved in 5,000 troops from the 135th Motorized Rifle Division. On 15 March, three T-62 tanks from one of its tank battalions crossed the frozen river to get behind the PLA, but the lead tank of Major Leonov ('Bort' No. 545) hit a mine or was hit by RPG fire and was disabled. The crew bailed out, albeit with casualties; however, the tank remained intact on the Chinese side of the river. The Soviet retaliation included the combat debut of another new weapon – the BM-21 multiple rocket launcher. Its battalion of 12 launchers (that was the TO&E [Table of Organization and Equipment] of that time frame) fired a full salvo into what they thought was a Chinese divisional artillery group; it turned out to be a cantonment area of two infantry regiments and the casualties were frightening; one report indicated 1,200 killed and 2,800 wounded. Fighting continued until the end of the month.

In better times China had obtained a licence for local production of the T-54 tank, which they built as the Type 59. But with the degraded relations in the 1960s no such deals were forthcoming, and the capture of a T-62 was seen as a boon to the PLA. They now had possession of a brand-new T-62 tank with only relatively minor damage. It was sent back to Beijing where it was copied by Chinese factories with the military giving it the index number WZ-122.* After testing, the PLA did not see a need for the tank and it was not accepted for service. It is believed the T-62 located in the Military Museum of the Chinese People's Revolution in Beijing is the original captured T-62 tank, albeit having been rebuilt using Chinese components.

There were two offshoots of the WZ-122 project. When the Chinese designed their improved Type 59 (T-54) tank, the Type 69, the first version of the tank (Type 69-I) was armed with a new 100mm smoothbore gun which looked a bit like a downsized U-5TS gun. It was a failure in service

---

*   The Chinese referred to their tanks as 'Type XX' in a manner similar to that used by the Japanese in WWII. But each tank also had an industrial production code: the Type 59 (T-54 copy) was the WZ-120; the Type 69 series the WZ-121; the T-62 copy WZ-122; and the Type 98 the WZ-123.

and the Chinese went back to their copy of the 100mm D-10TS gun with the Type 69-II. There was also an effort, possibly called the WZ-122B, to mount their copy of the U-5TS on a modified and lengthened Type 62 light tank chassis but this also seems to have been rejected.

WZ-122A San Ye (1970)

The WZ-122A San Ye was a reworked T-62 developed in 1970, based on the Soviet T-62 tank captured at Damansky Island in 1969 but with hydro-pneumatic adjustable suspension and a 690hp diesel engine.

WZ-122B San Ji (1971)

The WZ-122B San Ji was a major modernization of the WZ-122A developed in 1971. It was basically a new tank, now on a lengthened chassis with six road wheels, hydro-pneumatic adjustable suspension and 690hp engine, a new turret and 120mm smoothbore armament.

CH'ONMA MEDIUM TANKS (NORTH KOREA)

The DPRK was the only country to purchase a production licence to build the T-62 tank, which they dubbed the 'Ch'onma'. The licence was apparently obtained in the early 1980s as the version they received details on was the T-62 Model 1972 with the 12.7mm DShKM mount added to the turret. Some information indicates they may have actually received an earlier model T-62 from Syria and tried to reverse engineer that tank with little success. Reportedly more than 1,200 were built in five different models.

Recent information has clarified a number of points on the DPRK tanks. A Korean People's Army Museum was opened in Pyongyang in 2012 and it contains a number of tanks, including some of their more recent models. It appears that all weapons projects in the DPRK receive a 'Juche' (self-reliance) item number similar to Soviet Obiekt numbers for tracking vehicles as well as a service name and designator. Based on this museum the following data can be surmised as there is no solid source to provide accurate information:

- **Ch'onma-ho I** (Western name) – copy of the T-62 Model 1972 with reportedly thinner armour;
- **Ch'onma-ho II** – T-62 but fitted with a laser rangefinder on the turret and spaced armour 'boom shield' protection around the turret;
- **Ch'onma-ho III (Juche 89 – Ch'onma-89)** – 38 metric tonnes; a thermal sleeve added for the 115mm gun as well as fittings for explosive reactive armour, laser rangefinder, and modified fire control system with improved night vision equipment;
- **Ch'onma-ho IV (Juche 90 – Ch'onma-214)** – 38 metric tonnes; added composite armour protection to the glacis and turret front, a ballistic computer and an integrated fire control system. Carries new radios and also a 750hp engine. Also mounts studs for ERA and fitted with track skirts;
- **Ch'onma-ho (Juche 92 – Ch'onma-215)** – 39 metric tonnes; more armour upgrades similar to Russian T-72S and T-90S; now mounts smoke grenade launchers to include four firing rearwards;
- **Ch'onma-ho VI (Juche 93 – Ch'onma-216)** – stretched chassis with six T-62 type road wheels and composite armour protection against HEAT projectiles. Developed as the prototype of the successor tank.
- **Pokpo'ong (Juche 98 – Seon'gun-915)** – 44 metric tonnes, new hull based on T-72 design but using T-62 components; dimensions 3.502 metres in width and 2.416 metres high; 1,200hp engine and probable 125mm gun; 14.5mm AA machine gun; twin 'Bul'sae-3' ATGM launcher over main gun; mount to fit twin 'Hwa'Seong Chong' MANPADS missiles; modular armour protection; ERA fit; new fire control system with laser rangefinder and external sensors; four movement sensors; latest version (Model 2018) also appears to mount twin 30mm grenade launchers in front of the commander. This tank was previously incorrectly called the 'Pokpo'ong' or Model 2002 tank.

All of these tanks were still based on the T-62 hull and running gear with few deviations. Even on the tanks with more modern-looking turrets, side views show that under it all is still a cast T-62-style turret with the other fittings attached to it; one top view clearly showed the roof of a T-62 turret with sheet metal fairings attaching to it. Oddly enough the latest evolution, the Seon'gun-915, appears to mount a 125mm gun but retains both the original T-62 layout (gunner and commander on the left, loader on the right).

Ch'onma tanks have been sold to three countries: Ethiopia, Iran and Egypt. But while the latter reportedly purchased 50 Ch'onma tanks on the grounds they liked the Soviet T-62, the Korean-built ones were so poor (bad welding, poorly assembled engines, weak components) they returned them and demanded their money back.

T-62 UZBEKISTAN UPGRADE

In very recent years, the former Soviet republic of Uzbekistan developed upgrades for both the Soviet Russian built T-62 and the Soviet Ukrainian built T-64 tanks. The hull has significantly raised vertical side armour panels protecting the fuel tanks and lower turret surfaces, while the turret is provided with 'Kontakt-5'-type KDZ armour, 902B smoke dischargers. Whether work progressed beyond prototype stage is unknown.

CONCLUSION

While there is still some life in the T-62 – and the Russians continued to find it useful in some circumstances in the 21st century, especially in mountainous terrain, the T-62 was officially removed from Russian Army service in 2013. Internationally, large numbers of T-62 tanks continue to serve in various armies, with the T-62 being a common sight during the most recent and ongoing war in Syria. The T-62 received a new lease of life in the Russian Federation in 2019–20 when a number of T-62s that had not been scrapped were rebuilt for reserve driver-training purposes.

This radically modified T-62 is an older T-72A rebuilt in the Ukraine to test if T-62 road wheels will work on a T-72 chassis!

CHAPTER FIVE

SERVICE AND COMBAT USE OF THE T-62 MAIN BATTLE TANK

INTRODUCTION

The first pre-series 'Establishment Lot' of 25 T-62 tanks entered service with the PriCarpathian Military District (PrikVO) for long-term service evaluation trials in late 1961, with full series production commencing in June 1962. The T-62 proved particularly enigmatic, however, being in service with the Soviet Army for three years before anyone outside of the country got a good look at the new 'wonder weapon'. The official public debut of the T-62 tank was when 20 T-62 tanks of the Kantemirovskaya Tank Division paraded across Red Square on 9 May 1965, the 20th anniversary of the end of World War II in Europe. Though it had actually appeared earlier, in both 1965 and 1966, the 7 November 1967 50th anniversary of the 'Great October Socialist Revolution' is often erroneously quoted as being the tank's public debut. The T-62 was subsequently fielded during the massive Operation *Dnepr* exercises in 1967. The tank was originally expected to have a relatively short production and service life as the Kharkov-designed Obiekt-432 (the future T-64) was at the time the preferred future 'universal' or main battle tank, but the significant delays in the development of the more complex T-64, coupled with the fact that the T-62 proved to be a more than adequate design in its own right, significantly lengthened the tank's service life. Over the more than half a century that the tank has been in service, the T-62 has seen a number of combat operations both with the Soviet Army and successor Russian Army, as well as in the hands of several other nations around the world.

During the Cold War years, the T-62 was judged in 'the West' (as then defined) to be inferior to NATO tanks primarily due to the results of combat in the Arab-Israeli 'Yom Kippur' War in October 1973, where Egyptian and Syrian tank losses including the T-62 owed as much to the lack of training and enthusiasm of the participants as it did technical merit or lack thereof. The IDF made use of captured T-62 tanks without re-gunning them as they had done with some T-54 and T-55 tanks, and clearly considered the tank worthwhile to retain in inventory while the unique calibre ammunition supplies lasted.

A T-62 M1962 of the 235th Guards Mozyrskiy tank regiment of the 40th Guards Pomeranian Tank Division, which took part in Operation *Danube*, Prague, Czechoslovakia, August 1968. Temporary white crosses were applied over the tank turret and hull for quick identification of friendly forces. (Andrey Aksenov)

It would be many years before a more balanced understanding of the T-62 would emerge based on its service in the Soviet Army. The combat debut of the T-62 would be against the Chinese in 1969 during border clashes along the Ussuri River, which formed the Sino-Soviet border in the region. The tank would be extensively used in Afghanistan from the invasion in December 1979 until the Soviet disengagement a decade later, with the tank being modified and upgraded based on experience gained during that long war, often fought in mountainous terrain unsuitable for armoured vehicles.

As regards how the T-62 was perceived by Soviet tank crews, the overall impression provided by former Soviet tankers was particularly positive. The tank was considered as very reliable, relatively simple to service and to maintain in the field, and was regarded by crews as a powerful tank in its time. The tank suffered from some air supply and filtration problems in dusty conditions such as encountered in the Middle East, but nothing more than for tanks of other countries operating in the same conditions.

The tank was also extensively used during the Iran-Iraq War of 1980–88, where the T-62 was

A number of T-62s were used during Operation *Dunay* – the invasion of Czechoslovakia in August 1968.

pitched by Iraqi forces against Iranian M60 and Chieftain tanks.

The T-62 remained in service into the first decade of the 21st century, with the tank also being used extensively by Russian MVD internal security forces at the outbreak of the second war in Chechnya.

At the time of writing, the last Russian combat use of the tank was in South Ossetia during the short war against Georgia in August 2008, with the tank having been formally decommissioned from Russian inventory in early 2013 before being re-commissioned at the end of the second decade of the 21st century for driver-training purposes. Internationally, the tank is at the time of writing on active service with federal SAA forces in Syria and remains part of the arsenal of many other nations worldwide.

1968 – OPERATION 'DUNAY' (DANUBE) – THE INVASION OF CZECHOSLOVAKIA

The first foreign excursion of the T-62 was when the Soviet Union and allied Warsaw Pact forces invaded Czechoslovakia (the CSSR) to suppress the 'Prague Spring' Movement on the night of 21 August 1968, with several T-62 regiments from the Group of Soviet Forces, Germany, among the units participating in the invasion. While no actual combat took place, photos show the T-62 among crowds of Czech citizens during some of the few resistance efforts against Warsaw Pact units. In addition to the annual Red Square parade runs, this was the first 'photo opportunity' for Western intelligence units to see the T-62 relatively close up.

1969 – DAMANSKY ISLAND INCIDENT – THE COMBAT DEBUT OF THE T-62

As covered in Chapter Four, the combat debut of the T-62 was in 1969 during a border incident with China in the Soviet Far East, the outcome of which would be a significant factor in the operational future of the T-62 tank. Several regions along the Sino-Soviet border remained disputed territory between the two nuclear powers during the 1960s, and the incident was part of a general escalation that came close to a nuclear confrontation between the Soviet Union and China. Tensions had been high throughout the decade, and an armed clash finally occurred in the spring of 1969 on the Soviet-occupied Damansky Island* located near the Chinese shore of the Ussuri River, which forms the border between the two countries in the region. The skirmish on Damansky Island was the first direct clash between Soviet forces and another major power since the end of World War II in 1945.

Following an altercation between Chinese PLA troops and Soviet Border Guards on the night of 2 March, there was a far more major clash between the same units on 15 March, when 700 Chinese troops crossed from the Chinese shore of the still-frozen Ussuri River and seized Damansky Island. Chinese intelligence had suggested the small island, less than 1km² in total area, was patrolled by approximately 40 border guards in armoured personnel carriers (the BTR-60PB). Soviet Border Guards had, however, been reinforced on the Soviet shore of the river three days prior by tanks of the 135th Pacific Fleet Red Banner Motorized Rifle Division (MRD). The tanks were in turn backed by a regiment of BM-21 'Grad' multiple rocket launchers, and 122mm howitzers.

On the morning of 15 March, three T-62 main battle tanks of a Separate Tank Battalion within the 135th MRD moved across the frozen river to Damansky Island in support of the Soviet Border Guards. During the battle,

---

* Damansky Island was named after the Russian Stanislav Damansky who died nearby in 1888 while surveying the route for building the Trans-Siberian railway.

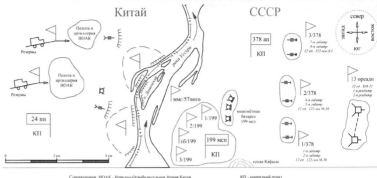

the lead tank, turret or 'Bort' No. 545, was destroyed; either by a mine or a Chinese RPG-2 according to conflicting sources. The crew attempted to bail out, but the tank commander, Demokrat Leonov (who was actually the commander of the 57th Border Troop Detachment and the senior officer in charge) was killed by a Chinese sniper as he exited the burning tank from the turret hatch. The loader, Private Aleksei Kuzmin, rescued other injured crew members via the hull floor emergency hatch, but also subsequently died of his injuries. The other two T-62 tanks broke off the engagement and the T-62 was abandoned in 'no man's land' under enemy fire.

A subsequent attempt to tow the damaged T-62 tank back to the Soviet lines under heavy Chinese fire resulted in Junior Sergeant A. Vlasov also being killed. Soviet troops then made an attempt to destroy the abandoned tank by mortar fire, lest it fall intact into Chinese hands. The tank was at the time still considered a 'secret' design as regards its exact capability, and moreover had a full ammunition complement on board, and as such was a major and unexpected loss.

In retaliation, Soviet artillery – including the combat debut of the BM-21 'Grad' multiple rocket launcher – fired salvoes 7km into Chinese territory. With a T-62 tank and other vehicles destroyed, Soviet forces killed, and BM-21 'Grad' salvoes being directed into 'mainland' China, the Chinese concluded that they had miscalculated, and that rather than combatting lightly armed border guards, the Soviet Union had clearly given instruction for the Soviet Army to engage directly with the Chinese PLA. The Chinese

TOP LEFT Damansky Island, in the Ussuri River between Siberia and China.

TOP RIGHT A map of the combat action, which took place there in March 1969. While the upshot was a Chinese disengagement, the Soviets lost a brand-new T-62 to the Chinese and the Chinese suffered as many as 4,000 casualties.

ABOVE T-62 tank 'Bort' No. 545 after recovery from the frozen river by the Chinese. The tank hit a mine, was shelled by mortar fire and also suffered damage during recovery.

142

RIGHT Tank No. 545 after restoration, today on display at the Beijing military museum.

BELOW RIGHT Some of the Soviet motorized rifle troops at Damansky Island. This battle was also the 'baptism of fire' for the BTR-60PB and the new 9K51 'Grad' 40-round 122mm multiple rocket launcher. These troops are probably from the 135th Motorized Rifle Division.

broke off the engagement. Soviet losses during the incident were 58 killed; Chinese losses are not reliably known, but at least several hundred were killed in the particularly lethal Soviet barrage, confirmed by the military graveyard on the Chinese shore near the island.

The Russians had meantime been unable to recover the damaged T-62 tank, which remained on the territory the Chinese had seized. Conflated Soviet-era information originally suggested that the tank had either sunk through the ice on the river or had become embedded to the extent it could not be towed from its resting position. Later published photographic evidence suggests the tank was on relatively firm ground when hit and subsequently abandoned under heavy Chinese fire. The only known photographs of the destroyed T-62 show the tank with heavily damaged tracks and road wheels, that could have been the result of mortar fire directed at the abandoned tank by Soviet artillery in an attempt to destroy it.

Regardless of the details of the actual loss of the tank, the same night that the T-62 was lost in combat, and unbeknown to the Russians at the time, Chinese 'razvedchiki' (reconnaissance or special forces) had removed the TSh2B-21 gun sight and several rounds of APFSDS ammunition from the abandoned tank. When the ice melted in early April, the Chinese towed the tank to their shore of the Ussuri River and shipped it out for full technical evaluation.* The captured Soviet T-62 tank, No. 545, is according to the Chinese the tank today displayed in the Military Museum of the Chinese People's Revolution in Beijing, China.

On 19 May 1991, the new post-Soviet Russian government and China agreed mutual land concessions along the former Sino-Soviet border, including the transfer of Damansky Island to China; it became known thereafter as the Chinese island of Zhenbao. The capture of the 'new' and at the time high-technology tank led in part to the decision to export the T-62 to the Middle East soon thereafter (albeit with initial ammunition restrictions) as from a surprise point of view the tank was a 'gonner'.

The T-62 captured on Damansky Island was used by the Chinese in the development of the Type-69 tank, and also as the basis for the WZ-122A, a Chinese attempt to series produce the T-62 tank type.

After the loss of the 'secret' T-62 tank to the Chinese, the design and in particular its innovative 115mm U-5TS smoothbore tank gun and sub-calibre APFSDS ammunition were largely compromised. Soon thereafter the decision was thereby taken to release the T-62 tank for export (albeit with ammunition restrictions) to the Middle East. This decision was made easier on the basis that the tank had at the outset also been envisaged by some in the Soviet high command as an interim design pending the much-delayed series production of the Obiekt-432 (the future T-64). Now that a new T-62 tank had been captured and evaluated by the Chinese the decision to release it for export and concentrate domestically on its T-72 replacement was given priority.

The first export batch of T-62 tanks left the Soviet Union for Egypt in 1971, with the country receiving some 400 tanks in the period 1971–72.

---

*   If the Chinese waited until the ice melted to tow the T-62 the short distance to the Chinese riverbank rather than towing it across the frozen ice, which assuming it would bear the weight would be simpler, then perhaps the T-62 did sink through the ice as per the original Soviet account. The only surviving photographs may also be of the tank after recovery by the Chinese, rather than where originally destroyed.

A T-62 M1962 of an unknown tank unit of the Egyptian 3rd Army during the Yom Kippur War, Sinai Peninsula, October 1973. (Andrey Aksenov)

The Damansky Island 'Chinese' T-62 scandal of 1969 was quickly followed by the 'Egyptian' T-62 scandal of 1971. On receiving their first batch of T-62 tanks, Egyptian tank crews, trained in the Soviet Union, noticed the 'minor detail' that the TSh2B-41 telescopic sight for the main armament was set for three types of ammunition, one of which – the sub-calibre APFSDS round, was conspicuous by its absence. The scandal escalated quickly, with Gamel Abdel Nasser Hussein (President Nasser of Egypt) sending a telex directly to Soviet Premier Leonid Brezhnev expressing his displeasure. The reason for the 'technical misunderstanding' was accounted for due to the export process not having had all the relevant ministries and authorities involved, and hence an 'oversight'. The APFSDS rounds were duly dispatched, and not long afterwards the T-62 would enter combat en masse in the Middle East. In 1972, the T-62 was also released for export to Iraq, Libya and Syria.

THE 'OCTOBER' OR 'YOM KIPPUR' WAR – 1973

The first major combat engagements involving the T-62 tank were during the October 1973 Arab-Israeli 'Yom Kippur' War. Egypt and Syria had both begun to purchase the T-62 tank when made available by the Soviet Union,

with both countries having by 1973 a variety of Model 1962, 1967 and 1972 production models in service. Prior to October 1973, Syria had ordered some 500 T-62 tanks, while Egypt had ordered 750 beginning from 1971, receiving the first 400 tanks in 1971–72. Both countries had assimilated them into service and allocated T-62 tanks to the armoured forces that were assigned to attack Israel in the Golan Heights occupied by Israel during the 1967 war, Gaza, the West Bank of the River Jordan and in the Sinai Peninsula. At the beginning of the war, Egypt had approximately 2,200 tanks including the aforementioned 750 T-62s. Syria had a total of 1,350 tanks, with a mix of T-62 and earlier T-55 and T-54 types.

The war began on 6 October 1973 – 'Yom Kippur' or the 'Day of Atonement', one of the holiest days of the Jewish faith, with Israel being attacked on several fronts, by Egypt in the Sinai, Syria on the Golan Heights, and by a coalition of less militarily committed countries including Jordan. The IDF began to frantically mobilize but initially only units in place on both major fronts were available; reserves were called up but were obviously not available for a number of days.

One of the earliest engagements was on 7 October, when the Israeli 460th Tank Brigade opened fire at long range on Egyptian T-62 and T-55 tanks, destroying 67 during a single engagement. The war would demonstrate

The IDF captured or recovered a few hundred tanks from both the Syrians and the Egyptians. These tanks are Syrian with the T-62 in the foreground most likely from the 81st Tank Brigade. Syria had all three variants of the T-62 of which this is a Model 1967.

remarkably different outcomes for the opposing forces depending on the tactical situation and terrain involved in individual engagements.

The Egyptian Army had at least two brigades of T-62 tanks (15th Independent Armoured Brigade attached to the 18th Infantry Division and 25th Independent Armoured Brigade attached to the 7th Infantry Division) as well as some other T-62 units. This meant around 190 T-62 tanks participated in the battles in the Sinai. While the 15th was essentially pinned in place, a counterattack on 16 October virtually destroyed the 25th Brigade with them losing 86 out of 96 T-62 tanks.

On the Golan Heights, the Syrian Army had the 91st Tank Brigade in their 1st Armoured Division and the 81st Tank Brigade in the 3rd Armoured Division, plus additional T-62s in the Assad Republican Guards. They made their attacks along a wide front with success in the north but faced stiff resistance in the centre from units like the 77th Tank Battalion of the 7th Armoured Brigade. This unit opposed the 1st and 3rd Syrian Armoured Divisions and eventually knocked out or damaged some 130 tanks (mixed T-54, T-55 and T-62 types) in an action detailed below that was later dubbed the Valley of the Tears. Later, the Israelis chased these units back into Syria, engaging the Iraqi 1st Mechanized and 3rd Armoured Divisions, inflicting massive losses on the latter in a matter of but 20 minutes. (Even so the 3rd 'Saladin' Armoured Division became the honour division of the Iraqi Army for 'striking a blow against the Zionist Entity' as they referred to Israel.)

On the northern front, there was a major battle near Kantari that started on 8 October, during which the Israeli 162nd and 252nd armoured divisions lost 120 and 170 tanks respectively, while the Israeli 600th Tank Brigade of the 162nd Armoured Division lost 24 tanks in 18 minutes during one engagement.

In the Sinai Peninsula, Egypt had assembled 400 tanks for the assault on the Bar-Lev defence line, with sand embankments breached in 81 places by the use of high-pressure water cannon purchased from Great Britain and Germany. During initial tank engagements in support of the Egyptian 7th and 19th infantry divisions in Sinai, the Israeli 190th Tank Brigade was decimated and its commander, Colonel Asaf Yaturi, was captured.

On 14 October, Egypt advanced in six spearheads in Sinai, with 1,200 T-54, T-55 and T-62 tanks against Israeli forces supported by 750 tanks. There followed the largest tank battle since Kursk in World War II, which was over within slightly over 24 hours, with devastating losses on both sides.

In the north, the 18th Egyptian Infantry Division supported by T-62 tanks broke through the lines of the Israeli 162nd Armoured Division, with 55 Egyptian tanks – all T-62s – lost in one day. According to Israeli sources a total of 264 tanks were lost during these engagements – including the Egyptian losses.

On 17 October one of the most famous battles of the war began in the Sinai Peninsula near a 20km^2 area of cultivated land known locally as the 'Chinese Farm'. At 0800hrs Israeli reconnaissance aircraft spotted a column of 100 T-62 tanks of the Egyptian 25th Armoured Brigade moving towards positions held by the 162nd Armoured Division. At 1445hrs the Israeli 217th and 500th Tank Brigades with a majority of American-supplied M60 tanks ambushed the road-bound column at a point where the Israelis had planted minefields on either side of the road. Some tanks in the trapped column pushed forward, others tried to turn around and retreat, with many tanks being destroyed in the adjacent minefields as they did so. By 1700hrs the Egyptian 25th Armoured Brigade had, per Israeli sources, lost 86 tanks, many in the minefields, for a loss of only four Israeli tanks.

This was an IDF press release photo of a captured T-62 but its ownership is harder to determine. It bears an Arabic serial number of 11177.

On the Golan Heights, Syrian forces mobilized three infantry and two tank divisions and a separate tank brigade against Israeli forces in the area, with approximately 900 of 1,500 available T-54, T-55 and T-62 tanks being deployed in action, of which 500 were deployed in the region of Katna-Kasave and 100 with the Syrian Republican Guard near Damascus. Israel had 180–200 tanks operating on the Golan Heights during the war.

The first tank battle was near El Kuneiter on the Golan Heights on the night of 6 October. Reconnaissance units of the 7th Israeli Brigade, which had only 35 tanks, located tank columns of the Syrian 81st Tank Brigade, at 2200. The resultant battle was fought at night between Syrian T-55 and T-62 tanks, fitted with infrared night vision equipment, and Israeli Centurion and M48 tanks which were reliant on white-light projectors, flares and tracer rounds. In the morning of 7 October, tanks of the Syrian 46th Tank Brigade joined the engagement, with another major night offensive including the Syrian 3rd Tank Brigade and the Syrian Republican Guard against the Israeli 7th Brigade on the night of 9 October. This latter action resulted in the loss of 230 Syrian T-55 and T-62 tanks – however, the Israeli 7th Brigade also lost 98 Centurion tanks from a total of 105 deployed in an action known by Israelis as the 'Valley of the Tears'. The last major tank battle during the war was on 20 October, with 120 Syrian T-62 tanks engaged against Israeli units. A ceasefire was agreed between Israel and Syria on that day.

Total tank losses during the 1973 Arab-Israeli War, according to Israeli sources, consisted of 2,400 Egyptian and Syrian tanks and 2,500 Israeli tanks, an almost 1:1 ratio. Directly after the war, there was a general assumption in the West that Soviet-delivered tanks, and their Arab crews, performed badly, but the figures suggest that, despite some known crew deficiencies, the Arabs and their Soviet-supplied tanks including the T-62 performed as well as their Israeli opponents during the war. One Israeli commander commented that Arab forces often just did not find the 'time and place' to use their Soviet-supplied tanks to better effect. Israel also approached Great Britain after the war with regard to procuring Chieftain tanks as a possible replacement for their destroyed M60s.

After the war was over, Kartsev, in his persona as a general-lieutenant (Kartsev only used the title on specific occasions such as foreign liaison trips) was sent to Egypt to review the combat performance of the T-62. His findings were that they used well-trained crews but these had been no match for the training of the IDF, just as the IDF found they were no match for the 9M14 'Malyutka' ATGM without infantry support. Kartsev and the Egyptians communicated in English as their common language.

Of the 2,400 Arab tanks lost to the IDF, some 400 tanks were either captured intact or with repairable damage. Israel recovered approximately 200 captured Egyptian and Syrian T-62 tanks of which 72 underwent capital rebuilt. These T-62s were incorporated into the IDF as the 'Tiran 6' with minor changes such as American-supplied VRC-type radios. These captured T-62 tanks were not popular with Israeli tank crews, however, as still being armed with the original 115mm U-5TS smoothbore gun, they had none of the compatibility that the T-54 and T-55 tanks did when re-gunned with US M68 copy of the British L7 gun. More significantly, Israel could not secure quantities of the unique 115mm-calibre ammunition for the tank, which limited its long-term employment. A number of T-62 tanks were transferred to the US Army for training and analysis, in such a sufficient quantity that the Army had to create an operator's manual in English for the tanks.

WESTERN SAHARA (MOROCCO AND THE POLISARIO) – 1975–91

Over the course of 16 years a splinter group fought to obtain independence of the Western Sahara area from Morocco. A handful of T-62 tanks wound up in the fight and still serve in the region today.

ANGOLAN CIVIL WAR – 1975–91

When the Portuguese were forced out of Angola, three groups – the MPLA, the FNLA and UNITA – fought with each other in order to take control of the country. In 1975 the Soviet Union, aided by its Cuban client state, sent in troops and weapons to help the MPLA take out the other two factions. Among the weapons used were T-62 tanks, and over the course of the war the FAPLA* (the military arm of the MPLA) had by 1985 received 175 T-62s, and ordered another 135 tanks in 1987. One of the largest battles involving tanks was intermittently fought from August 1987 until March 1988 south-east of Cuito Cuanavale, during which period FAPLA deployed 150 T-55 and T-62 tanks, with Cuban forces having 32 T-55 and T-62 tanks operational during the same period against UNITA and South African forces. In 1993 Angola received another 24 T-62 tanks with upgrades from Bulgaria.

---

*   FAPLA – People's Armed Forces for the Liberation of Angola.

A T-62 M1962 of the 5th Tank Battalion of the 7th Separate
Motor Rifle Brigade of Soviet troops based at Alkisar, Cuba – probably the
closest Soviet tank unit to US territory in the late 1970s. This tank received
RMSh tracks, and the wheels had strengthened bearings fitted to the front and
rear stations during repair. (Andrey Aksenov)

ETHIOPIAN-ERITREAN WAR – 1977–94

For more than 30 years, from 1961 to 1994, the Ethiopians and Eritreans
fought a war over the independence of Eritrea. Starting in 1977 the
Ethiopians acquired around 100 T-62s from the Soviet Union, which, as in
Angola, were originally operated by Cuban tank crews.

THE OGADEN WAR (ETHIOPIA – SOMALIA) – 1977–78

When Somalia invaded the disputed Ogaden region to take control of the
area for itself, the Soviets and Cubans came to the defence of the Ethiopians
with tanks and troops again operated by Cuban advisers. T-62s were integral
to both the Ethiopian Army and the forces brought in to defeat the Somalis.

LIBYA-CHAD WAR – 1978–87

During this running border conflict between these two nations the Libyans
used tanks to try to defeat the fast-moving 'technical' vehicles of the smaller

nation. Over the years from 1973 to 1978 they acquired around 900 T-62 tanks of all types. In 1986 the Libyans deployed T-62s in combat against Chad, but were not very successful, and the light forces of Chad were able to pick off a number of these tanks using MILAN ATGMs fired from pickup trucks.

THE SOVIET WAR IN AFGHANISTAN – 1979–89

In 1973, Afghanistan purchased 100 T-62 tanks from the Soviet Union, with the T-62 being the newest tank type in service when, in September 1979, Hafizullah Amin seized the premiership of the increasingly unstable country. Concerned for the potential spread of instability north into the predominantly Muslim Soviet republics, Soviet Premier Leonid Brezhnev and the Politburo reluctantly agreed military action, and on Christmas Day 1979 Soviet VDV troops landed in Kabul, captured and executed Amin, and installed their own choice of Babrak Kamal as president. At the same time Soviet ground troops invaded from the north across the Soviet Uzbek and Tajik republic borders.

The war would last nine years, and as with the American war in Vietnam would become increasingly unpopular at home as the losses mounted with no tangible result. Soviet forces began to pull out of Afghanistan in 1988,

A T-62M1 fitted with KTD-2 laser rangefinder, of the 24th Guards
Tank Regiment of the 5th Guards Motor Rifle Division, Shindand, Herat
province of Afghanistan, 1986. All vehicles of this regiment were painted
in the officially adopted light grey/black 'camouflage scheme for mountain areas'.
(Andrey Aksenov)

with the final armoured columns of the 40th Army leaving in February 1989
led by General-Lieutenant Boris Gromov.

Over the course of the war the Soviet armed forces suffered 14,553 killed
in action, 53,753 wounded in action and more than 415,000 casualties due
to injury, disease and poor sanitation. The Soviet Army acknowledged a loss
of 147 tanks of all types, mostly T-55s and T-62s. The T-55 and T-62 tanks
of the 40th Army in Afghanistan were sent into the country from the Central
Asian and Far Eastern Military Districts. The tanks faced the same difficulties
as other armoured vehicles operating in a country which features significant
expanses of mountain regions with narrow high-sided passes, absolutely not
ideal 'tank country', with tanks being vulnerable to mines and IEDs, and
RPG fire at close range; but with the main armament and coaxial turret
machine gun being limited in effectiveness in mountainous terrain. The
majority of early tank losses were due to RPG fire and roadside IEDs, the
latter often consisting of dud 250kg bombs dropped by Soviet aircraft buried
in the road with a wired detonator.

In Afghanistan, the T-62 became the default Soviet tank, often used as a
block-post on roads and even in hills. Soviet T-62 tanks were operated in
Afghanistan within the 24th Guards Tank Regiment and the 5th Guards
Motorized Rifle Division. The bulk of T-62 tanks were located in the 285th
Tank Regiment of the 108th Motorized Rifle Division, and the 234th Tank

Regiment of the 201st Motorized Rifle Division. T-62 tanks were also found within the 650th, 781st and 783rd Separate Reconnaissance Battalions among other units.

Due to the constant danger from mine explosions and concussion, tank crews constantly travelled in Afghanistan with hatches open. One of the priority modifications to the T-62 as a result of Afghan combat experience

Initially the Soviet Army used the T-62 as it came from either the USSR or from Afghan stocks. But as the war progressed the Mujahedin began using captured RPG-7s and the first improvised explosive devices (IED) to take them out.

ABOVE The T-62s proved to be the best tank in the mountainous terrain of Afghanistan. A wide-ratio 5-speed meant the drivers did not have to constantly shift gears, and its 115mm gun fired a heavier HE-FRAG round than the 100mm gun.

ABOVE RIGHT Later tests of both the T-64 and T-72 proved that their 7-speed close-ratio transmissions fatigued drivers too fast in the mountains so the T-62 soldiered on alone.

RIGHT Many times the tanks were used as 'block-post' installations to protect access routes from Mujahedin attacks. Here a T-62M1 with an improvised sun shield watches the hills for movement.

was the addition of hull floor stand-off armour to reduce the impact of such explosions, particularly on the driver-mechanic.

As a result of significant tank losses in the first year of operation, the T-55 and T-62 were both upgraded to 'M' specification, with 'BDD' turret armour packages, hull floor reinforcement and stand-off protection for the driver-mechanic, side skirts to protect against RPG fire and other protective measures. In later years, losses in Afghanistan continued, primarily due to large roadside IEDs, but losses to RPG fire dropped significantly. The modified T-62M, which featured significant armour upgrades including the aforementioned hull floor armour, was introduced as a direct result of early combat experience in Afghanistan.

The T-62 tank had a more powerful high-explosive round than the T-55, which made it more useful against fixed targets. The Soviets also found the wider engine power band and wide-range 5-speed transmission in the T-62 better suited to mountain combat than the narrow power band and 7-speed close-ratio transmission in the other two tanks. The latter contributed to driver fatigue, and as such were considered a liability under these circumstances.

The T-62 overall performed well in Afghanistan, during which a total of 1,340 tanks were listed as at one time or another 'out of commission' due to various combat or mechanical-related reasons, with some 385 T-62 tanks within that total designated as actual combat losses. The balance of repairable T-62 tanks underwent capital rebuild to T-62M standard as noted above and in many cases were sold on to third-world customers. Only Category V (irreparable) tanks were ever directly scrapped until the 1997 mass scrapping order by President Yeltsin, which many T-62s also survived. Despite the widespread use of mines and IEDs, T-62 losses to such weapons were in later years relatively low. General-Lieutenant Sergey Maev noted that the ratio of losses between mechanical breakdown and wear and combat damage was in the order of 20:1.

T-62 tanks began to be pulled out of Afghanistan from 1986, albeit the very last T-62 tanks departed with the final echelons of the 40th Army in 1989. There were two large-scale withdrawals from the country involving T-62 columns, with 110 T-62 tanks leaving between 15 May and 15 August 1988, and another withdrawal starting on 31 January 1989 with 202 T-62 tanks leaving Afghanistan – in both cases together with echelons of other armoured vehicles. During the Soviet occupation of Afghanistan, 179 T-62 tanks were also handed over to the Afghan Army.

THE IRAN-IRAQ WAR – 1980–88

During the 1970s, Iraq purchased T-62 tanks from the Soviet Union along with vehicles from other countries. The Shah of Iran meantime had tank forces including 400 American M60A1 and 300 British 'Chieftain' tanks. At the beginning of the Iran-Iraq War in 1980 Iraq had approximately 1,500 Soviet-supplied T-54, T-55 and T-62 tanks.

When Ayatollah Khomeni and his ideological supporters took over the country in 1979, the resulting chaos convinced Saddam Hussein he could eliminate them as a threat once and for all. Part of that was based on the large Shi'a minority in Iraq, and as the new government in Iran was made up of extremist Shi'ites, he felt he had to act to prevent them from bringing revolution to Iraq.

The war began on 22 September 1980, when Iraq invaded the oil-rich border region in south-west Iran. Reflecting the ever-evolving complexities of the region, during the war Iran was supported by Libya and Syria, with Iraq directly supported by Kuwait and Saudi Arabia, and also tacitly by both the Soviet Union and the United States.

When the war commenced, the Iraqi 3rd 'Saladin' Armoured Division had been refitted with T-62 tanks purchased from the Soviet Union as well as many other tanks from other countries such as Poland and Czechoslovakia. The country continued to build up their stocks and in most of the tank battles that took place the Iraqis inflicted losses of from 2:1 to 4:1 on the Iranians. There were several major tank engagements during the war, including a major battle near Susangerd in Iran between approximately 300 Iraqi T-62s and the reinforced 16th Iranian Tank Division with a similar number of Chieftain and M60A1 tanks. During that engagement, Iraq claimed 214 Iranian tanks destroyed and/or recovered (Iran claimed 88 tanks lost) with a conflated number of approximately 100 Iraqi tanks destroyed. Though as in most conflicts the numbers are disputed, it is clear that the Iraqi T-62s performed well against modern American and British tanks, with the 115mm U-5TS gun of the T-62 firing APFSDS ammunition able to penetrate the frontal armour of the 'next generation' Chieftain tank at standard engagement ranges. Iran is reported to have had as many as 875 Chieftain tanks in service during the entire war, of which all but approximately 200 were lost to combat and mechanical failure.

By the end of the war (which had bled most of the capital from both countries), Iraq had accumulated between 5,000 and 5,500 tanks. After the war ended, the Iranians purchased T-62s from other countries as well as new construction Korean-built Ch'onma tanks.

LEBANESE CIVIL WAR AND ISRAELI 'PEACE FOR GALILEE' OPERATION – 1982

When the Lebanese civil war began to spill over into neighbouring countries, both Syria and Israel took action to protect their factions in that nation of complex alliances. The Syrians backed the emerging Hezbollah, a radical Shi'a group, as well as the Palestine Liberation Organization (PLO). In early 1982, Syrian forces held 70 per cent of Lebanon including the capital city, Beirut, with the major concentration of armoured forces being in the Bekaa Valley. The Israelis came to the aid of the Lebanese Christians and the Maronite Phalangists who opposed them; apparently the two opposing groups decided the 'enemy of my enemy is my friend'. The Syrian 76th and 91st Armoured Brigades of the 1st Armoured Division and the 85th Independent Tank Brigade near Beirut and in the Bekaa Valley operated T-62 and T-72 tanks in Lebanon. Only a small number of the 1,100 T-62 tanks in Syrian inventory were located in the neighbouring country.

There were a number of tank-tank clashes between June 1982 and May 1983, most famously in the aforementioned Bekaa Valley area. On 8 June 1982 Israel Centurion tanks of the 460th Tank Brigade engaged the Syrian 424th Infantry Battalion, which was reinforced by a tank battalion with T-62 tanks. Three Centurion tanks were destroyed in the first minute of the engagement, with ten Centurion tanks lost as the battle continued through the night, where the T-62 tanks with their infrared night vision equipment had a significant advantage. The war also saw frequent engagements between T-62 and M60 tanks, with new players appearing, namely Syrian operated T-72 tanks and IDF-operated Merkava tanks. As might be expected, there are opposing claims of who knocked out who and how many tanks were destroyed, but Syria and the PLO would seem to have lost 334 tanks, while Israel lost over 30 per cent of the tanks committed to the conflict. The only known confirmed 'Merkava' kill was during the Lebanon war, destroyed by a Syrian T-62.

WARS IN THE CAUCASUS – 1988–93

From early in 1988 the Soviet Republic of Georgia began to suffer breakaway problems in two of its sub-republics, Abkhazia and South Ossetia. The regions resented the authoritarian government of Zviad Gamsakhurdia, the first democratically elected president of the republic. While all sides had access to tanks, including the T-62, there is no known recorded combat history of their use. Things quieted down once Eduard Shevardnadze, former Foreign Minister of the USSR, took over as president of Georgia.

THE GULF WAR (OPERATION *DESERT STORM*) – 1990–91

At the end of the Iran-Iraq War, Iraq was heavily in debt to a number of countries, the biggest debt holder being Kuwait. On 2 August 1990, Saddam Hussein found a new method of debt amortization when he invaded Kuwait, calling it 'Iraq's 19th Province' and having no right to exist as an independent nation. The UN called for him to withdraw, which was flatly refused. As a result, the US, UK, France, and many other countries, including Egypt and Syria, moved forces into Saudi Arabia to stage for combat operations to evict the Iraqis. The Coalition had approximately 5,100 tanks, with the Syrian contingent being equipped with T-72 and older T-62 tanks. The war would witness Iraqi T-62 and T-72 tanks pitched against Coalition tanks including the M1 Abrams and the British Challenger, and also against Syrian T-62s. Note that, while present, Egyptian and Syrian forces only promised to provide security to Saudi Arabia; they would not attack their former United Arab Republic member.

At that time the Iraqi Army had 34 divisions organized into seven corps, plus 12 Republican Guard divisions organized into two more corps. They numbered around 5,300 tanks of a variety of types, with over 3,500 located in the conflict zone, including the T-54, T-55, T-62, T-72, Chinese Type 59 and Type 69-II. The T-62s were known to be located in the following units:

- 6th Armoured Brigade, 3rd 'Saladin' Armoured Division
- 30th Armoured Brigade, 6th 'Sa'ad' Armoured Division
- 17th, 24th and 42nd Armoured Brigades, 10th 'al-Nasar' Armoured Division
- 37th Armoured Brigade, 12th 'al-Nu'man' Armoured Division

These units numbered around 660 T-62 tanks in their formations. Many of them had been upgraded by Iraqi workshops with armour protection for the two searchlights, Chinese 'zigzag' pattern side skirts, and some were even fitted with a Chinese-made laser 'dazzler' designed to disrupt the guidance on laser beam riding ATGMs.

After a protracted preparation phase, air combat operations started on 16 January 1991, with cruise missiles and air strikes against key Iraqi targets. Other than occasional ground probes by special operations forces no serious ground combat took place until the night of January 29/30.

The Iraqis were keenly aware that the US focused on satellite imagery to establish enemy order of battle, and as such made frequent night moves of units from place to place to disrupt their ability to accurately determine where armoured and infantry forces were deployed. On that night, Iraqi III Corps had two of its divisions, the 3rd Armoured and 5th Mechanized, change places on the battlefield. But both units missed their deployment sites in the dark. The 5th Mechanized ran into Saudi Arabia and the town of

Al-Khafji, getting into a skirmish with Saudi National Guard forces and forcing them out of the town. They were later dislodged by Saudi and Qatari forces, with heavy casualties.

The 3rd Armoured Division with its T-62-equipped 6th Armoured Brigade in the lead also missed their assigned positions, running into US Marine Corps positions near Al-Wafrah. Withdrawing each time they encountered fire, by dawn a number of tanks had run out of fuel and were abandoned. (The Iraqis did not like to use the auxiliary fuel tanks as long-range capability made them suspicious that the crews would defect to Saudi Arabia.) Two of these tanks were later displayed at the US Marine Corps Museum at Quantico, Virginia.

Full-fledged ground operations began on 20 February and lasted 100 hours. Over that time the Iraqis lost approximately 1,860 tanks (per US sources – far fewer per Russian sources) and armoured vehicles with assessments after the war that most were lost due to either direct fire or ATGM hits. Many of the T-62 tanks (an estimated 250 from a total inventory of 1,200 T-62 tanks) were lost, with the 6th Armoured Brigade virtually wiped out as they retreated across the gauntlet of every heavy armoured division in the Coalition.

The Iraqis later tried to put a brave face on their performance with the stories they passed on to the Soviets, who were unhappy at how easily Western technology defeated even T-72 tanks with ease. The story told by the Iraqis was this: 'On 26 February 1991 nine T-62 tanks from 16th "Dhu al Faqir" Infantry Division destroyed 5 M1A1 tanks from USMC 1st Tank Battalion and damaged 9 others without loss; Marines were lured into range by fake surrender and then soundly beaten; Iraqis successfully escaped after the Americans ran away.' This sounds good – except:

- The 16th Infantry Division did not have any T-62s in its inventory at the time, as it was only provided with one regiment (31 tanks) of T-55s.
- The USMC 1st Tank Battalion was only equipped with M60A1 RISE tanks at this time, not M1A1s. The only Marine unit with those tanks was B Company 4th Tank Battalion.
- This incident is what happened in Al-Khafji, when the lead elements of the 5th Mechanized Division drove into town with tanks in admin road march order (turrets reversed). The Saudis thought they were surrendering and went to greet them, at which point the Iraqis 'buttoned up', turned their turrets around, and destroyed several Saudi armoured vehicles. The Saudis were forced to withdraw until a counterattack retook the town.

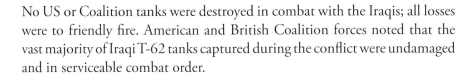

160

No US or Coalition tanks were destroyed in combat with the Iraqis; all losses were to friendly fire. American and British Coalition forces noted that the vast majority of Iraqi T-62 tanks captured during the conflict were undamaged and in serviceable combat order.

YEMENI CIVIL WAR – 1994–PRESENT

The states of Yemen – both North and South – have been in a near constant state of civil war since 1962, with the latest eruptions starting in 1994. Both sides have similar weapons and quite often those weapons change hands. A total of around 200 T-62 tanks (150 belonging to the government of Yemen, 50 to the Houthi rebels) were at one time in the country but there is no accurate way to trace losses or indeed current owners.

FIRST CHECHEN WAR – 1994–96

BELOW The First Chechen War (1994–96) was initially a disaster from a tanker's perspective but when hostilities renewed in 1999 the Russians were far-better prepared. Many of their T-62s were either M models or M tanks now also fitted with 'reshetka' grille armour. Here is a T-62M with the added grilles on the sides and around the rear of the turret.

BOTTOM Here is a Model 1967 fitted with grille armour but apparently missing most of the M-series package.

The Caucasus region, and in particular Chechnya, has always been a troubled region for Imperial Russia, the Soviet Union and now again the Russian Federation. This has been due to a combination of fierce nationalism, tribalism and a tendency towards violent criminality with little having changed since

Imperial Russia absorbed the region from the Chechens in the 1850s with the defeat of Imam Shamil. In 1994, with the Russian Federation suffering domestically after the collapse of the Soviet Union, a former Soviet VVS general-major, Dzhokar Dudayev, declared the republic the Chechen Republic of Ichkeria. At the start of the campaign Dudayev's forces inherited and operated ten T-62 tanks together with a number of wheeled BTR vehicles. After a period of sustained violence in the country, President Boris Yeltsin in December 1994 sent in a large task force of three *gruppirovki* (force groupings) to crush the separatists. The resulting war was carried on with no mercy being shown by either side in the conflict.

Russian tanks were dispatched to Chechnya, where their initial engagements were disastrous. At the turn of the year 1994/1995 a column of T-80 tanks awaiting orders in the capital, Grozny, ran out of fuel (the T-80s had no auxiliary power units) and elementary mistakes were made due to the crews not understanding their situation, with tank crews parked up in urban areas with hatches open finding that passing 'civilians' would lob grenades through the open hatches. As with all former Soviet citizens, Chechens had all served in the conscription Soviet Army and were versed in urban warfare tactics whereas the new Russian tank forces initially were not. Another basic problem encountered during the initial days of the conflict was that tanks fitted with ERA 'bricks' did not have the flyer plates installed as deployed, which resulted in the equipment being close to useless. This was quickly remedied.

The next 16 months was a bloodbath. In among the better-known T-80 tanks operated by the Russian Army in Chechnya were ten T-62 tanks operated by Russian Ministry of Internal Affairs (MVD) troops (internal forces known as Vnutrennie Voiska or 'VV' in Russian). A ceasefire was finally arranged in 1996 soon after the Chechen leader Dudayev was killed by an air strike directed onto his mobile phone signal.

The Russians suffered 5,500 killed in action, 16,000 wounded in action and thousands of other casualties due to illness or poor sanitation during the First Chechen War. There is no actual account of vehicles lost, but during the initial period General-Lieutenant Sergey Maev noted that the Russian Army lost 2,200 vehicles of all types due to combat, breakdowns, or failures of components (most were recovered and repaired).

CONFLICT IN DAGESTAN – 1997–98

During the war in Chechnya there was inevitable spill-over into Dagestan which has always had a better relationship with Moscow. The 93rd Mechanized Regiment from the Internal Troops (VV) of the Russian Ministry of Internal Affairs (MVD) were used to help restore order.

SECOND CHECHEN WAR – 1999–2003

The Russians took the lessons of the First Chechen War to heart, and as Yeltsin felt the fault of the debacle was on him he set up his protégé, Vladimir Putin, to come in as the new president and fix the problem. Putin, a former KGB 'apparatchik', became Prime Minister in 1999 and was then elected president in 2000. He had no problems fixing both the internal situation in the Russian Army and preparing to bait the Chechens into violating the ceasefire.

A T-62M1 with 'reshotka' slat grille anti-RPG protection, of the
70th Guards Tank Battalion of the 42nd Guards Motor Rifle Division,
as configured during the five-day war in South Ossetia, August 2008. (Andrey Aksenov)

The Chechens may have had a chance to get things right under Dudayev, but under their new leader, Shamil Basayev, and his vicious foreign deputy, Omar Ibn-al-Khattab, things got worse and Sharia law was implemented. This ignored the fact that, pre-1994, 44 per cent of the population in Chechnya were ethnic Russians and Orthodox Christian.

In August 1999 Russian intelligence operatives were alleged to have baited Basayev and Khattab into attacking Dagestan on the mistaken belief that the population of Dagestan wanted to be part of the new Icherkia. This was a false premise, and after the Chechens suffered a brutal beating by the Dagestani forces, including by the 93rd Mechanized Regiment of the 100th Vnutrennie Voiska (VV) internal security troops division of the Ministry of Internal Affairs (MVD).

The Russians re-invaded Chechnya in October with new tactics and organizations. The primary tanks used during the Second Chechen War were the T-62M and T-62MV and the T-72 tanks fitted with ERA. T-62 tanks in Chechnya were primarily operated by the 160th Guards Tank Regiment of the Siberian Military District (SVO) under the command of Colonel A. Budanov, within the 42nd Guards Motorized Rifle Division.

During the Second Chechen War, the Russian armed forces revived the 'fire carousel' tactic first used in street fighting in Europe in late 1944

and early 1945 to defeat the Chechens when they stood their ground. Tanks supporting infantry would move up one at a time to direct support fire range but out of range of most anti-tank weapons. The tanks would only carry ammunition in the most protected parts of the hull, and would fire at targets designated by the infantry, and when 'dry' would reverse out of range while a second tank would move up. They would continue this until the operation was completed, which was one reason that tank losses dropped dramatically.

Casualties were hard to determine as there were three claims by the Russian government, the 'Soldiers' Mothers' movement, and of course the Chechens. A realistic number would be somewhere between the official 4,557 and the 13,000 killed in action from the 'Soldiers' Mothers'. The Chechen claim of 'more than 110,000 killed' is ludicrous. There are once again few reports of tank losses that are substantiated, as the Russians put out few and the Chechens constantly claimed to have blown up dozens of tanks. After the initial 'active' phase of the war, T-62, T-62M and T-62MV tanks remained in Chechnya with the 42nd Guards MRD. During both the first and second wars in Chechnya, T-62 tanks were operated by Vnutrennie Voiska (VV) internal security troops of the Ministry of Internal Affairs (MVD).

AFGHANISTAN – 2001–PRESENT

Two events in September 2001 caused a massive upheaval in the perennially unstable nation of Afghanistan. One was the assassination of Ahmad Shah Masood, leader of the Northern Alliance and enemy of the hard-line Islamist Taliban. The other was a result of the attacks on the US in New York and Washington, as a consequence of which the US launched the 'War on Terror' against several countries in the Middle East beginning with ground and air operations in Afghanistan against the Taliban, and ostensibly also in search of Osama bin Laden.

A number of Afghan factions had access to former government weapons systems including T-62 tanks, which, as noted, have been used by those factions against each other. Around 250 T-62 tanks were delivered to Afghanistan between 1973 and 1991, but there is no way to establish how many remain in service.

IRAQ WAR (OPERATION *IRAQI FREEDOM*) – 2003–PRESENT

Saddam Hussein did not go quietly into the night after his crushing defeat in 1991, but kept playing shell games with his weapons of mass destruction programmes to confuse his enemies and also the West. While there was some oversight, in 1998 Saddam kicked out all of the UN inspection teams and appeared to restart his chemical, nuclear and biological weapons programmes. He also gave the impression that he was willing to ally with Al-Qaeda (unlikely given Saddam's desire to be in charge but he did keep his options open).

After an attempt to assassinate former US President George H.W. Bush, and given erroneous information by the CIA on the status of Saddam's programmes, as well as continuing demands for the Hussein family (Saddam, Uday and Qusay) to leave power which they ignored, and in spite of most of the world favouring a diplomatic solution, nearly 200,000 Coalition troops crossed into Iraq on 20 March 2003 and 21 days later declared initial victory. After four stands by Iraqi forces, all of which were defeated, most of the Iraqi Army (including the Republican Guards) simply melted away and abandoned their equipment. Once Coalition forces realized this, most of the tanks and armoured vehicles were moved to collection points. They were later returned to the new Iraqi Army in the post-Saddam environment. These included a number of surviving T-62 tanks.

Most of the rest of the war through 2011 consisted of guerrilla warfare by groups like the Fedayeen Saddam. Brutal fighting ensued in the cities such as Mosul and Fallujah, and the US did lose some Abrams tanks but this was due to either ATGM or RPG strikes when the tanks were serving as checkpoints and block-posts.

RUSSO-GEORGIAN WAR – 2008

There was a great deal of friction between Russia and Georgia over two districts, Abkhazia and South Ossetia. While the former basically ignored Georgian control, the government did not see Ossetia as either Russian or independent and was constantly sending troops in to suppress the breakaway province. By 2006 most Ossetian nationals had Russian passports, and considered themselves to be part of Russia, not Georgia.

The new Georgian president, Mikhail Saakashvili, saw it differently and in August 2008 decided to solve the problem once and for all by invading South Ossetia. On 7 August, following the Georgian shelling of the town of Tskhinvali, the Russians invaded both Abkhazia and South Ossetia. Mechanized forces poured into both provinces, and the Georgian forces were defeated in detail. While the war was pretty much over by the morning of 13 August, isolated fighting and incidents took place into September. On 8 September, the Russians declared both provinces independent and stationed permanent forces in those areas. The main Russian contingent operating T-62 tanks was the 42nd Guards MRD, the same combat-hardened unit, that had operated in Chechnya during the Second Chechen War.

The Georgians were beaten at every turn, starting with losing their nationwide cell phone structure (which was used for command and control) on the first day. Key weapon systems such as 9K58-2 'Smerch' and 2S7 'Peon' heavy artillery systems were picked off and eliminated and vast amounts of Georgian military hardware was destroyed. Many of the Russian columns were led by the trusty T-62M series tanks due to the mountainous terrain.

LIBYAN CIVIL WAR – 2011

After the Gulf War and the invasion of Iraq, Muammar Gaddafi opted to surrender all of his weapons of mass destruction materials and programmes to Western nations. While on his best behaviour being cognizant of the fate of Saddam Hussein in Iraq, there were other forces that decided his removal was nevertheless a better idea. But while there was a rebel movement to oust him, it turned out much too late to prevent a disaster and chaos caused by the fact the alternative nationalists were also not really the 'forces of democracy' that Western nations found to their liking.

External forces had nevertheless decided that Gaddafi had to go, and as a result, when he failed to step down per UNC Resolution 1973, NATO forces joined with rebels to crush Gaddafi loyalists and drive him from power. Gaddafi was subsequently caught and executed by rebels on video. By 2013 the country had collapsed into a nearly ungovernable mess, and both Al-Qaeda and the Muslim Brotherhood found a foothold in the shattered country.

Both government forces and rebels used the tanks in the military inventory, which may have included 170 remaining T-62 tanks.

SYRIAN CIVIL WAR – 2011

Under President Hafaz al-Assad, Syria was relatively stable but that was more due to his having an iron grip on the country than factional compatibility. When he died in 2000 and his son Bashar al-Assad took over as president, he promised reforms but they were not carried out for a number of reasons. In the summer of 2011 armed rebellion began and has continued to the present day.

While there are many different factions in the country, the worst one to appear was the Islamic State in Iraq and Syria or ISIS. At one point controlling some 20,000 square miles of Syria and Iraq, concentrated actions by Syria, Russia and the US have reduced them to small groups of fighters and eliminated what they were calling their 'caliphate'.

All of the groups except for the Russians have used various armoured vehicles including T-62 tanks used by the Syrian Army. Before the start of the new civil war around 1,000 T-62 and T-62M series tanks were in Syrian service, now joined by the T-90A and with even the T-14 'Armata' having been briefly tested in the country.

THE T-62 AND CONVENTIONAL FORCES EUROPE (CFE) TREATY RESTRICTIONS

T-62 tanks, which had been the default tank type operated by the Soviet Army in the mountainous territory of Afghanistan, were soon thereafter caught up in the arms reduction requirements related to the signing of the Conventional Forces Europe (CFE) treaty that came into effect on 19 November 1990. In accordance with the treaty, NATO and the Warsaw Pact agreed to reduce their respective levels of tanks, armoured vehicles, artillery, combat aircraft and other non-strategic weapons in Europe. Within three and a half years (specifically stated as 40 months) each side was to reduce their tank forces significantly. The Soviet Union was to reduce its tanks located in Europe (defined as west of the Ural Mountains) to 15,300 battle tanks within the specified time period, of which only 11,800 were to be located in active units, the balance to be in strategic reserve depots. The sheer landmass of the Soviet Union located east of the Urals, combined with the Soviet norm of rotating tanks out of storage for training and exercise rather than wearing out tanks on an ongoing basis, obviously gave tremendous scope for 'creative accounting'. The fact remained, however, that reducing the considerable Soviet tank park to the vastly reduced numbers committed to would mean the scrapping of some still particularly valid tank types, with the T-62 being a prime candidate for the forthcoming cull. Within the scope of the treaty as it applied to the Soviet Union, there were 2,021 T-62 tanks of various modifications – primarily T-62, T-62K, T-62M and T-62MK types – in the European part of the Soviet Union. The Soviet Union disbanded almost exactly one year later, already preceded by the Warsaw Pact. As such, by 1991, the raison d'être for the CFE treaty was less obvious. However, in the spirit of the times, the Russian Federation continued to scrap large numbers of tanks as agreed by the CFE treaty, including the T-62. By 1992, some 948 T-62 tanks remained in the 'European' part of the now former Soviet Union (i.e. west of the Ural Mountains), which included a significant number of tanks located in now independent Belorussia, Moldova and Ukraine. The numbers for 1993 are unclear, as the Russian Federation went through a period of significant political instability that year, including an attempted coup in Moscow that October which saw T-72 and T-80 tanks deployed on the streets of Moscow.

In 1994, 688 T-62 tanks remained in the 'European' part of the Russian Federation, a number that actually increased to 761 in 1995 due to tanks belonging to the Siberian Military District (SVO) being operationally deployed in Chechnya. By 1997, there were only 97 T-62 tanks recorded as left in the 'European' part of the Russian Federation, albeit the CFE treaty was by that time a historic agreement from a bygone age. A nuance was that, by this time, many T-62 tanks had been transferred to the Ministry of the Interior (MVD) and as such were not

A T-62 M1969 upgraded to M-1 standard during overhaul,
used by a tank unit of the Syrian Arab Army in the Aleppo province
of Syria, February 2020. (Andrey Aksenov)

included in CFE statistics. As the original Soviet T-62 numbers recorded in the CFE treaty amounted to only approximately 10 per cent of the T-62 tanks built, this begs the question as to where the balance that was not exported over the years disappeared.

During these years large numbers were located in tank 'kladbishye' or graveyards such as Strelnya near St. Petersburg and Stepnoy near Omsk, with as many as 1,500 T-62 and T-72 tanks sitting in open fields quietly rusting away in these two locations alone. Many tanks were located in strategic storage bases located to the east of the Ural Mountains. A not inconsiderable number were located in former Soviet republics such as Kazakhstan, Ukraine and Uzbekistan, with the only former Warsaw Pact country with a considerable quantity in service being Bulgaria. The remaining and significant missing balance is down to the fact that after the T-62 had been compromised in 1969 when a then secret tank had been captured by the Chinese, the decision to thereafter export the T-62 tank – minus a few essentials – led to the T-62 being one of the Soviet Union's export success stories.

T-62 – INITIAL FOREIGN ASSESSMENTS

As the T-62 never directly engaged NATO forces during the Cold War, there was never an ability to categorically analyse the likely outcome of direct tank engagement between well-trained Soviet tank crews using the full complement of original ammunition designed for the T-62 tank and any given NATO adversary country.

The historical Western perspective on the T-62 tank was largely based on initial Israeli evaluation of the T-62 tank, as a result of direct combat experience against Egyptian- and Syrian-crewed tanks in the 1973 'Yom Kippur' War. Significant numbers of captured T-62 tanks were taken into service with the Israeli Defence Forces (IDF) as the 'Tiran-6'. Approximately 20 T-62s were later provided to the US Army via Israel and used for 'OPFOR' (opposing forces) training, but the initial NATO assessment of the T-62 was Israeli rather than American or British in origin.

The Israelis were equipped with American-supplied M48 and M60 and British Centurion tanks to which they compared the captured T-62s. It was via Israel that the US also received its first T-62 tank, which was delivered complete with ammunition to the US, much to the chagrin of US customs authorities. The Israelis used the T-62 in considerable numbers, but in contrast to captured T-54 and T-55 tanks, the T-62 retained the original 115mm U-5TS armament.

Israeli observations included that the tank was significantly smaller than the M48, M60 and Centurion tanks, with limited ammunition stowage and relatively cramped crew conditions. The low silhouette of the T-62 (and hence resultant far smaller target) compared with US and British tanks was, however, considered a major advantage, and the 115mm U-5TS was acknowledged by the Israelis as being a powerful tank gun especially when firing the APFSDS sub-calibre ammunition at standard engagement ranges.

The main criticism made by Israeli tankers was the crew layout, with the turret cramped even by T-55 standards; however, the Israelis acknowledged the Soviet norm of selecting tank crews by height in domestic use. The turret layout was noted as a concern. This was in particular because, with the commander and gunner both located on the left side of the turret, and with the driver-mechanic located within the hull also on the left, all three crew members could theoretically be killed by a single shell. This was a possibility, but the situation on the Centurion was no different other than that the crew were all on the right side of the tank. The Israelis noted that the loader, located on the right, had a tough time moving the exceptionally long and heavy 115mm unitary rounds, eased only slightly if he happened to be left handed.

As regards the armament, overall gun depression (-4 degrees) was noted as insufficient compared to Western tanks, a consequence of the low-profile turret compared to the M48 (-9 degrees) and M60 (-10 degrees). Soviet tank commanders could, however, place the tank according to terrain and use the underditching beam to increase gun depression when firing from fixed positions if such fire was required.

The driver-mechanic was cramped and had a tougher time compared to those operating Western tanks, with more effort required for gear changes compared with the automatic gearboxes to which Israeli crews were accustomed, but the effort was considered relative in Soviet terms.

Even the Israelis acknowledged, however, that the T-62 was powerfully armed with a long reach, and any individual flaws would be more than compensated for by Soviet production numbers in a NATO versus Soviet Union/Warsaw Pact scenario, particularly when total T-54, T-55 and T-62 production numbers were compared with NATO combined capability. Total T-62 production alone was for instance ten times that of the British Chieftain tank, while the Iraqis lost more T-62 tanks during the two Gulf Wars lasting a matter of weeks than the total number of tanks fielded by the British Army during the Cold War. The T-62 was a powerful tank, reliable and proven, and available in multiples of any Western design. That it remains in service now nearly six decades after it entered production is testament to the capability of the original design.*

ABOVE LEFT The IDF added twin pintle mounts for an M2 .50-calibre machine gun to the turret.

ABOVE The IDF bins and other fittings have been removed to make it look more like the Soviet version.

---

* With extracts courtesy of 'The T-62 Jubilee Tank' by David Fletcher in *Classic Military Vehicle*, December 2007, pp. 68–71.

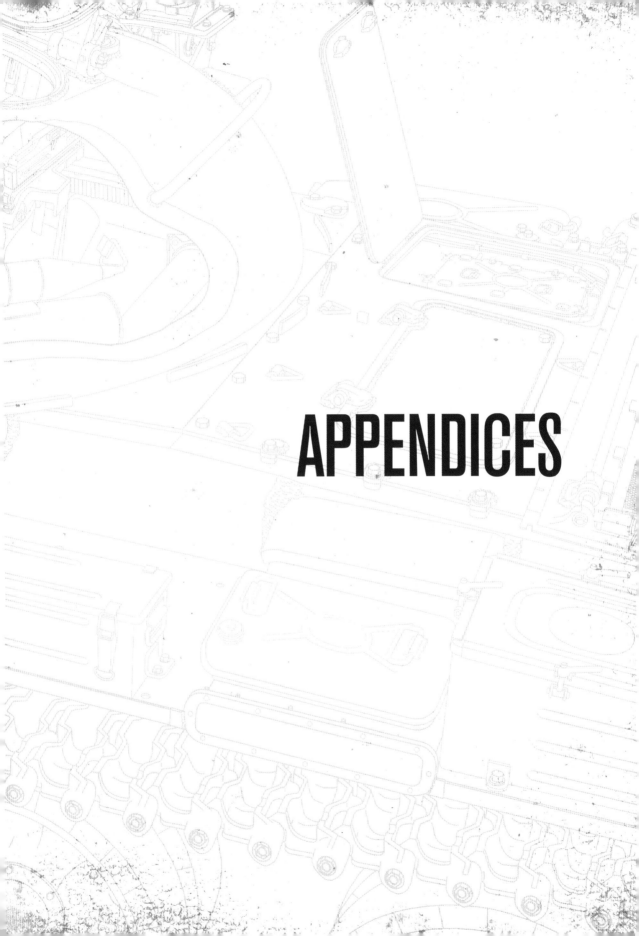

APPENDICES

APPENDIX ONE
TIMELINE FOR T-62 TANK DEVELOPMENT

Date	Item	Source	Vehicle	Remarks
8 October 1951	Ord 184-k	NKTM	–	Morozov removed from his position as chief designer at the UVZ and moved back to Kharkov; Kolesnikov named as chief designer at the UVZ
20 May 1952	–	NKTM	–	Conference held to review the future development of armoured vehicle technology; requirements for the 'NST' laid down
18 June 1952	–	NTK GBTU	–	Gen-Lt Orlovskiy tasks NKTM Makhonin and Glavtank head Kucherenko with laying out the parameters for a new medium tank
12 September 1952	Res 4169-1631	SM CCCP	Obiekt-141 Obiekt-430	Development of a T-54 tank fitted with a stabilized 100mm D-54 gun is authorized
16 October 1952	Dis 26917-rs	SM CCCP	4TD	Proceeding with the development of this specific engine is authorized
10 March 1953	–	NKT GBTU	–	Proposals for the NST are presented by Plant No. 75, Plant No. 183 and VNII-100
28 March 1953	Res 928-398	SM CCCP	Engine	Creation of a new diesel engine for the new proposed medium tank is authorized
29 September 1953	Res 2498-2031	SM CCCP	NST	Proposals to continue work on the NST are authorized
1 January 1954	–	–	–	Both Plant No. 75 and Plant No. 183 are to present their draft plans for the new medium tank
March 1954	–	Plant 9	–	The 100mm D-54T high-power gun is created by F. F. Petrov
2 April 1954	Res 598-265	SM CCCP	Obiekt-140	Creation of a new medium tank to succeed the T-54 is authorized
October 1954	–	–	–	Yari Baran is transferred from the UVZ to Kharkov and Kartsev takes over Obiekt-140, which he assigned to I. A. Nabutovskiy and V. N. Venediktov
October 1954	–	UVZ	Obiekt-139	Prospective T-54M with 100mm D-54TS gun begins factory testing
22 December 1954	–	MTMP MoD	NST	Plant No. 75 has the best design but Plant No. 183 has a more viable one that can be built faster; both must continue to work on their projects
24 February 1955	Res 374-205	SM CCCP	T-54M	Obiekt-139 authorized with 100mm D-54TS gun
6 May 1955	Res 880-524	SM CCCP	Obiekt-140 Obiekt-430	Approved technical concepts for the new medium tank and authorized prototype construction
24 November 1955	–	NTK GBTU	Obiekt-140 Obiekt-430	Work on both prototypes examined and both projects approved for advance
30 December 1955	–	NTK GBTU	Obiekt-140	Final project presented for approval
21 January 1956	–	SM CCCP	Obiekt-150	Meeting held on the topic of missile and gun armed tanks
5 April 1956	–	NTK GBTU	Obiekt-140	UVZ told to ensure complete satisfaction of all parameters to include a better transmission, engine cooling, comfort for the crew, etc.
3 September 1956	Appr	NTK GBTU	Obiekt-140	Plans for development submitted
25 September 1956	Appr	NTK GBTU	Obiekt-140	Plans approved and prototypes ordered
May 1957	–	Plant 75	Obiekt-430	Factory prepares first hull and turret
15 May 1957	–	–	Obiekt-140	First prototype begins factory testing
28 May 1957	–	SM CCCP	Obiekt-150	The development of missile tanks and tank destroyers authorized
July 1957	–	UVZ	Obiekt-142 Obiekt-165	On an initiative project UVZ creates a new tank using the 100mm D-54TS gun on a modified T-54B chassis. Later NTK GBTU re-designates it Obiekt-165
August 1957	–	Plant No. 75	Obiekt-430	Prototypes begin factory testing
20 August 1957	–	UVZ	Obiekt-140	First prototype noted as assembled and second one is underway
September 1957	–	UVZ	Obiekt-140	Obiekt-140 has serious problems with engine cooling, air cleaner, and lubrication needing major reworking
November 1957	–	UVZ	Obiekt-140 Obiekt-142	Kartsev asks to terminate Obiekt-140 in favour of a tank using most of the components of the T-54B tank which is designated Obiekt-142

December 1957	–	UVZ	Obiekt-140	Second prototype finished but third one way behind schedule
31 December 1957	–	NTK GBTU	Obiekt-150	Initial concept for the vehicle approved
6 June 1958	Res 609-294	SM CCCP	Obiekt-140 Obiekt-142 Obiekt-430	Obiekt-140 and Obiekt-142 officially terminated in favour of Obiekt-430; Obiekt-430 ordered to undergo range testing
November 1958	–	UVZ	Obiekt-166	Kartsev suggests swapping the 100mm D-54TS for the new 115mm 2A20 gun
December 1958	–	UVZ	Obiekt-142 Obiekt-165	First prototype of the new tank is assembled while the factory is gearing up for T-55 production
18 December 1958	–	GAU	Obiekt-150	'Drakon' missile selected for use in the tank destroyer
31 December 1958	–	MoD	Obiekt-165	Authorized work on 'Improved Combat Qualities of the Medium Tank'
13 January 1959	–	GKOT	Obiekt-165 Obiekt-166	Kartsev proposes fitting the new tank with a 115mm smoothbore gun vice the D-54TS
February 1959	–	NTK GBTU	Obiekt-166	Obiekt-166 will now be considered a tank destroyer and planning is for the production of 50 vehicles in 1960
24 March 1959	–	GNIAP GAU	Obiekt-430	Testing of the 100mm D-54TS gun at the Rzhev range
April 1959	–	UVZ	Obiekt-150	First prototype begins fitting the missile launcher to the chassis
21 July 1959	Res 831-371	SM CCCP	Obiekt-166	Creation of a T-55-based tank armed with a 115mm gun authorized
31 August 1959	–	GKOT	Obiekt-166	Technical project for a 115mm-gunned tank destroyer is approved; Kucherenko refers to it as a 115mm armed medium tank
September 1959	–	GRAU	–	First prototype armour-piercing fin-stabilized discarding sabot rounds developed
7 September 1959	–	NIIBT	Obiekt-150	First prototype arrives for testing
October 1959	–	UVZ	Obiekt-165	First two prototypes assembled
24 December 1959	–	SM CCCP	Obiekt-430	Intensive testing of the prototypes commences in 1960
26 January 1960	–	NIIBT	Obiekt-430	Three prototypes commence range testing
27 January 1960	–	NIIBT	Obiekt-165	Testing carried out from 6 to 27 January 1960 for firing trials on the new hull and turret; results similar to T-55 resistance
March 1960	–	UVZ	Obiekt-166	Two prototypes assembled
27 May 1966	–	NIIBT	Obiekt-165 Obiekt-166	Firing testing against the hulls and turrets carried out in which wholly cast turret shows good resistance
22 June 1960	–	SM CCCP	Obiekt-150	IT-1 prototype demonstrated for the Politburo
10 July 1960	–	NIIBT	Obiekt-430	Range testing reveals massive problems with Obiekt-430 in regard to cooling, engine reliability, tracks, stabilizer, and running gear
September 1960	–	NIIBT	Obiekt-166	Prototypes are satisfactory other than a low rate of fire of 4rpm due to heavy 115mm rounds
23 November 1960	–	GKSMOT	Obiekt-165 Obiekt-166	UVZ to investigate fitting 'podboy' NBC liners to these tanks as in the new T-55A Model
30 November 1960	–	GBTU	Obiekt-432	Marshal Blagonravov approves work on a developed version of Obiekt-430, Obiekt-432
January 1961	–	CG Ground	–	Marshal Chuykov finds out the US is now using the British 105mm gun and plans are to install it in the Leopard 1 and (erroneously) in the AMX-30; he immediately demands the 115mm gun go into service
17 January 1961	Res 141-58	SM CCCP	Obiekt-432	Commencement of work on the Obiekt-432 tank with 115mm 2A21 gun is authorized
24 January 1961	Ord 173rs	SM CCCP	GTD-3T	Work on the turbine tank engine for the T-54 or similar tanks is authorized
14 February 1961	–	NTK GBTU	Obiekt-165	Makhonin notes that the tank has failed to meet the TTT requirements and is 740kg overweight; this must be corrected
18 May 1961	–	GBTU	Obiekt-432	Committee examines a wooden mock-up of Obiekt-432 and makes recommendations for improvement
27 May 1961	–	NTK GBTU	Obiekt-166	Makhonin approves Obiekt-166 for acceptance for service but notes shortcomings must be corrected
7 July 1961	–	MoD GKOT	Obiekt-165 Obiekt-166	Marshal Malinovskiy and Smirnov approve of the new tanks

August 1961	–	UVZ	T-62	Establishment lot of 25 tanks ordered into production
12 August 1961	Res 729-305	SM CCCP	Obiekt-166	Obiekt-166 accepted into service as the T-62 tank destroyer
19 September 1961	–	CG Ground	Obiekt-430	Marshal Chuykov approves Obiekt-430 as a concept but says it must be used to develop a new tank
24 October 1961	Res 957-407	SM CCCP	Obiekt-432	Concept is approved and three prototypes ordered built by April 1962
25 October 1961	Res 972-416	SM CCCP	Obiekt-612	Plant No. 174 tasked to develop a T-62 with an automatic transmission
October 1961	–	UVZ	Obiekt-167	First prototype built
13 November 1961	–	UVZ	Obiekt-150	Kartsev reports on the status of the vehicle
December 1961	–	UVZ	Obiekt-167	Second prototype built; both tanks are to mount the new 125mm gun but it is not yet available
1 January 1962	–	UVZ	–	Plant shuts down to convert over to T-62 production; this takes six months to complete
9 January 1962	–	SM CCCP	Obiekt-165	Obiekt-165 accepted into service as the T-62A Medium Tank
15 March 1962	–	Plant No. 75	Obiekt-432	First running mock-up undergoes running testing
1 April 1962	–	UVZ	Obiekt-167	Both prototypes undergo factory testing from November 1961 to April 1962; tank judged superior to the T-62
June 1962	–	Plant No.75	Obiekt-432	Running mock-up fitted with its turret and armament
16 June 1962	–	MO CCCP	T-62	The T-62 will not require a fixed bow 7.62mm machine gun and the requirement is eliminated
July 1962	–	UVZ	Obiekt-167Zh	Work starts on fitting an autoloader and the 2A21 version of the 115mm gun into Obiekt-167
July 1962	–	UVZ	Obiekt-167M	Work starts on fitting the new 125mm gun into Obiekt-167
July 1962	–	UVZ	Obiekt-167D	Work starts on fitting a 'podboy' NBC liner into Obiekt-167
1 July 1962	–	UVZ	–	T-62 enters mass production
4 July 1962	Res 693-291	SM CCCP	Obiekt-432	Plant No. 75 is authorized to build an establishment lot of ten Obiekt-432 tanks, which are seen as the new medium tank
21 July 1962	–	GKSMOT	Obiekt-167	Ustinov, Chuykov and Makhonin reject Obiekt-167 (apparently as Ustinov sees it as a threat to Obiekt-432)
27 July 1962	–	GKSMOT	Obiekt-167	A special meeting decides that Obiekt-167 is superior to the T-55 and T-62 and all foreign tanks
August 1962	–	GKSMOT	Obiekt-167 Obiekt-432	Ustinov has decided that Obiekt-432 is more suitable and that Obiekt-167 is not worthwhile due to the costs involved, so it is rejected
22 October 1962	Res 1096-460	SM CCCP	T-62 T-62A	Both tanks are to be built in parallel with each other
December 1962	–	UVZ	T-62P	Two T-62s with 'podboy' liners built and sent for testing but found to severely impact room for the driver
27 December 1962	–	SM CCCP	Obiekt-432	Factories will switch to build Obiekt-432 and terminate production of others: Plant No. 75 to cease T-55 production in 1964 and the UVZ to cease T-62 production in 1966; support vehicles will switch to use the Obiekt-432 hull at the same time
2 March 1963	–	UVZ	T-62P	T-62 tanks with 'podboy' liner are cancelled
28 March 1963	Res 395-141	SM CCCP	Obiekt-432	Plant No. 75 to now increase establishment lot to 25 tanks and build 200 in 1964, 500 in 1965 and up to 700 in 1966 as well as terminate T-55A production in 1964
11 April 1963	–	UVZ	Obiekt-167T	Prototype is first presented with the GTD-3T engine
15 April 1963	–	Plant 75	Obiekt-432	There are 177 findings on Obiekt-432, 122 on the vehicle, 20 on the engine and 35 on the lubrication system
22 May 1963	–	CG Ground	Obiekt-432	Polyboyarov reports to Chuykov on the progress of testing; report is glowing but omits failings
June 1963	–	NIIBT	Obiekt-150	Testing shows 70 per cent accuracy with ten missile shots (one miss, two failures)
28 October 1963	Res 2235rs	MO CCCP	T-62	The T-62 will be the sole variant of this tank built

29 October 1963	Res 2238rs	MO CCCP	T-62A	Production of the T-62A terminated as tank seen as unnecessary
26 February 1964	–	GKOT	Obiekt-167M	Proposal for Obiekt-167 upgrade with 125mm D-81 gun, 'Zhelud' autoloader, 780HP V-2 type engine and improved components (T-62B proposal)
March 1964	–	NTK GBTU	T-62	Work begins to modernize the T-62 tank
11 March 1964	Ord 51	MO SSSR	T-62K	T-62K command tank accepted for service
May 1964	–	UVZ	–	UVZ gets two prototype 125mm D-81 guns for experimentation
June 1964	–	NIIBT	Obiekt-432	Obiekt-432 fails check testing and more development is recommended
June 1964	–	NIIBT	T-62	Testing begins to find a better OPVT system for use on the T-62 with new covers for the radiator air intakes
5 August 1964	Ques 199	VSNKh	GTD-3TU	Development of a more economical turbine for use in Obiekt-166TM
14 September 1964	–	SM CCCP	Obiekt-150	Firing demonstration for Khrushchev
1965	–	Plant No. 174	Obiekt-612	From 1962–65 Omsk tests fitting an automatic transmission into a T-62 with three modes of operation: automatic, semi-automatic and manual
18 January 1965	–	UVZ	Obiekt-167T	Obiekt-167T with the GTD-3T engine undergoes testing
10 February 1965	Order 24	VPK VSNKh	Obiekt-167T	Further testing is halted and the project is terminated
June 1965	–	UVZ	T-62M	Five prototype T-62M tanks built; each has the Obiekt-167 road wheels and rollers, RMSh tracks, V-36 engine and stronger shock absorbers
January 1966	–	UVZ	T-62M	Testing shows the tanks are faster and have better economy than production tanks but suspension is less durable
1966	–	UVZ	Obiekt-166TM	Prototypes built and tested with the GTD-3TU turbine engine
September 1966	–	UVZ	T-62Zh	UVZ ready to build new T-62 tanks fitted with the 115mm 2A21 gun and Zhelud autoloader but terminated as they are to instead build T-64A
October 1966	–	NIIBT	Obiekt-166M-1 Obiekt-166M-2	Two prototypes of an improved suspension for the T-62 are tested; -1 uses standard running gear, -2 uses Obiekt-167 road wheels with return rollers
5 November 1967	–	UVZ	Obiekt-166TM	Prototype T-62 fitted with the 125mm D-81 gun and Zhelud autoloader tested and demonstrated for Zverev who is irate at first and then wants it in the Obiekt-434 tank (Morozov shoots that down)
3 September 1968	Res 703-261	SM CCCP	IT-1	IT-1 accepted for service with the Red Army
25 July 1981	–	SM CCCP	T-54 T-55 T-62	Resolution passed 'On Measures to Provide Complex Modernization of the T-55 (T-55A) and T-62 Tanks' under which 785 T-62 tanks are upgraded to T-62M and T-62M-1 standards
1983	–	SM CCCP	T-62D	T-62 tank fitted with 'Drozh' active protection system is accepted for service with the Red Army
1985	–	SM CCCP	T-62MV	T-62M tanks retrofitted with first-generation ERA

APPENDIX TWO
T-62 TANKS PRESERVED IN MUSEUMS

Until relatively recently, there were few T-62 tanks to be found in museum collections, with the first outside the Soviet Union being as a result of tanks captured during the Arab-Israeli 'October' or 'Yom Kippur' War of October 1973. The first major batch of T-62s to reach the West was courtesy of Israel, which provided a number of T-62 tanks captured during the 1973 Arab-Israeli War to the US for evaluation, some of which duly ended up in military museum collections.

In recent years, however, the T-62 has seen extensive combat, again particularly in the Middle East, and there are now a significant number of T-62 tanks in museum collections worldwide. In particular, the two Gulf Wars against Iraq resulted in a large number of T-62 tanks also being delivered to Western countries courtesy of Coalition forces.

In the Russian Federation, a significant number of T-62 tanks of various modifications can now be seen in military museum collections and also within open collections located in parks and individual plinth-mounted memorials.

The list below is not exhaustive, but is representative of the large number of T-62 tanks in museum collections worldwide.

Country	City/Town	Location	Tank Type	Origin	Comments
China	Beijing	Museum of the Chinese Revolution	T-62 (2)		Includes tank No. 545 captured at Damansky Island in 1969
France	Saumur	Saumur Tank Museum	T-62		
Germany	Baumholder	US Base	T-62	Ex Iraq	
	Koblenz	Technical Museum	T-62		
	Munster	Tank Museum, Munster	T-62 M-1972		
Great Britain	Bovington, Dorset	Tank Museum	T-62	Ex Iraq, first Gulf War	Former Gate Guardian at the museum
	Shrivenham	Defence College of Management and Technology	T-62MV		Non standard ERA array fitment
Israel	Golan Heights				
	Latrun	Military Museum	T-62 (2)		
			Tiran-6		
	Tel Aviv	Military Museum	T-62		
Syria	Damascus?	Unknown museum	T-62		
Ukraine	Kiev	Great Patriotic War Memorial Museum	T-62 (2)		
		Officers Tank School	T-62		
United States	Aberdeen, Maryland	Aberdeen Proving Ground	T-62	Israel (ex Egypt/Syria)	
	Quantico	US Marine Corps Base Museum	T-62 (2)	Ex Iraq	

Russian Federation				
City/Town	Location	Tank Type	Origin	Comments
Aksai		T-62M		
Bor (Nizhny Novgorod)	Museum of Military Tekhniki	T-62		
Bryansk	Partizsanskaya Polyanna	T-62		
Chelyabinsk	Museum of Military Glory	T-62		
	City centre	T-62		
Chita	Memorial Park	T-62		
Ekaterinburg	Museum of Urals Military Glory	T-62		
Irkutsk	Museum of Military Glory	T-62		
Kachkanare		T-62M		
Kazan		T-62		
Khabarovsk	Military Museum	T-62M		
Krasnodar	Kolosisti village	T-62		
Krasnogorsk (Moscow)	Muzei Tekhniki Vadim Zadorozhny	T-62/T-62M1/ T-62MV		
Kubinka (Moscow)	Kubinka Tank Museum			
	Patriot Park	Obiekt-167T/ IT-1/T-62M/T-62MV		
	Railway Station	T-62M		
Kursk	Prospekt Pobedy	T-62		
Maloyaroslavets		T-62		
Mariinsk		T-62		
Moscow	Suvorov Academy	T-62		
	'Obiekt' small arms indoor range on NE of Ring Road (MKAD)	T-62		
Nizhny Tagil	UVZ Museum	T-62/ Obiekt-167/ IT-1		
Norilsk		T-62M		
Novokuznetsk		T-62		T-62 M-1975 with KTD-1
Omsk	Officer's Tank School	T-62MV		
	Omsk region	T-62		
Padikovo (Moscow)	Museum of Russian Military History	T-62		M-1965 production
		T-62M1		Cutaway training tank
Prokharovka	Prokhorovka Military History Museum	T-62		
Saratov	Museum of Military Glory	T-62		
Skormovo	Monument to Leonid Kartsev	T-62		Memorial at Kartsev's birthplace
Slav Gorodye (Altai)		T-62		
Smolensk		T-62		
St. Petersburg (Nevsky Pyatachok)	Leningrad Blockade Breakthrough Museum	I-62M	M1?	

Russian Federation (continued)				
City/Town	Location	Tank Type	Origin	Comments
Toliatti	Muzei Tekhniki	T-62 (2)		
Topolin (Omsk)		T-62		
Ussuriysk		T-62M		
Verkhnyaya Pyshma (Ekaterinburg)	Museum of Urals Military Glory	T-62		
Zmeinogorsk (Altai)		T-62		

APPENDIX THREE
PRODUCTION NUMBERS FOR THE T-62 AND RELATED VEHICLES

Year	T-62	T-62K	T-62A	IT-1**	Totals
1961	25	–	–	–	25
1962	270	–	5	–	275
1963	1,069	31	–	–	1,100
1964	1,521	79	–	–	1,600
1965	1,450	50	–	–	1,500
1966	1,420*	?	–	–	1,420
1967	1,505*	?	–	–	1,505
1968	1,957*	?	–	?	1,957
1969	1,970*	?	–	?	1,970
1970	2,280*	?	–	?	2,280
1971	2,215*	?	–	?	2,215
1972	2,209*	?	–	?	2,209
1973	1,620*	?	–	–	1,620
Total	19,019	627	5	220	19,651***

Notes: * Includes T-62K Model production tanks
** Apparently not held as part of summary T-62 production
*** The Soviet Army only received 19,484 T-62 tanks of all models. The remaining 167 tanks were probably those sold to Egypt in 1971 or demonstrators sold in single tank lots to other countries for evaluation.
Questions marks denote that there was production of the tank in these years, but the numbers per year are unknown, only the total quantity.

T-62M CONVERSIONS BY YEAR	
Year	Number
1981	10
1982	25
1983	50
1984	100
1985	600
Total	785

Note: No numbers for post 1985 modifications are available, but based on CFE Declarations (see below) more than 1,000 T-62s were upgraded to M status. There were also a number lost in Afghanistan during the late 1980s which are not reflected in the CFE totals.

STATUS OF SOVIET T-62 TANKS WEST OF THE URALS AS OF 1 NOVEMBER 1990
(CONVENTIONAL FORCES IN EUROPE DECLARATION, VIENNA, AUSTRIA)

Tank	Category I	Category II	Category III	Category IV	Category V	Total
T-62	1,555	1,322	798	11	233	3, 919
T-62K	110	57	50	0	53	270
T-62M	181	126	115	0	55	477
T-62MK	2	2	2	0	0	6
T-62M	113	113	112	0	0	338
T-62M1	60	60	60	0	0	180
Totals	2,021	1,680	1,077	11	341	5,190

Note: The numbers here differ somewhat from the known production numbers as they include all tanks in that category which were extant and counted under the CFE rules, and most of those were built after 1965. There was no explanation given as to why there were two T-62M categories but the second one may be T-62MV types with 'Kontakt 1' ERA. Also note that no T-62D 'Drozd' tanks were declared in this area whereas some 716 T-55AD/T-55AMD types were included.

APPENDIX FOUR
OBIEKT NUMBERS OF THE T-62 AND RELATED DEVELOPMENTAL TANKS

Number	Description
139	T-54 tank up-gunned with 100mm D-54TS gun and fitted with a single sight, the T2SA 'Udar' day/night gunner's sight
140	Completely new design of medium tank mounting the 100mm D-54TS gun in a new chassis with six road wheels, three return rollers, and the 'V'yuga' stabilizer
141	T-54 tank up-gunned with 100mm D-54TS gun and fitted with the single-axis 'Raduga' stabilizer and normal T-54/T-55 sights
142	Redesigned T-54B chassis with a new turret and the chassis extended 386mm as well as mounting the 100mm D-54TS gun
150	IT-1 missile armed tank destroyer using a modified T-62 hull and the 3M7 'Drakon' guided missile
165	T-62A tank, basically the Obiekt-142 tank with a new, smoother profile turret and other improvements but still mounting the 100mm D-54TS (2A24) gun
165K	Command tank prototype, 1960
165M	Prototype with V-36 engine developing 580hp. Modified running gear with no sixth wheel station, modified OPVT system
165P	Prototype with improved PAZ system, 1961
166	T-62, basically identical to Obiekt-165 but with a new 115mm U-5TS 'Molot' gun; modified twice during its production run and finally fitted with an AAMG
166D	T-62D mounting the 'Drozd' active protective system against ATGMs
166K	T-62K commander's tank with HF radio, generator and 11-metre antenna carried
166KN	Command version of T-62, R-112, TNA-2 navigation system, PAB-2A artillery plotter (series produced as T-62K)
166M	Modified T-62 tank with elements of the Obiekt-167 suspension and a V-36 diesel engine
166M-1	T-62 fitted with elements of the Obiekt-167 suspension but using standard T-62 fittings and five road wheels, 1964
166M-2	T-62 fitted with the complete Obiekt-167 suspension, 1964
166M-6	Prototype for the T-62M production tanks
166P	T-62 fitted with a complete 'podboy' nuclear radiation liner, 1961
166T	T-62 fitted with the GTD-3T 700shp turbine engine
166TM	T-62 fitted with the GTD-3T engine and Obiekt-167 suspension
166Zh	T-62 fitted with the 115mm 2A21 separate loading ammunition gun and the 'Zhelud' autoloader
167	Further development of the T-62 with a new suspension of six smaller aluminium road wheels, three return rollers, RMSh tracks, a new engine and other refinements
167D	Improved PAZ system, 1960
167M	Obiekt-167 fitted with the 125mm D-81T (2A26) gun and the 'Zhelud' autoloader; proposed for acceptance as the T-62B
167P	Obiekt-167 fitted with the 'podboy' nuclear radiation lining
167T	Obiekt-167 fitted with the GTD-3T and then GTD-3TU gas-turbine engines
167TU	Obiekt-167 with GTD-3TU 800hp gas-turbine engine adapted for low temperature use, 1964
169	T-62 with 902B 'Tucha' smoke discharger set as being developed for the T-72
167Zh	Obiekt-167 fitted with the 115mm 2A21 separate loading ammunition gun and 'Zhelud' autoloader; crew reduced to three; 2A21 is 125mm
167 Malyutka	Obiekt-167 with 9K11 Malyutka ATGM, 1963
612	T-62 fitted with an automatic transmission by Plant No. 174
619X	T-62 modified for use with PST-63 pontoon ferry (619B was the designation used with Ob.432)
626B	T-62 modified for use with Obiekt-80 assault hydrofoil

APPENDIX FIVE
T-62 EXPORT CLIENTS

The T-62 began to migrate from Soviet units to the third world (only Bulgaria in the Warsaw Pact ever bought and used them) in the early 1970s and is still moving around today among third world countries. Many of them have been donated or sold from one country to another, captured in combat, or changed sides due to defections or revolutions. It is still in second-line service with the Russian armed forces for use in mountainous terrain such as Chechnya.

LEFT A number of T-62s were captured during *Desert Storm*, and the USMC had two on display at their museum in Quantico, VA. Here is one of them – both tanks were from the 6th Armoured Brigade, 3rd 'Saladin' Armoured Division.

CENTRE FAR LEFT The tank had all normal Model 1972 features plus the armoured covers over the searchlights added by Iraqi workshops.

CENTRE LEFT The vehicle was number 22A of the 2nd Regiment of the brigade. Centre markings were white – 1st, yellow – 2nd, black – 3rd subunits.

BOTTOM It did not sport the usual serial number painted on the glacis and its own UVZ serial is unreadable.

RIGHT This is the glacis of the other T-62, also a Model 1972. It has a history here: its factory serial number was N02VT0460, built in February 1971; its Iraqi Army serial was 'Al Jaish (Army)' 211217; but the new 'owners' welded a tag on saying it was now the property of A Company, 8th Tank Battalion, USMC.

CENTRE RIGHT Another T-62 Model 1972, this one at the Bovington Tank Museum in England.

CENTRE FAR RIGHT The markings have been repainted but not accurately. It is number 2 but it looks as if it may also have been a 6th Armoured Brigade tank.

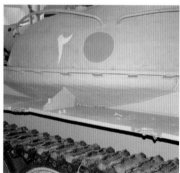

BELOW This one has six fasteners for 12.7mm ammo canisters but in a different pattern than most. It would be awkward for the loader to reach the front one without exiting the tank.

BOTTOM The commander's OU-3 light still has its 'flip down' armoured door protecting it.

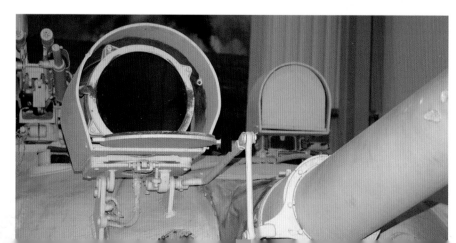

ABOVE LEFT The tank has had all of the external fittings on the left fender (as well as the mud guard) either knocked off or removed.

ABOVE All of the viewers and cables are still in situ.

LEFT Another repainted T-62 Model 1972 outside at Bovington. This one is in better nick as it still has all of its external fittings.

CENTRE LEFT All that is missing from this tank is the DShKM machine gun and some minor fittings.

BOTTOM For some reason the splash guard has been moved up behind the lights even though the brackets for it are still in place.

TOP The cleaning rod bin is missing as is the auxiliary oil tank over the exhaust outlet.

BELOW RIGHT The auxiliary fuel tanks and one set of brackets are missing. This was not uncommon as many senior Iraqi commanders were afraid if the tanks had a full 700km road range crews would defect! It also has a non-standard tow hook bolted to the rear plate.

FAR RIGHT When displayed, now many years ago, the T-62 made an imposing 'Gate Guard' for the museum entrance!

CENTRE Oddly enough, while a Model 1972, the tank has a Model 1961 engine deck. It is unclear if the Iraqis did this modification or the British.

BOTTOM The tank has a complete Model 1961 engine deck with the OPVT-54B type sealing frame around the radiator grille area.

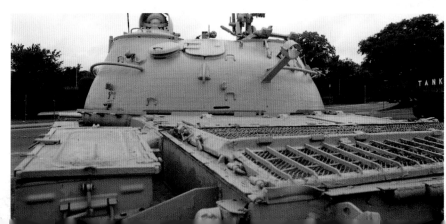

Note that while only 19,019 were built by the USSR, due to second-, third- and even fourth-hand transfers and DPRK Ch'onma production the numbers add up to far beyond the 19,019 built by the Soviet Union.

Country	Original Number	Remarks
Afghanistan	255	Tanks were delivered between 1973 and 1991 but have been reduced by combat and are in the hands of various factions
Algeria	300	Reported as in service in 2017
Angola	364	Multiple orders starting in 1980 and ending in 1994. Only 18 listed as still in service
Belarus	459	Number is as of 1992; by 2000 numbers were down to 170 but now all are either sold off or scrapped
Bulgaria	250	Only Warsaw Pact state to use them; withdrawn and disposed of before 2000
Cuba	400	Ordered in 1976 and 1984; 380 listed as still in service
Czechoslovakia	1+	Evaluated the tank but did not accept or produce it
Democratic People's Republic of Korea	500 (2,000)	500 T-62s were ordered from the USSR in 1970–75; remainder are domestically produced Ch'onma tanks in six versions
Egypt	1,300	Multiple orders between 1971 and 1975; 500 listed as still in service
Eritrea	Unknown	Small number donated by Ethiopia
Ethiopia	100+	Began ordering from the USSR in 1977 and acquired others second hand; around 100 still in service
Iran	315	Purchased from Libya, Syria and DPRK Ch'onma tanks. Around 50 are still in service
Iraq	2,850	All tanks ordered between 1973 and 1989 but status is unknown; many may have been sold off to other countries and about 450–500 were lost during the 1991 Gulf War
Iraqi Kurdistan	170-	Around 100–120 with PUK Peshmerga and 50 with KDP Peshmerga
Israel	120	Captured during the Yom Kippur War and 1982 Lebanese campaign; some converted to Tiran-6 status
Kazakhstan	280	T-62M models reported as of 2007
Lebanon	<64	Received mixed group of T-55 and T-62 tanks from Iraq via Jordan in 1988–89
Libya	900	All ordered between 1973 and 1978; some sold and others now in the hands of various factions inside Libya
Mongolia	250	Orders started in 1973; all apparently still in service
People's Republic of China	1+	Captured one T-62 in March 1969 and apparently copied it for evaluation as the WZ-122; not accepted for service
Russia	2,000	Inherited at the break-up of the USSR but more may have been stored east of the Urals and not counted by CFE measures; some still in second-line service due to mountain terrain performance
Syria	1,000	1,000 ordered between 1973 and 1984; now fielding T-62M tanks obtained from Russia to make up for combat losses; Syrian rebel groups have some tanks captured from government forces or surrendered by troops changing sides
Tajikistan	10	Only seven reportedly remain in service
Turkmenistan	7	Last reported number from this country
Ukraine	400	Inherited at the break-up of the USSR; most sold or scrapped; none in service after 2000; some offers of a T-62AG with TDF series engine (either 5TDF or the newer 6TD) and T-64-type transmission have been made but no word on production or sales
United States	~20	Obtained a small number of T-62s from Israel and perhaps Egypt for evaluation; used in Opposing Forces (OPFOR) detachments for training purposes after evaluation
USSR	19,019	Total produced but many sold or given away; numbers were down to 12,900 in 1985 and 11,300 (5,190 in the CFE covered area) in 1990 but were disseminated to the various new republics when the USSR broke up in 1991
Uzbekistan	170	Reported as of 2017
Vietnam	200–220	Purchased from the USSR after the end of the Vietnam War
Yemen (North)	16	Former Soviet tanks
Yemen (South)	270	Purchased from the USSR
Yemen (Houthi)	56	Purchased from Bulgaria in 1994

RIGHT The IDF presented the US with a large number of T-62s, mostly Model 1972 tanks. As a result, they published formal photographs like one of these two, which were widely distributed.

CENTRE This US-ownership T-62 Model 1972 – with a US matching unit for an AN/VRC radio fitted to the old Soviet whip antenna mount – was part of the US III Corps OPFOR Detachment at Fort Hood, TX.

BOTTOM A bit of a diversion. In 1983 one of the authors had to reenlist in the US Army, but, as a senior NCO, had only the choice of where to reenlist with no other options. He selected the commander's cupola of the III Corps OPFOR T-62, and his command went along with it. Here he is after the ceremony with company commander CPT Martha McCord Downey and the US flag and reenlistment NCO.

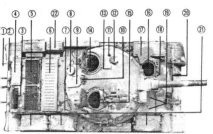
FIG. 1-6. T-62A: **AERIAL VIEW**

FIG. 1-7. ENGINE AND POWER TRAIN DECK LIDS

FIG. 1-8. ENGINE RADIATOR

1 SPARE FUEL DRUM BANDS
2 LOG
3 ENGINE PORT
4 COOLING PORT
5 ENGINE LOUVERS
6 ENGINE LOUVERS COVER FOR SNORKELING
7 REAR FUEL INTAKE PORT
8 TURRET VENTILATOR
9 SPENT SHELL EJECTION PORT
10 TURRET IDENTIFICATION LIGHT
11 ANTENNA MOUNT
12 ARMORED HOUSING FOR GUNNER'S PERISCOPE
13 GUNNER'S VISION BLOCK
14 TANK COMMANDER'S CUPOLA
15 LOADER'S CUPOLA
16 DRIVER'S COMPARTMENT
17 DRIVER'S HATCH
18 DRIVER'S VISION BLOCKS (2)
19 FRONT INTERNAL FUEL CELLS
20 WAVE DEFLECTOR
21 AUXILIARY FUEL TANKS
22 AUXILIARY OIL TANK

ABOVE LEFT The US Army had so many T-62s, nearly all operational, that they had to produce an operator's manual to run the tanks for training purposes. Here is the introductory page with items called out.

ABOVE CENTRE As the US Army has a bugaboo about servicing the vehicles, a call-out of how to access the components (here the radiator and transmission) was a must.

ABOVE RIGHT US Army view of the T-62's engine bay.

BELOW LEFT Driver's control panel with US Army call-outs.

BELOW RIGHT Driver's compartment with control call-outs.

FIG. 2-3. INSTRUMENT PANEL

1 BILGE PUMP TOGGLE
2 OIL PUMP-AIR START SWITCH
3 SMOKE SCREEN SWITCH
4 REAR MARKER SWITCH
5 I.R. HEADLIGHT SWITCH
6 SERVICE DRIVE LIGHT SWITCH
7 FRONT MARKER LIGHT SWITCH
8 HORN
9 ELECTRIC STARTER
10 ENGINE HOUR GAUGE
11 TACHOMETER
12 OIL PRESSURE GAUGE
13 OIL TEMPERATURE GAUGE
14 WATER TEMPERATURE GAUGE
15 VOLTMETER-AMMETER
16 FUSE BOX
2-4

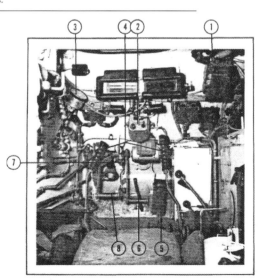
FIG. 2-5. DRIVER'S COMPARTMENT

1 PURGE PUMP AIR BLEEDER BUTTON
2 GYRO COMPASS
3 SPEEDOMETER
4 STEERING LATERALS
5 ACCELERATOR PEDAL
6 BRAKE PEDAL
7 PARK BRAKE
8 CLUTCH PEDAL
9 GEAR SHIFT LEVER

RIGHT Gunner's sight and control call-outs.

CENTRE Gunner's sight adjustment controls.

BOTTOM LEFT US Army instructions for proper adjustment for track tension in the T-62.

BOTTOM RIGHT Location of the adjustment mechanism on a T-62.

FIG. 3-21. TELESCOPE AND PERISCOPE
        PREPARED FOR RIGHT EYE USE

1 GUNNER'S VISION BLOCK
2 IR POWER SUPPLY
3 MANUAL TRAVERSE HANDLE
4 GUNNER'S CONTROLS
5 TPN BORESIGHT WRENCH

FIG. 3-20. TELESCOPE AND PERISCOPE
        PREPARED FOR LEFT EYE USE

1 AZIMUTH ADJUSTMENT
2 ELEVATION ADJUSTMENT

3-13

FIG. 3-19. TELESCOPE IN TANK

1 RANGE KNOB
2 MAGNIFICATION LEVER
3 FILTER LEVER
4 GUNNER'S CONTROLS

NORMAL TRACK TENSION 60-80mm ABOVE 1st ROAD WHEEL

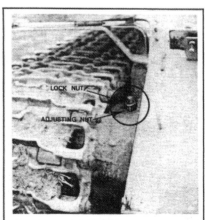

FIGURE 4-27 TRACK TENSION ADJUSTING NUT

ABOVE The 'poster child' for the US Army T-62 manual, a T-62 Model 1972 in the possession of the 203rd MI Battalion (Technical Intelligence) at APG in Maryland. This is serial number N06VT1487 built in June 1971.

LEFT An inoperative T-62 Model 1972, ex-Syrian, as an exhibit in front of the Ordnance Museum at APG. This tank is now at the Armor and Cavalry Museum at Fort Benning, GA.

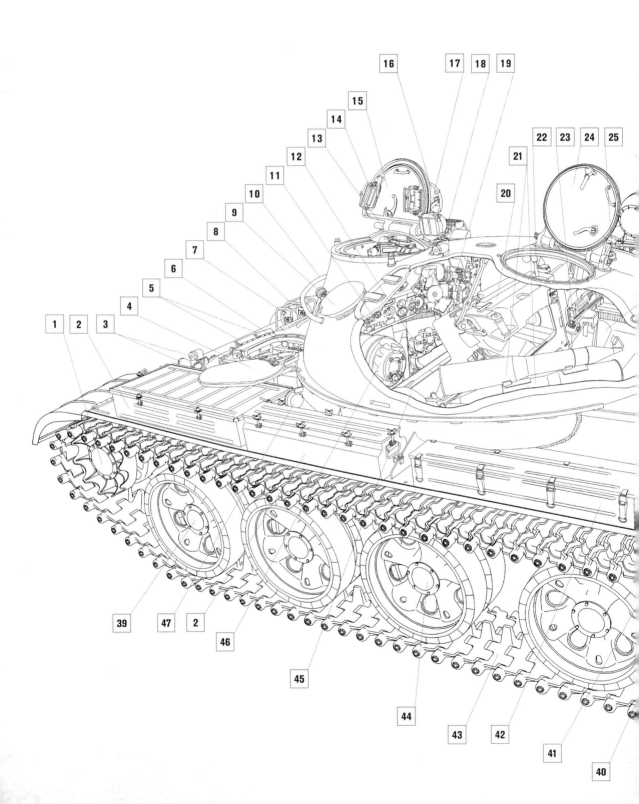

1	Idler wheel		**12**	Front external fuel tank/ammunition stowage
2	Spare part and instrument box		**13**	TKN-2 commander's sight
3	GST-64 night-positioning light		**14**	TNP-165 periscope vision block
4	Driver's hatch		**15**	Commander's cupola hatch
5	Driver's periscope		**16**	OU-3GK IR light
6	Dashboard		**17**	FG-126 rear light
7	FG-125 IR headlight		**18**	TPN-1-41-11 night sight
8	FG-127 headlight with night-driving device		**19**	TSh2B-41 telescopic gun sight
9	Ventilation system air intake cover		**20**	Gun breech
10	Turret handrail		**21**	Turret ammunition stowage
11	R-123 radio		**22**	'Meteor' gun stabilization system
			23	7.62mm PKT coaxial machine gun
			24	Loader's hatch
			25	Loader's Mk 4 periscope
			26	L-2G IR light
			27	Fume extractor
			28	U-5TS 115mm gun barrel
			29	Rear fuel tank
			30	Rear ammunition stowage
			31	Engine hatch
			32	Engine air filter
			33	External fuel tanks
			34	Radiator armoured cover
			35	Engine fan armoured flap
			36	Attachment points for additional 200 l-fuel barrels
			37	Unditching log
			38	Sprocket wheel
			39	Wheel with strengthened bearing (first and last stations)
			40	Exhaust pipe
			41	Spare engine oil tank
			42	Gun-cleaning kit box
			43	RMSh-type tracks
			44	'Starfish' type wheel
			45	Spent case extractor
			46	Air filter and ventilation system
			47	Horn

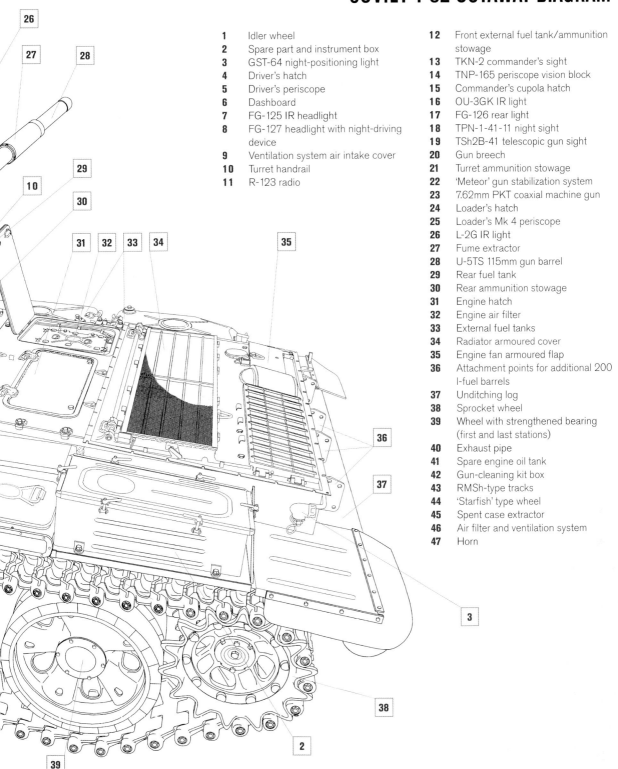

APPENDIX SEVEN
SOVIET/RUSSIAN COMMUNICATIONS SYSTEMS AND DEVELOPMENT

By the time the T-62 entered service, the Soviet Army was upgrading their first-generation VHF FM sets for better transmission characteristics on the battlefield.

They were initially fitted with the R-113 set. While it was limited in frequency range (20–22 MHz) it was coupled to the improved R-120 intercom system and was a great step forward in tank unit communications. Battalion-level commanders received tanks with two of these sets, and regimental commanders received tanks that were also fitted with the improved R-112 HF AM set (frequency range 1.5–4.2 MHz) and an 11m telescopic antenna for use while stopped. This gave them reliable battlefield area communications via the R-113 and up to 100km with Morse code on the R-112.

But the limited frequency ranges resulted in what radio operators call being 'stepped on' with too many units using the same narrow frequency bands. In the late 1960s, new equipment was developed and issued, starting with the R-123 radio set and R-124 intercom system. The R-123 was a much better set with up to four frequency pre-sets and increased output, but most welcome was its expanded frequency range of 20–51.5 MHz which both permitted wider use and also easy coordination with motorized rifle and artillery units and their dedicated radio sets – the artillery used the R-108 from 28–36.5 MHz and motorized rifle the R-105 (36–46.1 MHz). These were fitted to new production T-62 tanks and T-62K command tanks.

Initially battalion commanders had two R-123 sets, but with the pre-set frequency option (four previously selected frequencies) in the R-123 they soon received an HF set instead. While at first they used the R-112 as before, later it was upgraded to the newer R-130 HF AM/SSB (frequency range 1.5–10.99 MHz). The R-130 was optimized for what are referred to as single sideband 'skywave' communications where the signal is bounced off the ionosphere and now a battalion commander could communicate up to 350km with the right antenna and weather conditions.

As the early T-62s came in for midlife rebuilding, they generally all received the aforementioned communications upgrades so, by the 1970s, most of the tanks had the R-123/R-124 and R-130 configurations.

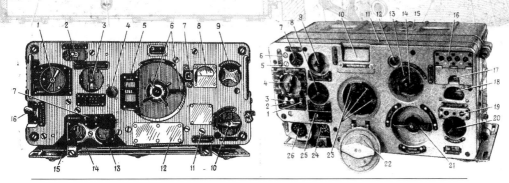

ABOVE LEFT A drawing of an R-113 showing its controls.
ABOVE RIGHT The more common R-123 transceiver that replaced the R-113 and was retrofitted to most Soviet tanks.
BELOW LEFT A complete set of communications equipment with the R-123 and R-124 intercom system as well as their antenna set.
BELOW RIGHT The amplifier used for boosting the R-123's signal to a full 10 watts.

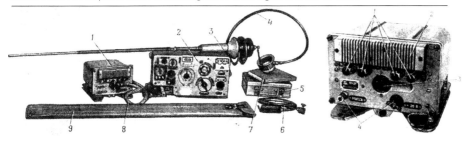

In the 1980s the Soviet Union began to adopt its first solid-state radio sets, and of course that meant new radios for the tactical level. The new tactical set was the R-173 which was even more advanced with a frequency range of 30–79.90 MHz (similar to NATO and US sets). It could store up to ten preset frequencies and also could be used for both analogue and digital communications systems. It was paired with the improved R-174 intercom system. The HF command sets were upgraded to the R-134 HF AM/SSB series radios (frequency range 1.5–29.99 MHz). As older T-62 tanks were upgraded to M status with new engines, fire controls, ATGM capability and other improvements they also received these new radio sets.

While the T-62 remains in service with the Russian military today (most recently reactivated as a training tank), as many of the tanks are still in service with foreign clients, hence new and modern communications suites are also offered, most involving the use of the new R-168 family of digital radio sets. These have a broad range of frequencies depending on model but the main VHF versions now cover 30–108 MHz.

With full upgrades such as reactive armour, laser rangefinders, the 1K13 fire control system, a new engine, tracks, survival equipment and electronics, the T-62 is still a very effective second-tier combat vehicle and the preferred mount of the Russian Army in mountainous terrain.

Note that most Soviet tankers used the 'Shlemofon', which was a padded helmet with built-in headsets and a strap-on throat microphone; a chest switch was used for transmitting on the selected radio set. But the throat microphone needed to be relatively tight to work properly and if not adjusted correctly the user tended to sound somewhat like 'Donald Duck' when speaking.

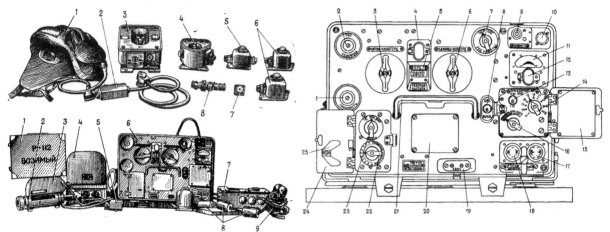

TOP LEFT The additional kit used with a radio set – the 'Shlemofon' helmet and headset, chest switch and individual connector boxes with the crew internal selectors and the commander's internal/external switch.
ABOVE LEFT The complete equipment set for the R-112 HF AM commander's set for battalion and regimental commanders.
ABOVE RIGHT Controls for the R-112. Number 5 is the frequency indicator in kilohertz.
BOTTOM LEFT The two-cycle gasoline generator provided in command tanks that was situated to the right rear of the driver. Information provided says it needs a 25:1 fuel to oil mixture to operate.
BOTTOM RIGHT While showing a T-55, the 11m commander's antenna on a command tank mounted in this manner.

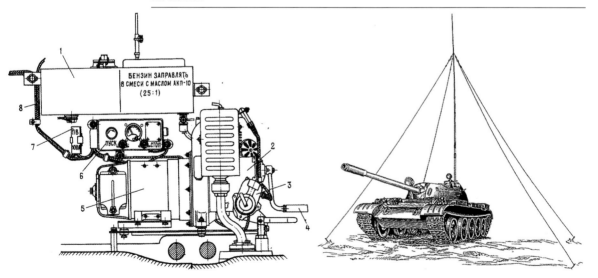

APPENDIX EIGHT
SOVIET BALLISTIC SETS AND TABLES

While politically the Soviet Union witnessed some internal extremes and dynamic movements, when it came to engineering and science the Soviet Union and its designers were very methodical, thorough, and practical. One such methodology was the determination of a set of ballistic standards and their application to all weapons of a given calibre and gun barrel specification.

Soviet weapon designers from the outset understood that all guns using similar ammunition and barrel length would have nearly identical ballistic tables and results. It made no difference if it was a machine gun, automatic cannon, mortar, howitzer or gun – all weapons of that calibre with that length barrel would fire with near-identical performance. Also irrelevant was its platform – field gun, tank, railway or ship. So tables were created based on the types of ammunition used and were therefore standardized by all arms plants to permit easier development of sights, equipment, accessories and most of all ammunition.

The sets were given a specific number and when developing sights or other accessories the relevant factory would have a set standard to use at once. For example, a 7.62mm machine gun firing 7.62x54mm cartridges, no matter whether it was a DT, SGM, SGMT or PKT type, would all use the same set of ballistics – Set 11. Likewise the 14.5mm KPV and KPVT would use Set 14.

The 76.2mm guns on the wartime tanks with a 41.5-calibre-long barrel – either the F-34 or the ZiS-5 – used Set 7. The early T-34-85 tanks used Set 15 but with more powerful ammunition it was upgraded to Set 16.

The T-54 and T-55 used three different sets of ballistic tables. The very early models used Set 20 but the production versions used Set 22. Later, when HEAT ammunition and then sabot (APDS) rounds were introduced, they used Set 32.

These sets are part of the designator for the sight and that tells the crew and the support staff what reticule is installed in the telescopic or direct fire sight. For example, the T-34-85 used either a TSh-15 or TSh-16 sight based on the production date and type of ammunition used. A T-10 used the TSh2-27 with the number indicating the table for the post-war 122mm gun whereas the T-10M used a T2S-29-14 day sight and a TPS-1-29-14 night sight; Set 29 was for the 122mm M-62 gun with improved ballistics and Set 14 indicated the coaxial 14.5mm KPVT heavy machine gun.

The T-62 used the 115mm U-5TS (2A20) 'Molot' gun which received a new ballistic set designated Set 41. This gun used the TSh2B-41-11 telescopic

198

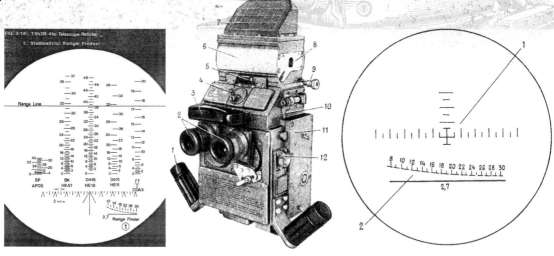

ABOVE LEFT This is the US Army translated reticule from the gunner's TSh2B-41u sight with all of the options translated into English. The flat trajectory for APFSDS rounds is on the left, the 7.62mm machine gun on the right.
ABOVE CENTRE The commander's TKN-3 sight. While it had day/night capability it was not as capable as the gunner's sight.
ABOVE RIGHT And here is why: the commander's sight was only capable of ranging a target and not selecting a weapon or ammunition. It only had a gauge for a 2.7m-high target – the Soviet estimate of the height of an M48, M60 or Centurion tank.
BELOW LEFT The complete gunner's night sight complex to include the sight and the searchlight.
BELOW RIGHT The 3UBM5 and 3UBM6 rounds and their projectiles showing the casing markings and the difference in size and shape.

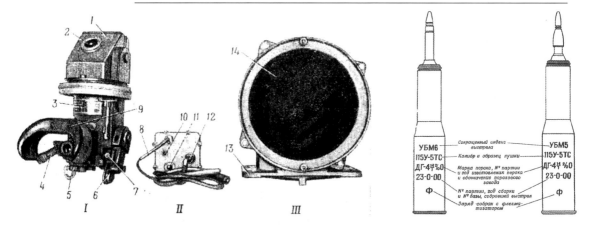

sight and the TShN-41-11 periscopic night sight. These sights were calibrated for use with high explosive-fragmentation (OF) ammunition, high explosive anti-tank (BK) ammunition, and armour-piercing fin-stabilized discarding sabot (BM) ammunition plus the 7.62mm machine gun. When the tanks upgraded in 1981 to carry the 9K116-2 ATGM system firing either the 9M117 'Sheksna', the 9M117M 'Kan' or 9M117M1 'Arkan' missiles, and its 1K13 sight, the main telescopic sight was changed to the TShSM-41U.

TOP LEFT An older 3UBM4 round with its casing cut away and the projectile with its sabot in place, on display at the Museum of Russian Military History, Padikovo.

CENTRE LEFT Comparison of the 3UBM4 and 3UBM5.

LEFT Another shot of the 3UBM4 projectile. The fins were usually cast into the projectile and would mark the target with six slits where they penetrated.

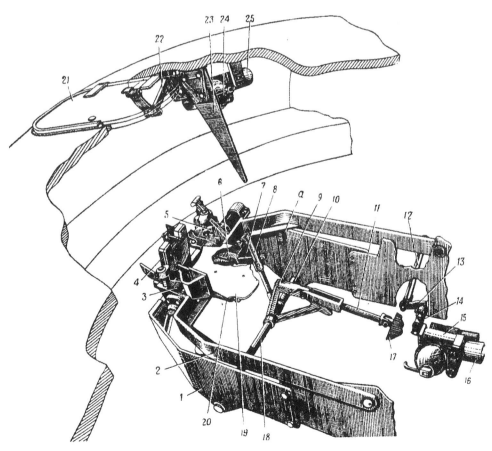

LEFT Schematic of the automatic casing ejector. When the casing strikes the follower (23) the door is opened for the casing to be tossed out.

RIGHT 3UBK3 HEAT round with the BK-4 projectile.

CENTRE RIGHT 3UOF1 HE-FRAG round with OF-11 projectile.

FAR RIGHT A shot of the door opened for ejection.

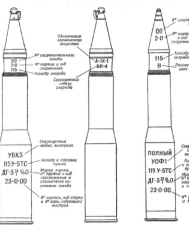
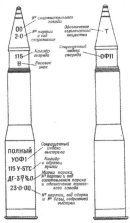

Bespoke reticules were installed that provided the deviation distance and lead percentage at range for each type of ammunition to cover the ballistic drop of the projectile and compensate for its velocity over distance. A different number and shift was needed for each one.

The 115mm U-5TS used the following ammunition types:

Round	Projectile	Type	Muzzle Velocity	Remarks
3UBM3	3BM3	APFSDS	1,650mps	300mm RHA @1,000m
3UBM4	3BM4	APFSDS	1,615mps	250mm RHA @1,000m
3UBM5	3BM6	APFSDS	1,680mps	240mm @2,000m
3UBM9	3BM21	APFSDS (tungsten core)	1,600mps	330mm RHA @2,000m
3UBM13	3BM28	APFSDS-DU*	1,650mps	380mm RHA @2,000m
3UBK3	3BK4 3BK4M	HEAT	955mps	440mm RHA
3UOF1	30F11	HE-FRAG	905mps	2.64kg HE
3UOF6	30F18	HE-FRAG	800mps	2.8kg HE
3UOF37	30F27	HE-FRAG	800mps	3.13kg HE
3UBK10-2	9M117 'Sheksna'	HEAT (ATGM)	400–500mps	550mm RHA Penetration
3UBK10M-1	9M117M 'Kan'	HEAT (ATGM)	400–500mps	600mm RHA Penetration
3UBK23-2	9M117M1 'Arkan'	Tandem HEAT (ATGM)	400–500mps	850mm RHA Penetration after ERA
Note: * Depleted uranium penetrator				

APPENDIX NINE
OPVT UNDERWATER TANK DRIVING EQUIPMENT

By the time the T-62 entered service in 1961, Soviet industry had managed to field a useful and effective system for underwater driving. As water obstacles are encountered roughly every 15–20km, with most being less than 5 metres deep, being able to wade across them was seen as essential to maintaining the offensive. The solution was introduced at UVZ in 1958 on the final production versions of the T-54B tank, and then immediately adapted for use on the later T-55 as it entered series production. Initially the T-62 Model 1961 used the OPVT-155 system then in production for the T-55.

The equipment – *Oborudovaniye dlya Podvodnogo Vozhdenniya Tanka* (OPVT) or equipment for underwater driving of tanks – was to permit the tank to autonomously cross a water obstacle of up to 700 metres' width with a depth of 5 metres or less and also permit the tank to emerge from the water combat ready with a safe crew. It provided air to the crew and engine, prevented water from flooding and stalling the engine while underwater, ensured the tank could move underwater in a given direction, and provided for the tank to be completely combat ready when it would egress from the water.

To this end the OPVT-155 system consisted of a number of components:

- A two-section snorkel tube roughly 3.8 metres long when assembled;
- An exhaust flapper valve providing one-way flow of the exhaust;
- Covers for the radiator air intake which fastened to a combing around the radiator air intakes, radiator air exhaust;
- A hinged domed steel cover over the fan exhaust grille;
- Covers for the gun muzzle, gunner's sight aperture, machine gun port, and antenna feed and base;
- Cover for the air feed to the transfer case (guitara);
- Sealing for the turret, ventilator, ZIP bins and hatches;
- A bilge pump at the rear of the hull fitted with a one-way valve to bail out water collecting on the floor of the engine compartment (apparently introduced on the T-55);
- Life jackets and rebreathers for crew escape if necessary;
- A GPK-48 gyrocompass for underwater navigation.

The intent was to carry all of this equipment on the tank, but it is not obvious if that was completely possible. At this time a two-section snorkel,

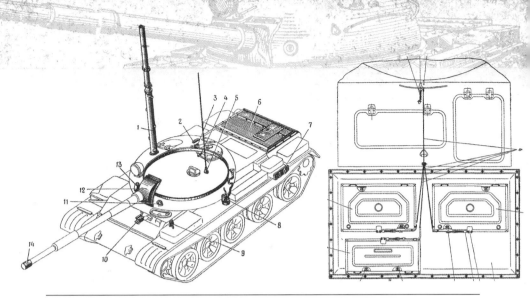

TOP LEFT A schematic drawing of all of the elements necessary for underwater driving with the T-62. This is a Model 1961 that still used the old OPVT-54B grille cover with frame around the engine grilles and a flip-open metal hatch for running prior to water entry. (Andrey Aksenov)

TOP RIGHT An interesting drawing from an early Model 1967 manual. Apparently while the radiator air intakes and exhaust were now to be fitted with folding metal covers, the engine deck was to be retained and as such a lever with bell crank was to be used with a cable system to pop the locks on the three hatches when the vehicle exited the water. The actual system employed when fielded used hinged hatches with a cover and a smooth engine deck and a series of rods and bell cranks down the left side of the engine deck. (Andrey Aksenov)

BELOW LEFT Drawing of where the major fittings are carried. 1 is for the two-section snorkel when preparing for fording, 2 is the folded engine grille cover strapped over the top of the engine access hatch, and 3 is the rail transport stowage position for the snorkel under the auxiliary fuel tanks. (Andrey Aksenov)

BELOW RIGHT The T-62 bilge pump, identical for all models. This exited the engine compartment under the turret overhang on the left side of the hull. (Andrey Aksenov)

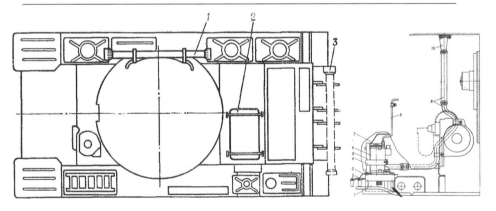

which in its collapsed state was about 1.75 metres long and 15cm in diameter, was installed in brackets under the 200-litre auxiliary fuel tanks.

To prepare the tank for crossing, all of the seals were checked first and drain plugs installed in the hull floor of the tank. The snorkel was removed, bolted together with seals between sections and base, the loader's MK-4 viewing device was removed from its mount, and the assembled snorkel was

attached in its place with bolts. Steps were mounted to the snorkel for the use of rescue personnel to climb up and contact the crew if the tank stalled. The covers were attached to their specific items with clamps and the flapper valve installed to the exhaust outlet.

The entire engine deck area was covered by a rubber-impregnated canvas cover that was bolted down to the edges of a frame. It had a fixed metal frame in the middle with a folding and sealing hatch cover to permit airflow on land without removing the cover. The engine radiator air intake had five moveable internal louvres that could be adjusted to cut off outside airflow but the cover prevented water ingress.

Once the tank was prepared, a seal around the inside of the turret race was inflated to prevent water entry into the tank. Some leakage was expected and charts told the crew what was acceptable; once the tank began crossing, the bilge pump would be turned on to evacuate water that did seep into the tank, but it was only after the tank exited the water that it could fully clear the engine compartment.

A T-62 Model 1961 fording shallow water with only one snorkel segment employed, but if in deeper water the only difference would be the second section added at the top.

The actual crossing usually required prepared banks on both sides of the obstacle or at least shallow approaches to the river or creek. The tank would move into the water in first gear at an engine speed of 1,500rpm to make the crossing. The driver would use the GPK-48 gyrocompass to keep the tank heading in the right direction. Once across the tank could fire on targets immediately if needed but this would destroy the muzzle and machine gun covers. The tank would start to overheat if the hatch over the engine deck was not opened soon after crossing, and the tanks could obviously not sit at idle for a long time with no air circulation.

For night crossings a cable would be dropped down the snorkel and a red light similar to the marker and tail lights fitted to the top so the commander could follow the progress of his tanks across the water.

There were, as might be expected, accidents during training and exercises and usually tow cables would be run to the tanks to ensure that if the tanks stalled they could be hauled out of the water. Often (as in East Germany) the places where training took place were purpose-built concrete basin-like structures to make it easy to enter, cross and exit.

Several changes in design took place over the years. One was the introduction of a larger training snorkel that bolted to the commander's cupola and allowed the crew easy exit if the tank stalled. Another was an antenna feed to the top of the snorkel for an antenna allowing communications to the tank via radio.

Both were developed for crew safety and also to reduce the number of accidents. If the driver-mechanic did not switch on the GPK-48 to give him a bearing, the worst problem was that the tank would turn 90 degrees towards downstream and go with the flow rather than across it.

Changes were made to the system used by the T-62 with, first, a pair of beams being provided to offer some relief to the canvas cover and allow some air circulation within the engine compartment when sealed. Later, a new cover with three steel hatches, one over each radiator air intake and one over the radiator air exhaust on the left side of the engine deck, was provided to improve airflow when waiting to cross.

In 1967 a new and final solution was developed and introduced. The engine deck was redesigned and the engine access and air cleaner access hatches were eliminated; the new deck was hinged at the front for access to service the engine and air cleaner. Twin hinged covers that hermetically sealed the radiator air intakes were installed on the new deck and a reinforced steel cover was provided to protect them when not in use. Another smaller cover was hinged at the rear of the radiator air exhaust on the left with the previously provided domed cover for the fan grille on the right (to prevent compressibility during fan operation). A new smaller flapper value for the exhaust was introduced, as was a new three-section snorkel with sections each about 1.25 metres long. The new snorkel was stowed at the left rear of the turret. Also, a GPK-59 gyrocompass replaced the GPK-48.

The new equipment was designated the OPVT-166 system, and in modified form was carried forward to use on the T-72 and T-90 series tanks as well.

A T-62 Model 1972 using the training snorkel. As the commander's cupola was identical to the T-55 series tanks and could be fitted with the training snorkel, the same device was used on the T-62.

APPENDIX TEN
COMPARATIVE TECHNICAL AND TACTICAL CHARACTERISTICS OF THE T-62, T-62M AND OBIEKT-167 TANKS

Technical Characteristics	Article 167	T-62 Model 1961	T-62M
General Data			
Combat Weight in metric tonnes	36.6	37 (OMSh) 37.5 (RMSh)	41.5–42
Crew	4	4	4
Dimensions in mm			
Width	3,300	3,300	3,566
Length of hull over fenders	6,365	6,630	6,630
Height (to roof of turret)	2258.5	2,248	3,039
Power to weight ratio, HP/metric tonnes	19.1	15.4–15.7	14.8–14.9 (V-55U) 16.4–16.6 (V-46-5M)
Ground clearance	482	471.5	450
Armament			
Type of Gun	2A20 (U-5TS)	2A20 (U-5TS)	2A20 (U-5TS)
Calibre	115mm	115mm	115mm
Type of gun	Smoothbore	Smoothbore	Smoothbore
Fire Control System Telescopic Sight Periscopic/Night Sight Missile Control Sight (day/night)	TSh2B-41-11 TPN-1-41 –	TSh2B-41-11 TPN-1-41 –	TShSM-41U – 1K13-1
Two-Axis Stabilizer	'Liven'	'Meteor' 'Meteor-M'	'Meteor-M1'
Coaxial machine gun: Type Calibre	PKT (SGMT) 7.62mm	PKT (SGMT) 7.62mm	PKT 7.62mm
Anti-aircraft Machine Gun: Type of Gun Calibre	–	–	(some vehicles) DShKM or NSVT 12.7mm
Basic Load Cannon rounds Missile Rounds Machine gun rounds AA Machine Gun Rounds	– 40 –2500 –	– 40 –2500 –	35 5 2,500 300
Armour Protection (thickness/angle of slope in degrees from vertical) mm/degrees			
Hull			
Upper Glacis Appliqué Lower Glacis Sides Skirts (steel reinforced rubber)	100/60 100/55 70/0	100/60 100/55 80/0	100/60 120+30 equivalent 100/55 80/0 10 skirts
Turret			
Front Appliqué	188/33	188/33	188/33 360+60 equivalent

Thickness of Armour (mm)

Hull

Upper glacis	200	200	200+
Lower glacis	175	175	175+
Sides	70	80	80+

Turret

Front	258	258	258+

Mobility

Maximum highway speed in kph	60	50	50
Average speed on dirt roads, kph	35–42	22–27	25–27
Maximum grade negotiated in degrees	Up to 30	32	32
Average ground pressure, kg/cm^2	0.73	0.75 0.77	0.85
Fording Depth in metres Unprepared Prepared (OPVT)	1.4 Unknown	1.4 5	1.4 5

Fuel Capacity in litres

Hull	715	675	675
Fenders	285	285	285
Auxiliary Fuel Tanks	2 x 200	2 x 200	2 x 200 (integrated into fuel system)
Range in km	550–700	450–700	450–700

Engine-Transmission Installation

Engine, type	V-26	V-55 or V-55V	V-55U or V-46-5M
Type	Diesel, liquid-cooled, with driven centrifugal supercharger	Diesel, liquid-cooled	Diesel, liquid-cooled, supercharged
Cycles	4	4	4
Number of cylinders	12	12	12
Disposition	V type, 60 degree	V type, 60 degree	V type, 60 degree
Maximum power, HP (kWt) Under Test Stand Conditions	700 (515)	580 (426)	V-55U – 620 V-46-5M – 690
Transmission	Strengthened, mechanical	Strengthened, mechanical	Strengthened, mechanical

Running Gear

Suspension, type	Individual, torsion bar	Individual, torsion bar	Individual, torsion bar
Dynamic travel of road wheel, mm	242	162	232
Spring element	Torsion	Torsion	Torsion
Shock absorbers, type	Hydraulic, Blade type	Hydraulic, Blade type	Hydraulic, Blade type
Track drive, type	Rear-mounted drive wheel	Rear mounted drive wheel	Rear mounted drive wheel
Track, type	RMSh	RMSh OMSh	RMSh
Number of links	Unknown	96 (OMSh) 97 (RMSh)	97
Number of road wheels	6	5	5
Diameter of road wheel, mm	750	810	810
Type of buffering of road wheel	Rubber tyre	Rubber tyre	Rubber tyre
Number of return rollers per side	3 x 250mm	None	None

COMPARATIVE TACTICAL AND TECHNICAL CHARACTERISTICS OF THE PROPOSED T-62B (OBIEKT-167M) AND THE T-64A TANKS		
Technical Characteristic	T-62B (Obiekt-167M)	T-64A (Obiekt-434)
General Data		
Year of Project Development	1962–64	1964–67
Combat weight, metric tonnes	39–40	36
Crew	3	3
Dimensions in mm: Length of hull Height (to roof of turret)	6,593 2258	6,540 2,170
Power to weight ratio HP/mt (kWt/mt)	20–19.5 (14.7–14.3)	19.4 (14.2)
Ground pressure, kg/cm^2	0.75	0.79
Armament		
Gun, type Calibre, mm Type of gun	2A26 (D-81T) 125 Smoothbore	2A26 (D-81T) 125 Smoothbore
Basic load (inc autoloader)	40 (19)*	40 (28)
Rangefinder	None	TPD
Primary armament stabilizer	'Liven'	2Eh23
Armour Protection (thickness/angle from the vertical) mm/degrees		
Glacis Side	80+105+20/68 70/0–80/0	80+105+20/68 80/0
Turret front	Comparable	
Mobility		
Maximum speed on highways km	60	65
Range on highways in km	500	500
Engine-Transmission Installation		
Engine, type	V-35	5TDF
Type	Diesel Liquid-cooled, Supercharged	Diesel Air cooled
Cycles	4	2
Number of cylinders	12	5
Disposition and angle	V type, 60 degrees	Horizontal
Maximum output, HP (kWt) Per stand testing	780 (574)	700 (515)
Running Gear		
Suspension, type	Individual, Torsion bar	
Springing element	Torsion	Torsion
Shock absorbers, type	Hydraulic, blade	Hydraulic, telescopic
Track drive, type	With rear mounted drive wheels	
Track, type	RMSh rubber buffered metallic	Twin pin rubber-metallic
Note: * In the production version used on the T-72 this was increased to 22 rounds.		

MODERNIZATION OF T-62 TANKS BY MODEL AND TYPE

Modernized Feature	T-62M	T-62M1	T-62M1-2	T-62MV	T-62D
'Sheksna' ATGM Complex	Yes	No	No	Yes	No
DShKM or NSVT AA MG*	Yes	Yes	Yes	Yes	No
Thermal barrel shroud	Yes	Yes	Yes	Yes	No
Additional Armour Protection:					
Hull	Yes	Yes	No	No	Yes
Turret	Yes	Yes	Yes	No	No
Belly	Yes	Yes	Yes	Yes	Yes
Improved Driver's Seat	Yes	Yes	Yes	Yes	Yes
KDZ Protection (ERA)	No	No	No	Yes	No
'Drozd' Active Protection	No	No	No	No	Yes
Neutron Protection	Yes	Yes	Yes	Yes	Yes
Side Skirts	Yes	Yes	Yes	Yes	Yes
'Soda' fire suppression	Yes	Yes	Yes	Yes	No
'Tucha' Smoke Grenades	Yes	Yes	Yes	Yes	Yes
V-55U Engine**	Yes	Yes	Yes	Yes	Yes
Updated Running Gear	Yes	Yes	Yes	Yes	Yes
R-173/R-173P/R-174 commo	Yes	Yes	Yes	Yes	Yes

Notes: * Only on those tanks with the Model 1972 turret.
** If the tank received a V-46-5M engine of 690HP the designators are T-62M-1, T-62M1-1, T-62M1-2, T-62MV-1 and T-62D-1 respectively.
In 1995 some T-62M tanks were retrofitted with 'reshetka' grille armour for use in Chechnya.

APPENDIX ELEVEN
GLOSSARY

AAMG	Anti-Aircraft Machine Gun
APFSDS	Armour-Piercing Fin-Stabilized Discarding Sabot projectile
ATGM	Anti-Tank Guided Missile
BDD	Bronya Desantogo Deystviya – Assault Operations Armour
BTS	Bronyevoy Tyagach Sredny or Sredny Tankovy Tyagach – Medium Tank Tractor
CFE	Conventional Forces in Europe
ChKZ	Chelyabinsky Kirovsky Zavod (ChTZ from 15 May 1958)
ChTZ	Chelyabinsky Traktorny Zavod imeni V. I. Lenina (ChKZ before 15 May 1958)
ERA	Explosive Reactive Armour
GABTU	Gosudarstvennoye Avtomotivnoye Bronetankirovannoye Upravleniye – Main Automotive and Armoured Vehicle Directorate
GBTU	Gosudarstvennoye Bronetankirovannoye Upravleniye – Main Armoured Vehicle Directorate
GKOT	Gosudarstvennyy Komitet Oboronnoy Tekhniki – State Committee on Defence Technology
Glavtank	12th Main Directorate for Tank Production of the Ministry of Transport Machinery Production
HEAT	High Explosive Anti-Tank
HE-FRAG	High Explosive Fragmentation
IDF	Israeli Defence Forces
IED	Improvised Explosive Devices
KB	Konstruktorskoye Byuro – design bureau
KBTM	Konstruktorskoye Byuro Transportivnoy Mashinoy – Design Bureau for Transport Vehicles (Omsk)

KO	Kontrol'naya Otdel' – control compartment
MBT	Main Battle Tank
MO	Ministerstvo Oboroni – Soviet (Russian) Ministry of Defence (MoD)
MRD	Motorized Rifle Division
MTO	Motorno-Transmissionaya Otdel' – motor transmission compartment
MTrM	Ministerstvo Trasportivnoy Mashinikh Promishlennosti (Ministry of Transport Machinery Construction)
NKVD	Narodny Kommisariat Vnutrenikh Del – People's Commissariat for Internal Affairs
NST	Novyy Sredny Tank – new medium tank
NTK	Nauchno-Tekhnicheskiy Komitet (Scientific Technical Committee)
OPFOR	US Army Opposing Forces units
OPVT	Oborudovaniye Podvodnoy Vozhdeniya Tanki – underwater tank driving equipment
PAZ	Protivoatomnoi Zashiti – anti-nuclear protection
PLA	People's Liberation Army of China
PLO	Palestine Liberation Organization
PPO	Protivo-Pozharnoye Oborudovaniye – fire suppression equipment
RPG	Rocket Propelled Grenade (launcher)
SACLOS	Semi-active Command Line of Sight
SM SSSR	Sovet Ministerov SSSR – Council of Ministers of the USSR
TDA	Termal'naya Dymovaya Apparata – thermal smoke generation apparatus
TO	Tankovyy Ognemet – tank flamethrower

TPU	Tankovoe Peregovornoe Ustroistva – tank voice communications system	VPK	Voenny Promishlennoi Kommissiei pri Soviet Ministrov SSSR – Military-Industrial Commissariat for the Council of Ministers of the USSR
TsK KPSU	Tsentral'ny Komitet Kommunicheskoy Partii Sovetskogo Soyuza – Central Committee of the Communist Party of the Soviet Union	VV	Vnutrenny Voisk (internal security troops)
UVZ	Ural'nyy Vagonstroitel'sviy Zavod (Urals Railway Wagon Construction Factory)	ZIP	Komplekt zapasnykh chastey, instrumentov, i prinadzhelnostey – set of spare parts, tools, and accessories

CONSTRUCTION PLANTS AND DESIGN BUREAUS

TsNII-6	Central Scientific Research Institutes for Flame Weapons, Moscow	Zavod No. 75	Kharkov Tank Plant (formerly Kharkov Diesel Engine Construction Plant)
TsNII-48	Central Scientific Research Institute for Armour, Leningrad	Zavod No. 174	Omsk Tank Plant (formerly in Leningrad)
TsNII-173	Central Scientific Research Institute for Artillery Stabilizers, Moscow	Zavod No. 183	Urals Railway Wagon Construction Plant, Nizhny Tagil (formerly Kharkov Steam Locomotive Construction Plant in Kharkov) (today Kharkiv)
VNII-100	Vsesoyuzny Nauchno-Issledovatelsky Institut (later VNII Transmash)		
Zavod No. 9	Artillery Plant No. 9, Perm (F. F. Petrov Bureau)	Zavod No. 393	Optical Plant, Krasnogorsk (the 'Zenit' Plant)

BIBLIOGRAPHY

BOOKS – RUSSIAN LANGUAGE

Babazhanyan, A. Kh., *Tanki I Tankovye Voyska* (2nd edition) (Voyennoye Izdatel'stvo, 1980)

Baranov, I. N. (general editor), *Glavnyy Konstruktor V. N. Venediktov: Zhizn' Otdannaya Tankam* (DiAl, Nizhny Tagil, 2009)

Baryatinskiy, M., *1945–2008: Sovetskiye Tanki v Boyu* (Yauza/Ehksmo, 2008)

Baryatinskiy, M., *Tanki v Chechnye – Sovetskaya Bronetankovaya Tekhika v 'Goryachikh Tochkakh' SSSR I SNG 1989–1998 gg.* (Zhelezhnodoroznoye Delo, Moscow, 1999)

Baryatinskiy, M., *Tanki XX Vek – Unikal'naya Ehtsiklopediya* (Yauza/Ehksmo, 2010)

Baushev, I. (editor), *Sozdateli Oruzhiya I Voyennoy Tekhniki Sukhoputnykh Voysk Rossii* (Pashkov Dom, Moscow, 2008)

Bryukhov, V. P., *Bronetankovye Voyska* (Golos Press, Moscow, 2006)

Bryzgov, V. and Yermolina, O., *Bronetankovaya Tekhnika – Fotoal'bom*; Gonchar' (Moscow, 1994)

Bubenin, V., *Krovavyy Sneg Damanskogo: Sobytiya 1967–1969 gg.* (Kuchkovo Pole, Moscow, 2004)

Chernyshev, V. L. (editor), *Tanki I Lyudi: Dnevnik Glavnogo Konstruktora Aleksandra Aleksandrovicha Morozova*; Internet Version published on http://www.btvt.narod.ru, 2006/2007 (translated by author)

Drogovoz, I. G., *Neob'yavlennye Voyny SSSR* (Kharvest, Minsk, 2004)

Drogovoz, I. G., *Tankovyy Mech SSSR 1945–1991* (P'yedestal, 1999)

Fes'kov, V. I., Kalashnikov, K. A. and Golikov, V. I., *Sovetskaya Armiya v Gody 'Kholodnoy Voyny' (1945–1991)* (Tomsk State University, Tomsk, 2004)

Ionin, S. N., *Bronetankovye Voyska SSSR-Rossii* (Veche, Moscow, 2006)

Karpenko, A. V., *Obozreniye Otechestvennoy Bronetankovoy Tekhniki (1905–1995 gg.)* (Nevskiy Bastion, St. Petersburg, 1996)

Karyakin, L. A. and Moiseyev, V. I., *Voyennye Tekhniki I Vooruzheniye Kitaya – Vyp. 1: Tanki* (Krasnaya Oktyabr, Saransk, Russia, 2002)

Kholyavskiy, G. L., *Ehtsiklopediya Bronyetekhniki – Gusenichnye Boyevye Mashiny* (Kharvest, Minsk, 2001)

Krivosheyev, G. F., Andronikov, V. M., Burikov, P. D. and Gurkin, V.V., *Velikaya Otechestvennaya bez grifa secretnosti. Kniga Poter'* (Veche, Moscow, 2009)

Lavrenov, S. Ya., *Sovetskiy Soyuz v Lokal'nykh Voynakh I Konfliktakh* (Astrel, Moscow, 2003)

Loza, D. F., *Skaz o Tankakh 'Sherman'* (Ostrov, St. Petersburg, 2001)

Minayev, A. V. (general editor), *Sovetskaya Voyennaya Moshch': Ot Stalina do Gorbacheva* (Voyennyy Parad, 1999)

Ministry of Defence Publications, *Izdeliye 434: Rukovodstvo po Voyskovomu Remontu* (Moscow, 1969)

Ministry of Defence Publications, *Rukovodstvo po Material'noy Chasti I Ehkspluatsii Tanka T-55* (Moscow, 1969)

Ministry of Defence Publications, *Rukovodstvo po Material'noy Chasti I Ehkspluatsii Tanka T-62* (Moscow, 1968)

Ministry of Defence Publications, *Tank T-55AM: Dopolneniye k Tekhicheskomy Opisaniyu I Instruktsii po Ehksplutatsii Tanka T-55* (Voyenizdat, Moscow, 1983)

Ministry of Defence Publications, *Tanki T-64B I T-64B1: Tekhicheskoye Opisaniye I Instruktsiya po Ehksplutatsii* (TO) Book 1 (Moscow, 1983)

Ministry of Defence Publications, *Tank T-72A: Tekhicheskoye Opisaniye I Instruktsiya po Ehksplutatsii* (TO) Book 2 Part 1 (Moscow, 1988)

Moskovskiy, A. G. (general editor), *75 Let Upravleniyu Nachal'nika Vooruzheniya* (Voyennyy Parad, Moscow, 2004)

Musalov, A., *Damanskiy I Zhalanashkol' 1969* (Exprint, 2005)

Polonskiy, V. A. (Chairman of the Editorial Group), *Glavnoye Avtobronyetankovoye Upraveniye: Lyudi, Sobytiya, Fakty v Dokumentakh 1946–1953 gg.* Book V (Ministry of Defence of the Russian Federation, Moscow, 2007)

Popov, N. S., Petrov, V. I., Popov, A. N. and Ashik, M. V., *Bez Tayn I Sekretov* (Prana, St. Petersburg, 1995)

Popov, N. S., Ashik, M. V., Bakh, I. V., Dobryakov, B. A., Dmitriyev, L. M., Il'in, O. K. and Petrov, V. I., *Konstruktor Boyevykh Mashin* (Lenizdat, St. Petersburg, 1988)

Popov. N. S., Yefremov, A. S. and Ashik, M.V., *Tank, Brosivshiy Vyzov Vremeni* (Kaskad Poligrafiya, St. Petersburg, 2001)

Ryabaushkin, D. S., *Mify Damanskogo* (AST, Moscow, 2004)

Safonov, B. S. and Murakhovskiy, V. I., *Osnovnye Boyevye Tanki* (Arsenal-Press, Moscow, 1993)

Shunkov, V. N., *Ehtsiklopediya Reaktivnoy Artillerii* (Poligrafkombinat Im. Ya. Kolasa, Minsk, 2004)

Solyankin, A. G., *Bronetankovaya Tekhnika Sovetskoy Armii – Al'bom* (Ministry of Defence Publishing, Moscow, 1983)

Solyankin, A. G., Zheltov, I. G. and Kudryashov, K. N., *Otechestvennye*

Bronirovannye Mashiny XX Vek: Tom 3 – Otechestvennye Bronirovannye Mashiny 1945–1965 (Tseykhgauz, Moscow, 2010)

Suvorov, S., *T-72: Vchera, Segodnya, Zavtra* (Tankomaster, Moscow, 2001)

Svirin, M., *Tankovaya Moshch' SSSR: Pervaya Polnaya Ehntsiklopediya* (Yauza/Ehksmo, 2009)

Ust'yantsev, S. and Kolmakov, D., *Boyevye Mashiny Uralvagonzavoda: Tank T-72*, Part 2 (Dom 'Media-Print', Nizhny Tagil, 2004) (translated by author)

Ust'yantsev, S. and Kolmakov, D., *Boyevye Mashiny Uralvagonzavoda: Tanki T-54/T55*, Part 3 (Dom 'Media-Print', Nizhny Tagil, 2006) (translated by author)

Ust'yantsev, S. and Kolmakov, D., *Boyevye Mashiny Uralvagonzavoda: Tanki 60-ikh* Part 4 (Dom 'Media-Print', Nizhny Tagil, 2007) (translated by author)

Vasil'yeva, L. and Zheltov, I., *Nikolay Kucherenko: Pyat'desyat Let v Bitve za Tanki SSSR* (Atlantida – XXI Vek/Moskovskiye Uchebniki, 2009) (translated by author)

Veretrennikov, A., Rasskazov, I., Sidorov, K. and Reshetilo, Y., *Kharkovskoye Konstruktorskoye Byuro po Mashinostroyeniyu imeni A. A. Morozova* (IRIS Press, Kharkov, 1998)

Veretrennikov, A., Rasskazov, I., Sidorov, K. and Reshetilo, Y., *Kharkovskoye Konstruktorskoye Byuro po Mashinostroyeniyu imeni A. A. Morozova* (Kharkov, 2007)

BOOKS – ENGLISH LANGUAGE

203rd Military Intelligence Battalion, *Department of the Army Operator's Manual for T-62* (undated)

Geraghty, T. *BRIXMIS: The Untold Exploits of Britain's Most Daring Cold War Spy Mission* (Harper/Collins, Hammersmith, London, 1997)

Hull, A., Markov, D. and Zaloga, S., *Soviet/Russian Armor and Artillery Design Practices: 1945 to the Present* (Darlington Publications, Darlington, Maryland, 1999)

Isby, D. and Nordeen, L., *M60 vs T-62: Cold War Combatants 1956–92* (Osprey Publishing, Oxford, UK, 2010)

Scott, H. F. and Scott, W. F., *The Armed Forces of the USSR*; (Westview Press, Boulder, CO, 1979)

Zaloga, S. J., *New Vanguard 158: T-62 Main Battle Tank 1965–2005* (Osprey Publishing, Oxford, UK, 2009)

PERIODICALS – RUSSIAN LANGUAGE

Bronekollektiysa (Moscow)
   No. 2/2004 – Srednyy Tank T-62; Mikhail Baryatinskiy
Krasnaya Zvezda (Moscow)
Modelist-Konstruktor (Moscow)
M-Khobbi (Moscow)
Tekhnika I Vooruzheniye (pre-1991 Soviet issues)
Tekhnika I Vooruzheniye: Vchera, Segondya, Zaftra (ISSN 1682-7507)
   (Moscow)
Continuing Series by M. V. Pavlov and I. V. Pavlov from January 2009 to at
   least April 2014: *Otechestvennye Bronirovannye Mashiny 1945–1965 gg.*

ARTICLES – RUSSIAN LANGUAGE

Baryatinskiy, M. and Mal'ginov, V., 'Sredniy Tank T-62' (T-62 Medium Tank),
   M-Khobbi, April 2006
Kos, I. I. and Sidorenko, R. V., 'Spravitel'naya Otsenka Nadezhnosti Srednikh
   Tankov' (Comparative Assessment of the Reliability of Medium Tanks),
   Vestnik Bronetankvoy Tekhniki, No. 1-1968
Zayets, A., 'Afganskiy Variant' (The Afghan Variant), *Voyennye Znaniya,* June
   1995, p. 23
Zayets, A., ' 'My Kakim-to Chudom Ne Lishilis' Tankov …' (It was a Miracle
   We didn't lose our Tanks), *Voyennye Znaniya,* March 1995, pp. 20–21

PERIODICALS – ENGLISH LANGUAGE

Armor (US Army)
AFV Profile (London)
   No. 23 – Soviet Mediums T44, T54, T55 & T62 – Major Michael Norman
   Classic Military Vehicle (UK)
International Defence Review
Jane's Defence Review

ONLINE SOURCES

'Gur Khan Attacks' – http://gurkhan.blogspot.com/
'Soldat.ru' – http://www.soldat.ru/
'Yuri Pasholok's Journal' – http://yuripasholok.livejournal.com/
'Andrei's BTVT Journal' – http://www,btvt.info

INDEX

References to images are in **bold**.